TRANSPORTATION — AMERICA'S LIFELINE

INFORMATION PLUS®
WYLIE, TEXAS 75098-7006
© 1983, 1985, 1987, 1989, 1991, 1993, 1995, 1997, 1999

EDITORS:
ABBEY M. BEGUN, B.A.
CORNELIA BLAIR, M.S.
MARK A. SIEGEL, Ph.D.

CHAPTER I

SHIPS — TRAVELING THE WATERWAYS

Shipping played a major role in the early growth and development of the United States. The first European settlers made their way to the New World by boat. Slaves were packed into the holds of slave ships and brought over to work the fields of the growing colonies. The very existence of the colonies and the young republic depended on the flow of passengers and vital goods on both inland and oceanic waterways. For almost two hundred years after the arrival of those first settlers, ships were the country's primary mode of transporting commercial cargo. From the mid-1800s through the early 1900s, ships brought millions of European and Asian immigrants to American shores.

Over the past 300 years, this has spawned the development of ocean, Great Lakes, and inland waterway ports. Together, the waterways, lakes, oceans, harbors, and ports form the network of the national waterborne transportation system. The system plays a vital role in the nation's trade and helps stimulate the economy by attracting new industries and providing jobs, income, and tax revenues.

The waterborne transportation system also includes the nation's many types of vessels, its piers and wharves, cargo handling equipment, storage facilities, and its connections to other types of transportation. In

TABLE 1.1

U.S. Port Terminal Facilities by Type and Location: 1995

Location	Total	Number of berths by type			
		General cargo	Dry bulk	Liquid bulk	Other
Total berths	4,990	1,271	1,758	1,118	843
Coastal region					
Total	3,179	1,197	710	628	644
North Atlantic	756	264	96	184	212
South Atlantic	343	204	40	56	43
Gulf	790	270	169	184	167
South Pacific	405	211	50	72	72
North Pacific	378	153	79	75	71
Great Lakes	507	95	276	57	79
River system					
Total	1,811	74	1,048	490	199
Mississippi	1,756	65	1,016	483	192
Columbia/Snake	55	9	32	7	7

SOURCE: Adapted from U.S. Department of Transportation, Maritime Administration, *U.S. Public Ports Annual Report* (Washington, DC: 1996), tables 17, 18.

Source: *Transportation Statistics Annual Report 1998 — Long-Distance Travel and Freight*, Bureau of Transportation Statistics, Washington, DC, 1998

addition, it provides the link for the exchange of goods and passengers between land and water.

A REVOLUTIONARY TECHNOLOGY

For thousands of years, the movement of ships depended on sails and oars. Had fate been kinder, John Fitch, rather than Robert Fulton, would be credited with leading the world from the age of wind and muscle power into the age of steam power. Fitch, an explorer, mapmaker, and surveyor by profession, launched the first fully operational steamboat in 1787. A year later, a 30-passenger boat was launched, and by 1790, a third steamboat was regularly carrying passengers and freight between Philadelphia and Burlington, New Jersey. Fitch took out patents in the United States and France for his invention and was granted the sole right to build and operate steamboats in the states of New Jersey, Pennsylvania, Delaware, New York, and Virginia. Although John Fitch had the patent, he could not capture the interest of the American public. He lost financial backing for his enterprise and died in 1798, considered a failure by most.

Instead, it was Robert Fulton who popularized the steamboat that would spark the imagination of the nation and the world. His steamship, the *Clermont,* cruised up the Hudson River in 1807 to instant success and a place in the history of navigation. The potential of a boat that could move upstream or downstream, with or against the currents, independently of the direction of the wind or the strength of oars, was finally recognized. On May 22, 1819, the steam-powered *SS Savannah* crossed the Atlantic Ocean.

The steamboat is perhaps most closely associated with the mighty Mississippi River. The well-dressed river boat gambler who traveled the river on powerful steamboats is almost as familiar a folk figure as the cowboy riding the range.

THE CANAL AGE

In 1817, the New York State Legislature began a period of intensive canal building by authorizing construction of a watercourse between the Hudson River at Albany and Lake Erie at Buffalo. The canal was such a financial and commercial success that it became celebrated in song and folklore as the "Erie Canal" (rather than "Clinton's Big Ditch," as opponents of Governor DeWitt Clinton had called it). Financed, built, and operated solely with state funds, the waterway returned its $8 million construction cost within seven years of its completion in 1825. By using the 338-mile canal rather than overland routes, the cost of hauling a ton of freight between Buffalo and New York City was reduced from $100 to $10 and travel time from 26 days to six days.

While several canals had previously been constructed, the success of the Erie Canal prompted other states with navigable waterways to make a serious commitment to canal building. Unfortunately, many of the new canals were not as successful as the Erie. Lack of capital for construction and maintenance, mismanagement, corruption, and overbuilding created huge debts that many states were never able to pay off.

INTEREST FADES . . .

Economic depression, lack of readily available coal to fuel steamboats, and the coming of the railroads signaled the end of America's reliance on boats and waterways as a major form of transportation. By the early 1900s, American ships were carrying less than 10 percent of the country's trade, and only one American trans-Atlantic line was in operation.

World War I generated a brief resurgence in shipbuilding. The federal government, which up to this time had shown no real interest in the shipping industry, realized that the country was practically without ships for transporting arms and troops to the fighting fronts in Europe. To correct the situation, Congress passed the Shipping Act of 1916, creating the Emergency Fleet Corporation, which built 2,318 vessels between 1918 and 1922. Most of these ships were delivered too late to serve in the war (which ended in 1918) and were often so poorly designed and constructed that they could not be used for any other purpose.

. . . AND IS RENEWED — THE MERCHANT MARINE ACT OF 1936

The Great Depression of the early 1930s created another slump in shipbuilding and transport, but as the

TABLE 1.2

U.S. Waterborne Traffic by State in 1997[1]
(Millions of Short Tons and Change from 1996)

Rank	State	Domestic Tons	Domestic %	Foreign Tons	Foreign %	Total[2] Tons	Total[2] %
1	Louisiana	277.8	1.0	215.2	-1.9	493.0	-0.3
2	Texas	121.9	-0.4	300.7	14.3	422.6	9.6
3	California	74.5	-13.5	97.3	2.4	171.8	-5.2
4	Ohio	112.0	7.5	22.2	15.2	134.2	8.7
5	Florida	79.3	4.3	45.1	9.0	124.5	6.0
6	Pennsylvania	76.2	6.6	43.0	17.1	119.2	10.2
7	Washington	61.6	5.9	56.2	-4.4	117.8	0.7
8	Illinois	105.5	-3.7	3.9	-11.5	109.3	-4.0
9	New York	60.3	5.0	43.2	14.3	103.5	8.7
10	New Jersey	61.1	7.7	36.8	-12.8	97.9	-1.1
11	Alaska	82.2	-3.2	12.2	9.7	94.4	-1.7
12	Kentucky	87.3	7.0	0.0	0.0	87.3	7.0
13	Michigan	69.1	4.5	13.8	-2.9	82.9	3.2
14	Indiana	79.5	3.1	2.6	-20.5	82.1	2.2
15	West Virginia	79.5	-4.2	0.0	0.0	79.5	-4.2
16	Virginia	24.3	-0.5	53.4	-13.2	77.7	-9.6
17	Alabama	46.7	-3.6	24.9	-2.5	71.6	-3.2
18	Minnesota	48.7	6.4	6.6	2.3	55.3	5.9
19	Maryland	19.7	7.4	30.1	1.9	49.8	4.0
20	Mississippi	26.1	9.5	23.7	5.9	49.8	7.8
21	Tennessee	47.5	8.0	0.0	0.0	47.5	8.0
22	Virgin Islands	20.4	-10.1	24.9	26.1	45.3	6.7
23	Wisconsin	31.7	1.1	6.9	3.3	38.5	1.5
24	Oregon	17.2	1.3	19.5	-1.4	36.7	-0.1
25	Missouri	31.5	9.1	0.0	0.0	31.5	9.1
26	Puerto Rico	13.7	-8.3	14.5	-3.4	28.2	-5.9
27	Massachusetts	14.0	9.0	13.5	2.6	27.5	5.8
28	Delaware	18.7	5.1	5.6	-30.0	24.3	-5.8
29	Hawaii	13.0	-7.3	8.4	15.5	21.3	0.5
30	Georgia	3.8	2.0	17.2	5.8	21.0	5.1
31	Maine	2.9	-4.2	17.1	11.8	20.0	9.1
32	Connecticut	16.4	5.2	3.3	22.5	19.7	7.7
33	South Carolina	4.8	8.2	14.7	23.6	19.5	19.4
34	Iowa	13.6	-7.6	0.0	0.0	13.6	-7.6
35	North Carolina	6.4	-5.5	7.1	-1.0	13.5	-3.2
36	Arkansas	13.4	-2.1	0.0	0.0	13.4	-2.1
37	Rhode Island	5.6	25.7	3.9	1.8	9.5	14.6
38	Oklahoma	4.0	18.9	0.0	0.0	4.0	18.9
39	New Hampshire	1.0	10.8	2.9	5.2	4.0	6.6
40	Idaho	1.6	22.3	0.0	0.0	1.6	22.4
41	District of Columbia	0.7	-5.5	0.0	0.0	0.7	-5.5
42	Guam	0.4	-2.2	0.0	0.0	0.4	-2.2
43	Nebraska	0.3	-22.4	0.0	0.0	0.3	-22.4
44	Kansas	0.3	-58.7	0.0	0.0	0.3	-58.7

1. Includes shipments, receipts and intrastate commerce.
2. Total may not equal column sum due to rounding.

Source: *The U.S. Waterway System — FACTS*, Navigation Data Center, U.S. Army Corps of Engineers, Alexandria, VA, 1998

country began to recover, the government took a renewed interest in shipping. In 1936, Congress passed the Merchant Marine Act, declaring it national policy to foster the creation of a merchant marine fleet capable of handling domestic and foreign commerce and of serving in time of war.

The fleet was to be owned and operated "insofar as practicable" by private U.S. concerns. The federal government would provide subsidies to private companies to make up the difference between the cost of building and operating ships in the United States and the often much lower costs of these activities in foreign countries. Freight rates and trade routes were placed under federal jurisdiction. A Maritime Commission was formed to survey the state of the merchant marine fleet and develop a long-range program to meet future needs.

BETTER PREPARED

Within five years of the passage of the Merchant Marine Act of 1936, the United States was again at war. This time, however, the country's maritime fleet

FIGURE 1.1

Major Waterways and Ports in the United States

TABLE OF MILES BETWEEN COASTAL AND GREAT LAKES PORTS

	ANCHORAGE	DETROIT	DULUTH-SUPERIOR	HONOLULU	HOUSTON	JACKSONVILLE	LOS ANGELES	NEW ORLEANS	NEW YORK	NORFOLK	PANAMA CITY, PAN	PORTLAND, OR	SAN FRANCISCO	SAN JUAN	SEATTLE
DETROIT	8903														
DULUTH-SUPERIOR	9710	726													
HONOLULU	2477	8471	9278												
HOUSTON	6703	3907	4633	6271											
JACKSONVILLE	6676	2709	3516	6244	1272										
LOS ANGELES	2220	6725	7532	2233	4525	4498									
NEW ORLEANS	6559	3617	4424	6127	490	1083	4381								
NEW YORK	7135	2071	2878	6703	1919	788	4957	1710							
NORFOLK	6944	2253	3060	6512	1718	587	4766	1509	294						
PANAMA CITY, PAN	5117	3786	4593	4685	1586	1559	2939	1442	2018	1827					
PORTLAND, OR	1520	7674	8481	2331	5474	5447	989	5330	5906	5715	3888				
SAN FRANCISCO	1882	7056	7863	2091	4856	4829	371	4712	5288	5097	3270	652			
SAN JUAN	6153	2982	3789	5721	1766	1121	3975	1557	1399	1252	1036	4924	4306		
SEATTLE	1420	7830	8637	2409	5830	5603	1144	5486	6062	5871	4044	362	807	5080	
TAMPA	6376	3390	4116	5944	746	755	4198	472	1402	1201	1259	5147	4529	1249	5303

(continued)

FIGURE 1.1 (Continued)

Major Waterways and Ports in the United States

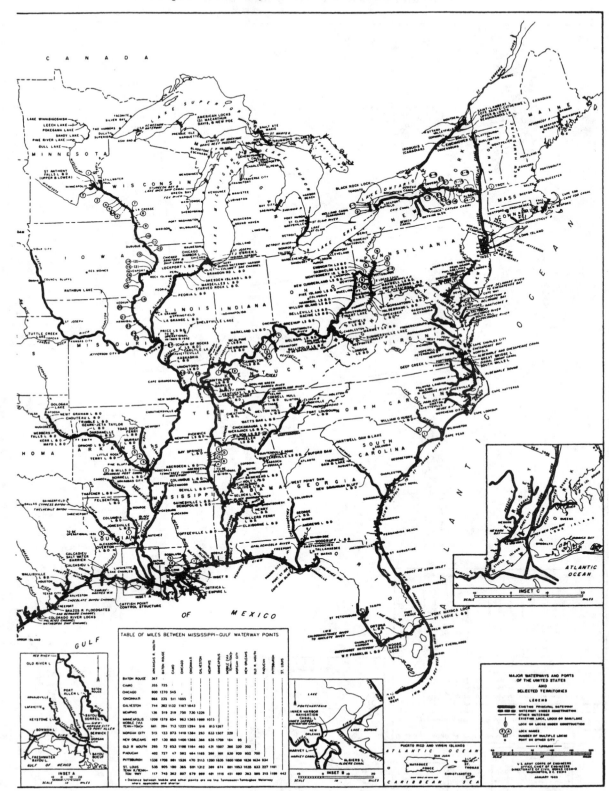

Source: *Waterborne Commerce of the United States: Part 5 — National Summaries,* Department of the Army Corps of Engineers, Water Resources Support Center, New Orleans, LA, 1997

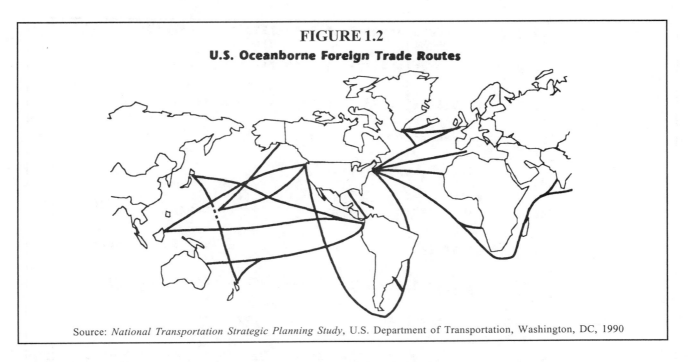

FIGURE 1.2
U.S. Oceanborne Foreign Trade Routes

Source: *National Transportation Strategic Planning Study*, U.S. Department of Transportation, Washington, DC, 1990

was in much better condition. The federal government took full control of almost all shipping operations under the War Shipping Administration. Between 1942 and 1945, 5,592 merchant ships were built, half of which were the mass-produced, cheaply made Liberty ships, often derisively referred to as "tin cans." These new ships, along with those purchased, captured, and acquired from private owners, were instrumental in securing an Allied victory.

After the war ended, the War Shipping Administration was dissolved and merchant fleets returned to private control. The government sold off excess ships for a total of almost $2 billion, while retaining some vessels in reserve fleets for emergency use. These reserve fleets were called into action in both the Korean and Vietnam wars.

THE MARITIME ADMINISTRATION (MARAD)

In 1950, the Maritime Commission was disbanded and replaced with the Federal Maritime Board and the Maritime Administration (MARAD) under the U.S. Department of Commerce. The Maritime Administration performs many functions. It maintains the National Defense Reserve Fleet, administers government subsidies to ship builders and operators, promotes and provides technical assistance for the development of port facilities and intermodal transportation systems, and operates the U.S. Merchant Marine Academy at Kings Point, New York.

TODAY'S WATERBORNE TRANSPORTATION SYSTEM

Ports and Harbors

The nation's port system consists of two basic parts: harbor works and port facilities. By definition, *harbors* provide ships and boats shelter from wind, high waves, and storms. The U.S. Army's Corps of Engineers currently maintains 757 commercial harbors, most of which are located on the nation's four major coastlines — Atlantic, Gulf, Pacific, and Great Lakes. *Ports*, on the other hand, allow the loading and unloading of both freight and passengers. Not all harbors have port facilities. Federal policy has generally supported the growth of the nation's public ports. While Congress has declared that every town and city located on federally improved harbors and waterways should have at least one public terminal for shipping, port development has traditionally relied on local and private initiative.

The United States has the world's largest port system. According to the Corps of Engineers, there are 4,990 ports and other ship facilities. There are 3,179

TABLE 1.3

Merchant Fleets of the World

OCEANGOING SELF-PROPELLED VESSELS OF 1,000 TONS AND ABOVE

AS OF JANUARY 1, 1999
(Tonnages in Thousands)

FLAG OF REGISTRY	TOTAL NO. OF SHIPS	TOTAL GRT TONS	TOTAL DWT TONS	TANKER NO. OF SHIPS	TANKER GRT TONS	TANKER DWT TONS	DRY BULK NO. OF SHIPS	DRY BULK GRT TONS	DRY BULK DWT TONS	CONTAINERSHIP NO. OF SHIPS	CONTAINERSHIP GRT TONS	CONTAINERSHIP DWT TONS	ROLL-ON-ROLL-OFF NO. OF SHIPS	ROLL-ON-ROLL-OFF GRT TONS	ROLL-ON-ROLL-OFF DWT TONS	CRUISE/PASSENGER NO. OF SHIPS	CRUISE/PASSENGER GRT TONS	CRUISE/PASSENGER DWT TONS	OTHER** NO. OF SHIPS	OTHER** GRT TONS	OTHER** DWT TONS
ALL COUNTRIES	27,825	489,300	755,435	6,781	182,147	317,337	5,726	158,096	277,242	2,382	53,569	61,237	1,432	25,763	13,467	283	6,659	1,172	11,224	63,865	84,604
UNITED STATES (Privately-Owned)	261	9,544	13,213	126	4,698	8,403	15	350	604	87	3,026	3,028	26	917	518	1	20	7	26	533	655
UNITED STATES (Govt. Owned)	189	2,702	3,528	28	491	866	.	.	.	4	71	70	32	697	718	11	147	109	114	1,296	1,745
PANAMA	4,485	95,844	145,769	985	27,396	47,516	1,302	40,474	70,880	475	11,910	13,303	241	6,394	2,572	43	1,274	202	1,439	8,396	11,196
LIBERIA	1,644	60,462	97,232	698	32,820	57,859	453	18,860	29,932	181	4,421	5,087	57	1,869	731	38	1,753	206	217	2,738	3,618
GREECE	737	24,595	44,072	262	13,398	25,516	307	8,976	16,093	47	1,297	1,405	18	131	97	17	171	51	86	622	909
BAHAMAS	1,042	26,301	40,944	249	12,952	23,670	158	4,962	8,691	50	989	1,044	60	1,092	851	57	1,308	250	468	4,978	6,638
MALTA	1,312	23,712	39,311	352	10,294	18,758	368	8,605	14,711	45	685	774	57	616	365	3	27	6	487	3,484	4,697
CYPRUS	1,431	23,068	36,059	179	4,308	7,386	478	11,210	19,423	122	2,335	2,780	30	349	219	9	90	29	613	4,776	6,222
SINGAPORE	879	19,884	31,436	384	9,592	16,690	134	4,616	8,512	161	3,100	3,622	35	1,152	481				165	1,514	2,130
NORWAY (NIS)	655	19,420	30,373	289	11,134	19,642	105	3,930	6,994	5	96	119	73	1,902	1,037	12	550	61	171	1,808	2,519
CHINA, PEOPLE'S REPUBLIC OF	1,476	14,845	22,342	248	2,071	3,251	338	8,659	15,115	95	1,357	1,652	19	218	218	3	135	24	773	4,531	6,177
JAPAN	698	22,342	12,278	68	182	280	209	5,651	9,736	29	690	873	124	1,351	694	6	7	2	88	314	1,754
PHILIPPINES	534	7,826	19,694	96	1,152	1,968	172	5,462	9,736	11	187	221	42	599	329	1	7	2	203	1,248	3,506
SAINT VINCENT & THE GRENADINES	784	13,745	10,507	43	3,785	7,045	142	3,146	5,462	28	187	221	39	448	316	2	6	.	477	2,677	3,506
MARSHALL ISLANDS	112	6,342	10,901	97	2,936	5,110	41	1,555	2,809	20	871	937	3	67	30	.	.	.	5	65	80
INDIA	289	6,293	10,586	9	346	642	124	4,190	4,759	40	914	1,024	3	127	43	2	9	2	62	448	607
HONG KONG, CHINA	191	6,067	10,190	73	583	1,039	109	3,942	7,785	13	108	142	19	242	177	2	32	5	30	490	696
TURKEY	518	5,767	9,556	19	178	272	167	3,942	6,844				15	192	97				244	882	1,351
GERMANY	514	7,400	9,243	17	901	1,554	54	2,346	4,344	293	6,280	7,978	11	2	1	9	550	15	185	717	891
CHINA, REPUBLIC OF (TAIWAN)	184	5,305	8,342	266	901	2,235	54	1,155	1,700	75	1,919	2,237	1	71	46	3	4	.	37	138	206
RUSSIA	1,446	6,732	8,244	266	1,549	2,235	113	2,933	2,933	24	268	299	11	425	156	9	32	15	1,025	3,658	3,951
KOREA (SOUTH)	427	5,098	7,931	106	483	829	105	2,933	5,305	45	808	944	11	105	55	3	4	.	157	444	695
BERMUDA	98	4,776	7,846	33	2,728	4,758	20	1,172	2,248	19	595	589	62	1,237	727	4	52	12	17	179	196
ITALY	352	5,569	7,741	193	2,242	3,515	33	1,525	2,867	14	377	393	62	1,237	39	2	8	1	139	157	227
MALAYSIA	370	5,014	7,338	112	2,187	3,024	58	1,447	2,545	48	667	817	11	76	39	.	.	.	32	629	911
BRAZIL	168	4,101	6,894	76	1,877	3,171	45	1,789	3,179	6	134	166	9	187	150	.	.	.	21	168	228
ISLE OF MAN	149	4,101	6,756	72	2,496	4,409	22	810	1,494	21	398	474	13	197	117	.	.	.	160	199	261
DENMARK (DIS)	309	4,878	6,654	66	1,289	2,182	13	521	967	61	2,478	2,834	9	134	91	.	.	.	47	457	580
IRAN	121	3,207	5,637	24	1,624	3,141	45	994	1,676	3	10	12	11	3	5	.	.	.	12	576	803
FRENCH ANTARCTIC TERRITORY	73	2,589	4,413	35	1,621	3,088	1	17	27	11	409	462	11	112	82	.	.	.	12	96	140
KUWAIT	46	2,360	3,837	28	1,939	3,341	4	87	123	5	182	191	.	.	.	1	348	43	12	222	278
NETHERLANDS	411	3,387	3,814	59	441	685	4	358	577	39	1,249	1,336	12	125	75	1	10	3	290	1,136	1,552
INDONESIA	491	2,310	3,497	123	817	1,297	24	294	473	12	86	111	13	54	49	.	.	.	318	984	1,460
ANTIGUA & BARBUDA	414	2,414	3,145	10	28	42	20	294	473	93	1,060	1,346	18	86	63	.	.	.	273	947	1,220
THAILAND	285	1,848	2,970	89	367	661	38	501	836	12	119	160	8	133	36	1	5	1	145	153	1,311
NORWAY	124	1,853	2,952	39	197	337	6	15	19	2	15	17	8	80	44	.	.	.	71	153	149
ROMANIA	190	1,950	2,904	8	350	623	38	846	1,378	6	51	54	2	4	5	.	.	.	133	813	1,129
BELIZE	414	1,719	2,584	64	621	1,051	24	247	422	25	998	1,088	19	350	147	10	358	56	318	1,067	1,460
UNITED KINGDOM	140	2,459	2,506	55	710	740	4	44	69	4	114	128	3	32	30	27	3	1	27	83	95
AUSTRALIA	52	1,775	2,418	15	63	95	27	901	1,499	1	14	18	9	43	37	2	2	.	64	15	21
EGYPT	113	1,216	1,935	16	212	368	22	613	1,054	1	99	114	10	141	63	4	4	.	11	332	458
FRANCE	52	1,235	1,906	25	881	1,570	1	2	.	4	99	.	6	15	7	1	.	.	11	62	156
POLAND	83	1,182	1,889	2	13	19	51	1,091	1,808	.	.	.	.	.	.	.	.	.	38	230	54
VANUATU	167	1,356	1,809	64	112	160	30	734	1,253	12	119	160	6	279	99	2	5	.	35	242	298
SWEDEN	73	2,124	1,612	18	534	873	6	25	32	.	.	.	53	1,324	689	.	.	.	39	285	215
CAYMAN ISLANDS	98	1,057	1,549	11	215	358	12	455	813	2	15	17	7	43	23	.	.	.	210	227	352
BULGARIA	264	1,058	1,495	22	151	267	35	546	855	6	56	67	7	77	61	.	.	.	39	227	299
UKRAINE	60	1,331	1,456	24	63	95	10	207	342	7	32	28	11	102	68	8	1	.	210	832	940
SAUDI ARABIA	123	1,152	1,357	30	344	593	1	12	20	7	222	217	9	276	253	1	94	22	19	299	373
PORTUGAL	63	66	1,232	5	422	703	14	187	333	4	21	26	5	32	7	1	6	2	70	203	277
CROATIA	63	792	1,232	5	9	12	14	187	333	5	82	98	2	7	.	.	.	.	29	173	225
MEXICO	46	791	1,164	38	656	1,004	21	516	889	4	124	147	.	.	.	1	7	6	3	4	8

Source: *Merchant Fleets of the World*, U.S. Department of Transportation, Maritime Administration, Washington, DC 1998

8

FIGURE 1.3
A General Cargo Vessel

Source: *Maritime Industry: Cargo Preference Laws — Estimated Costs and Effects*, U.S. General Accounting Office, Washington, DC, 1994

major U.S. seaport berths, and 1,811 river berths located in 21 states on the U.S. inland waterway system. The East Coast maintains 34.5 percent of the U.S. seaport berths, followed by the Gulf Coast with 24.9 percent and the West Coast with 24.6 percent. The Great Lakes have 15.9 percent of the berths. (See Table 1.1.)

Naturally, the states involved to the greatest degree in waterborne commerce are those located on major waterways. Table 1.2 shows the waterborne commerce of the various states in 1997. Louisiana and Texas led the 50 states in the amount of waterborne commerce, followed by California, Ohio, Florida, Pennsylvania, Washington, Illinois, and New York.

Larger U.S. Seaports

Global trade is expanding, and every major port in the country is spending or proposing to spend large amounts of money to attract more cargo. Nationwide, ports are expected to spend a record $6.5 billion between 1997 and 2001 on expansion and infrastruc-

ture projects, according to the American Association of Port Authorities. (In the previous 50 years, a total of $16 billion was spent on the nation's ports.) The funds will be spent on modern berths, huge cranes, rail lines, and roads to handle the post-Panamax vessels — 1,000-foot cargo ships that require harbors at least 50 feet deep. (They are called post-Panamax vessels because they are too large to pass through the Panama Canal.) Some of the port cities planning expansion include

- New Orleans, Louisiana — Consultants have recommended a $1 billion Millennium Port complex on the Mississippi River to accommodate an expected sixfold increase in container cargo through 2030.

- Savannah, Georgia — A $70 million container berth with two enormous cranes was recently completed, and port officials plan to deepen the Savannah River to 48 feet to accommodate large container ships. Moreover, a proposed $20 million, 150-acre rail yard would allow four trains to be loaded each day.

FIGURE 1.4
A Bulk Carrier Vessel

FIGURE 1.5
A Tanker

Source of both figures: *Maritime Industry: Cargo Preference Laws — Estimated Costs and Effects*, U.S. General Accounting Office, Washington, DC, 1994

- New York and New Jersey — The Port of New York and New Jersey, the largest port in the Eastern United States, plans to start a $621 million project to deepen a major channel to 45 feet from its current 40 feet.

- Houston, Texas — A 720-acre Bayport container complex is planned for completion by 2001.

- Texas City, Texas — A $300 million terminal to be built on 375 acres has been proposed.

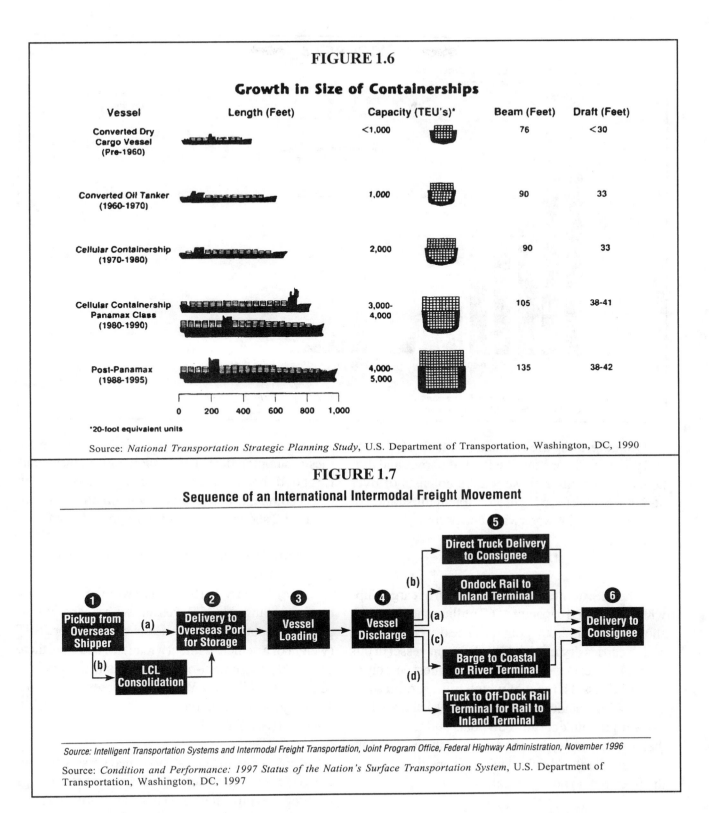

FIGURE 1.6

Growth in Size of Containerships

Vessel	Length (Feet)	Capacity (TEU's)*		Beam (Feet)	Draft (Feet)
Converted Dry Cargo Vessel (Pre-1960)		<1,000		76	<30
Converted Oil Tanker (1960-1970)		1,000		90	33
Cellular Containership (1970-1980)		2,000		90	33
Cellular Containership Panamax Class (1980-1990)		3,000-4,000		105	38-41
Post-Panamax (1988-1995)		4,000-5,000		135	38-42

0   200   400   600   800   1,000

*20-foot equivalent units

Source: *National Transportation Strategic Planning Study*, U.S. Department of Transportation, Washington, DC, 1990

FIGURE 1.7

Sequence of an International Intermodal Freight Movement

1 Pickup from Overseas Shipper — (a) → **2** Delivery to Overseas Port for Storage → **3** Vessel Loading → **4** Vessel Discharge

(b) → **1** Pickup from Overseas Shipper → LCL Consolidation

5 Direct Truck Delivery to Consignee

(b) Ondock Rail to Inland Terminal

(a) **6** Delivery to Consignee

(c) Barge to Coastal or River Terminal

(d) Truck to Off-Dock Rail Terminal for Rail to Inland Terminal

Source: Intelligent Transportation Systems and Intermodal Freight Transportation, Joint Program Office, Federal Highway Administration, November 1996

Source: *Condition and Performance: 1997 Status of the Nation's Surface Transportation System*, U.S. Department of Transportation, Washington, DC, 1997

- Long Beach, California — The Port of Long Beach, the largest container port in the United States, plans to spend about $850 million on expansion by 2001. In addition, the federal government is being asked to contribute up to $20 million to deepen the harbor entrance to more than 70 feet.

Inland Waterways

The United States has a total of approximately 11,703 miles of commercially navigable inland waterways. More than half are on the Mississippi River system and its tributaries (6,651 miles), with most of the

11

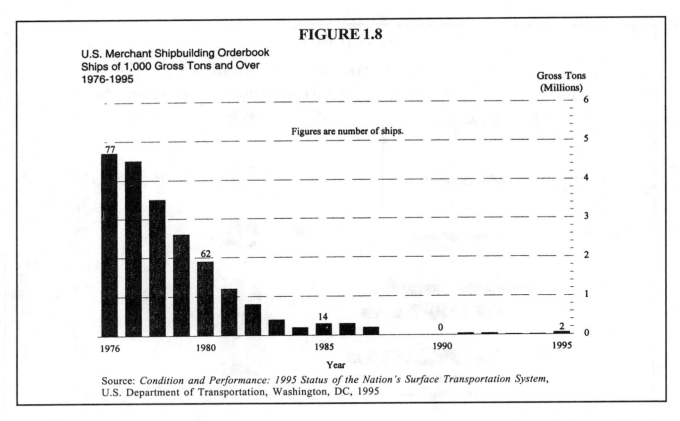

FIGURE 1.8

U.S. Merchant Shipbuilding Orderbook
Ships of 1,000 Gross Tons and Over
1976-1995

Gross Tons (Millions)

Figures are number of ships.

77

62

14

0

2

1976   1980   1985   1990   1995

Year

Source: *Condition and Performance: 1995 Status of the Nation's Surface Transportation System,*
U.S. Department of Transportation, Washington, DC, 1995

rest running along the coasts of the Gulf of Mexico and the Atlantic ocean. The fleet of barges and tugboats that navigate these waters consists of over 36,000 vessels. (See Figure 1.1 for an.illustration of the nation's major waterways and ports.)

Domestic Fleet

The U.S. domestic fleet is made up of cargo ships with a combined capacity of 67 million short tons. (A short ton equals 2,000 pounds.) The dry cargo barge, which carries dry materials, is the main vessel in this fleet. The Great Lakes fleet consists almost entirely of dry bulk vessels, most of which transport ores and grains. Also included in the fleet are tank barges, which carry liquid bulk cargo. Towboats and tugboats, as their names imply, push and pull dumb vessels (non-self-propelled) and rafts. They are considered part of the fleet, but do not carry cargo.

Deep-Sea Shipping

The nation's deep-sea water transportation system is made up of privately owned merchant ships, commonly termed the merchant marine deep draft fleet.

It consists of both the foreign trade fleet and the domestic shipping fleet. The foreign trade industry carries goods between U.S. and foreign ports and is in direct competition with all other international fleets. Figure 1.2 shows the primary foreign trade routes.

A Study of the Nation's Merchant Fleet

As of January 1, 1999, there were 281 privately owned oceangoing U.S. vessels with a carrying capacity of about 13.2 million deadweight tons, or DWT (weight of a vehicle without a load). In addition, there were 189 government-owned vessels with a total capacity of 3.5 million DWT. Each of these ships weighs 1,000 gross tons or more. (A gross ton is 2,240 pounds.) (See Table 1.3.)

However, many privately owned vessels belonging to U.S. citizens or corporations, carry foreign flags — "flags of convenience." These ships are registered in foreign countries such as the Bahamas, Honduras, Liberia, the Marshall Islands, or Panama because their laws are less restrictive, and the ships generally cannot be commandeered by the U.S. government during national emergencies.

Eighty percent of the privately owned vessels are actively engaged in commerce. Most of the federally owned vessels are in long-term storage, held in MARAD custody in case they are needed during a national emergency.

U.S.-flag oceangoing vessels play a small role in carrying the nation's international commerce. The United States ranks twenty-sixth, worldwide, in the total number of ships in its fleet, but eleventh in total DWT. By vessel type, the United States ranks thir-

TABLE 1.4
TOTAL LARGE MERCHANT VESSELS UNDER CONTRACT IN PRIVATE U.S. SHIPYARDS, As of July 1, 1998

NEW CONSTRUCTION[4]

	Total	Intermodal[1]	Freighters	Tankers	LNG	Dry Bulk[2]	Tug/Barge[3]
Government	0	0	0	0	0	0	0
Private	8	0	0	8	0	0	0
TOTAL	8	0	0	8	0	0	0

CONVERSIONS[4]

None

SHIPS COMPLETED[4]
(October 1, 1997 - July 1, 1998)

	Total	Intermodal[1]	Freighters	Tankers	LNG	Dry Bulk[2]	Tug/Barge[3]
Private	2	1	0	1	0	0	0

CONVERSIONS

	Total	Intermodal	Freighters	Tankers	LNG	Dry Bulk	Tug/Barge
Private	0	0	0	0	0	0	0

SHIP CONSTRUCTION CONTRACTS AWARDED DURING FISCAL YEAR 1998 (see Table 1.5 for full description)

Date	No. of Ships	Owner	Shipyard	Dwt.	Total Cost[5]	Scheduled Delivery Date
None						

[1]Includes the following types: RO/RO, LASH, Seabee, Containership, Partial Containership.
[2]Includes OBOs and Ore Carriers.
[3]Includes Tanker Barges.
[4]In commercial shipyards with facilities to build vessels 400 feet minimum length.
[5]Millions of dollars estimated.

KEY TO SHIP TYPES

B = Bulk	DB = Dry Bulk	OBO = Oil/Bulk/Ore
C = Cargo	F = Freighter	PT = Product Tanker
Ch = Chemical Carrier	I = Incinerator Ship	R = Research
Cn = Containership	L = Lighter-Aboard Ship (LASH)	RO/RO = Roll-on/Roll-off
Cn-p = Partial Containership	LB = Liquid Bulk Ship	T = Tanker
CT = Crude Tanker	LNG = Liquid Natural Gas	TB = Tug Barge
D = Dredge	O = Ore Carrier	TKB = Tanker Barge

KEY TO AIDS

CCF = Capital Construction Fund
CS = Construction Subsidy
MG = Mortgage Guarantee (Title XI)

Source: *U.S. Merchant Marine Data Sheet*, U.S. Department of Transportation, Maritime Administration, Washington, DC, 1998

TABLE 1.5

SHIP CONSTRUCTION CONTRACTS[1]

July 1, 1998

No.	Type (Propulsion)	Total Dwt.	Cost[2]	Government Participation	Owner	Scheduled Delivery Date
NEWPORT NEWS SHIPBUILDING						
5	PT(D)*	230,100	213.2	MG	Hvide Marine	1999

NOTE: Hvide Marine purchased ownership of tankers from Newport News after contract renegotiation with Eletson and Hvide Van Ommeren.

No.	Type (Propulsion)	Total Dwt.	Cost[2]	Government Participation	Owner	Scheduled Delivery Date
ALABAMA SHIPYARD						
1	Ch(D)*	16,000	26.7	MG	Dannebrog Rederi AS	1998
AVONDALE INDUSTRIES						
2	CT(D)*	250,000	332.0	CCF	Arco Marine	2000

CONVERSIONS

None

| GRAND TOTAL 8 | | 496,100 | 571.9 | | | |

*(S=Steam; D=Diesel; C=Coal Fired)
[1] In commercial shipyards with facilities to build vessel 400 feet minimum length.
[2] Millions of dollars estimated.
[3] Private contract--cost not available.

Source: *U.S. Merchant Marine Data Sheet*, U.S. Department of Transportation, Maritime Administration, Washington, DC, 1998

teenth in the number of tankers, ninth in tanker DWT, eighth in number of container ships, and sixth in containership DWT. (See Table 1.3.)

The domestic deep-sea fleet travels offshore along the nation's coasts, as well as to Alaska, Hawaii, Guam, Puerto Rico, Wake and Midway Islands, and the Virgin Islands. As of 1998, 122 ships operated in domestic ocean trade. Tankers carrying American petroleum products and coal make up the bulk of the domestic fleet. Less cargo is being hauled by the domestic ocean trades, due to the decline in production and shipments of crude oil from the Alaska North Slope. In 1997, the 263 million tons that moved in the domestic ocean trades were approximately 20 percent less than in 1988.

Types of Ships

The ocean transportation system operations are financed almost entirely from freight revenues. There are three categories of service: general cargo, dry bulk, and liquid bulk. General cargo, primarily finished products, is usually carried on regularly scheduled ocean freighters. (Figure 1.3). Dry bulk cargoes, such as grain, coal, and fertilizer, are shipped in specialized vessels under contract (Figure 1.4). Liquid bulk cargo, mainly petroleum products, are handled only by tankers and tank barge fleets (Figure 1.5). Most of the ocean-going ships are tankers.

Over the years, freight ships have grown dramatically in size, and so has their carrying capacity. Figure 1.6 illustrates the growth in the size and capacity of the nation's ocean-going ships over the past 35 years. Tankers that transport oil illustrate the increase in the size of ships. Oil tankers are bigger than ever before. In 1945, the largest tanker held 16,500 tons of oil; today the supertankers carry more than 550,000 tons. The age and vessel size of all ocean-going fleets vary considerably by vessel type, but all the newer ships are larger and more fuel-efficient and have smaller crews.

The Intermodal Process

The United States developed intermodal shipping, which plans and executes the movement of goods from point of departure to final destination, using containerized vessels, terminals, technology, and inland delivery systems. (See Figure 1.7.) This process not only reduces transportation and inventory costs, but reduces damage and theft as well.

Ships carry cargo in pre-loaded, standard-size containers, making loading and unloading faster and easier, and enabling more efficient transportation of cargo to and from the port area. One example of the container ship is the Roll-on/Roll-off ship, or RO/RO. Vehicles such as trucks and trailers that carry cargo can drive directly on and off a RO/RO ship. Most experts expect intermodal ships to continue to grow in size and DWT capacity.

A Tiny Part of the World's Ocean-Going Fleet

The American merchant fleet plays a very minor role in international shipping. By 1998, the total number of ocean-going ships weighing 1,000 tons and more registered as part of the U.S. merchant fleet had dropped to 470 ships (281 privately owned and 189 government-owned), down from 1,550 in 1970 and 2,926 in 1960. In 1998, the world fleet consisted of 27,825 ships. The U.S. fleet made up less than 2 percent of this figure, down from 8 percent in 1970 and 17 percent in 1960. (See Table 1.3.)

When compared to other nations' merchant fleets, the United States is at a distinct disadvantage for several reasons. Most international operators use lower-cost foreign shipyards for maintenance and repairs. They also save on fuel costs because they usually use more modern, efficient ships. Foreign operators can use smaller crews than the U.S. collective bargaining and safety requirements allow. Furthermore, they can employ low-priced labor from Third World nations. Total employment expenditures per day on a foreign ship with a non-U.S. crew are only 15 to 20 percent of the total cost for crew wages on an American ship of the same size and number of crew members.

TABLE 1.6

TOTAL WATERBORNE COMMERCE OF THE U.S., 1958-1997
(in short tons of 2000 pounds)

Year	Total	Foreign	Domestic
1958	1,004,515,776	308,850,798	695,664,978
1959	1,052,402,102	325,669,939	726,732,163
1960	1,099,850,431	339,277,275	760,573,156
1961	1,062,155,182	329,329,818	732,825,364
1962	1,129,404,375	358,599,030	770,805,345
1963	1,173,766,964	385,658,999	788,107,965
1964	1,238,093,573	421,925,133	816,168,440
1965	1,272,896,243	443,726,809	829,169,434
1966	1,334,116,078	471,391,083	862,724,995
1967	1,336,606,078	465,972,238	870,633,840
1968	1,395,839,450	507,950,002	887,889,448
1969	1,448,711,541	521,312,362	927,399,179
1970	1,531,696,507	580,969,133	950,727,374
1971	1,512,583,690	565,985,584	946,598,106
1972	1,616,792,605	629,980,844	986,811,761
1973	1,761,552,010	767,393,903	994,158,107
1974	1,746,788,544	764,088,905	982,699,639
1975	1,695,034,366	748,707,407	946,326,959
1976	1,835,006,819	855,963,909	979,042,910
1977	1,908,223,619	935,256,813	972,966,806
1978	2,021,349,754	946,057,889	1,075,291,865
1979	2,073,757,628	993,444,963	1,080,312,665
1980	1,998,887,402	921,404,000	1,077,483,402
1981	1,941,558,947	887,102,150	1,054,456,797
1982	1,776,740,579	819,730,983	957,009,596
1983	1,707,661,011	751,140,194	956,520,817
1984	1,836,020,619	803,338,133	1,032,682,486
1985	1,788,434,822	774,323,283	1,014,111,539
1986	1,874,416,280	837,223,503	1,037,192,777
1987	1,967,458,261	890,980,045	1,076,478,216
1988	2,087,993,484	976,220,985	1,111,772,499
1989	2,140,442,372	1,037,910,213	1,102,532,159
1990	2,163,854,373	1,041,555,740	1,122,298,633
1991	2,092,108,462	1,013,557,036	1,078,551,426
1992	2,132,095,154	1,037,466,130	1,094,629,024
1993	2,128,221,188	1,060,041,217	1,068,179,971
1994	2,214,754,086	1,115,742,828	1,099,011,258
1995	2,240,393,059	1,147,357,782	1,093,035,277
1996	2,284,065,249	1,183,386,621	*1,100,678,628
1997	2,333,142,046	1,220,615,132	1,112,526,914

*Beginning in 1996, fish was excluded for internal and intraport domestic traffic.

Source: *Waterborne Commerce of the United States: Part 5 — National Summaries,* Department of the Army Corps of Engineers, Water Resources Support Center, New Orleans, LA, 1997

THE SHIPBUILDING INDUSTRY — NEW HOPE

In the twentieth century, the U.S. fleet has experienced significant growth only during the World Wars. After World War II, new shipbuilding decreased sharply as naval ship orders declined. As a result of the suspension of federal construction assistance, the U.S. shipbuilding industry's commercial orderbook fell from 77 vessels in the mid-1970s to zero by 1990. This was the lowest activity level for the industry since before World War II. (See Figure 1.8.)

Additionally, a global economic recession during the 1980s and the excess inventory of ships, particularly oil tankers, contributed to a continuing decline of the shipping industry worldwide. Major shipbuilders in Europe and Japan also faced serious drops in demand but were able to turn to their governments for support. As a result, Japan and Korea are now the leading merchant ship builders, with a combined 64 percent share based on DWT. In 1998, the United States ranked twenty-sixth in terms of its orderbook.

U.S. shipyards delivered only one privately owned oceangoing vessel of 1,000 gross tons or larger in the fiscal years 1988-1993. However, between October 1997 and July 1998, two privately owned vessels —one intermodal-type vessel and one tanker — were delivered. As of July 1, 1998, there were eight privately owned commercial ships (tankers) under construction or on order. (See Table 1.4.) One ship was delivered in 1998, five are scheduled for delivery in 1999, and two are projected to be delivered in 2000. (See Table 1.5.)

National Shipbuilding and Shipyard Conversion Act

In 1993, the National Shipbuilding and Shipyard Conversion Act (PL 103-160) was passed, and U.S. shipyards began to compete once again in the domestic and foreign commercial shipbuilding markets. The National Shipbuilding and Shipyard Conversion Act includes a five-point revitalization plan:

- Extended government guarantees to finance vessels purchased in U.S. shipyards by foreign owners through the existing domestic loan guarantee program (Title XI).

- Efforts to ensure fair international competition.

- Improvement of commercial competitiveness.

- Elimination of unnecessary government regulation.

- Assistance in international marketing.

The act also funded research and development projects under MARITECH, which focuses on mar-

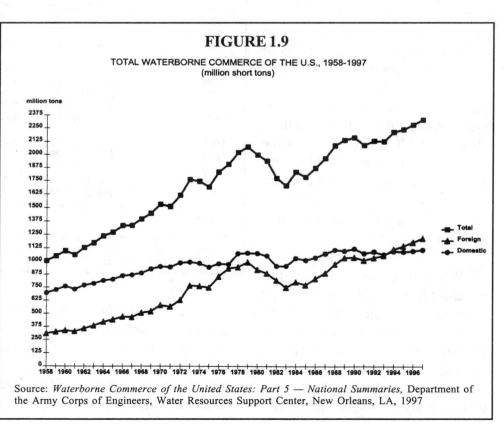

FIGURE 1.9

TOTAL WATERBORNE COMMERCE OF THE U.S., 1958-1997
(million short tons)

Source: *Waterborne Commerce of the United States: Part 5 — National Summaries,* Department of the Army Corps of Engineers, Water Resources Support Center, New Orleans, LA, 1997

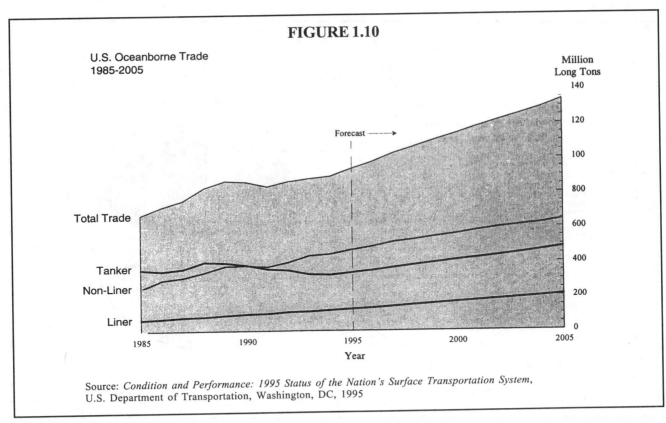

FIGURE 1.10

U.S. Oceanborne Trade
1985-2005

Million
Long Tons

Source: *Condition and Performance: 1995 Status of the Nation's Surface Transportation System*, U.S. Department of Transportation, Washington, DC, 1995

ket penetration and longer-term technology development. (MARITECH stood for "maritime technology" when the program was in its development. However, today it is used by itself.) The original MARITECH program ended in 1999, and MARITECH ASE (advanced shipbuilding enterprise) took its place.

The Title XI loan guarantee program allows MARAD to guarantee private sector debt financing, up to 87.5 percent of the cost of the vessel. The construction or reconstruction will be done in U.S. shipyards and includes both U.S.-flag vessels and foreign-flag vessels. The program extends to U.S. shipyard modernization and improvement projects.

A Dilemma

The merchant marine has been faced with a dilemma. Under Section 27 of the Merchant Marine Act of 1920, it is not permitted to buy less expensive foreign-made ships. By law, all waterborne commerce between ports throughout the United States and its territories must be carried on ships built and registered in this country and must be owned by U.S. citizens.

Realizing the extent of the problem facing the merchant marine, in 1996, the government adopted a ten-year Maritime Security Program (MSP). The program gives limited assistance to the U.S. merchant marine involved in U.S.-foreign commerce in an effort to help that industry become more competitive internationally. The Clinton Administration ordered an annual appropriation of $100 million to maintain a U.S.-flag presence in international trade and a U.S. shipbuilding capability.

In return, participating carriers would be required to enroll in an Emergency Preparedness Program to provide intermodal sealift support (a system for transporting persons or cargo by ship, especially in an emergency) in time of war or national crisis. Vessel owners would be required to provide ships, intermodal equipment, terminal facilities, and management services. This partnership would provide the government with cost-effective sealift capability, using commercial vessels to complement U. S. Department of Defense sealift programs.

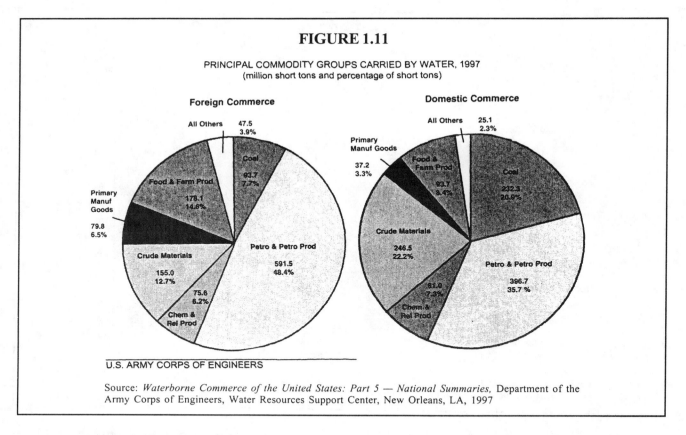

FIGURE 1.11

PRINCIPAL COMMODITY GROUPS CARRIED BY WATER, 1997
(million short tons and percentage of short tons)

Foreign Commerce

All Others 47.5 3.9%
Coal 93.7 7.7%
Food & Farm Prod 178.1 14.6%
Primary Manuf Goods 79.8 6.5%
Petro & Petro Prod 591.5 48.4%
Crude Materials 155.0 12.7%
Chem & Rel Prod 75.6 6.2%

Domestic Commerce

All Others 25.1 2.3%
Primary Manuf Goods 37.2 3.3%
Food & Farm Prod 93.7 8.4%
Coal 232.3 20.9%
Crude Materials 246.5 22.2%
Petro & Petro Prod 396.7 35.7 %
Chem & Rel Prod 81.0 7.3%

U.S. ARMY CORPS OF ENGINEERS

Source: *Waterborne Commerce of the United States: Part 5 — National Summaries,* Department of the Army Corps of Engineers, Water Resources Support Center, New Orleans, LA, 1997

WATERBORNE COMMERCE — ON THE UPSWING

In 1955, America's ports were handling about 1 billion tons of freight. At the end of the 1970s, the total tonnage was just over 2 billion tons of cargo each year, divided almost equally between foreign and domestic commerce. In 1983, in the midst of a recession, total U.S. tonnage dropped to a low of 1.7 billion tons and then rose again in 1990 to 2.16 billion tons. By 1997, tonnage rose to 2.3 billion tons, with the cargo fairly evenly divided between domestic and foreign. (See Table 1.6 and Figure 1.9.)

In 1994, experts projected that U.S. oceanborne trade would grow at an average annual rate of 4.5 percent up to 2005. Because the demand for shipping capacity is largely a function of the volume of international oceanborne trade, the demand for shipping services is expected to increase. By 2005, U.S. oceanborne trade is projected to be over 130 million long tons. (A long ton is 2,240 pounds, the same as a gross ton — see above.) (See Figure 1.10.)

What Is Carried?

The advantage of shipping by water is that ships can hold large amounts of goods. It should not be surprising, then, that coal and oil account for over half of what is shipped both in domestic and foreign commerce. Food and farm products also account for a significant percentage, as do crude materials (raw products such as iron or copper ore). (See Figure 1.11.)

THE FUTURE

Water transportation services that are available today are provided by a combination of public (federal, state, and local) and private funds, with private money contributing the larger share. This shared funding will likely continue if the industry is to survive and grow. A large portion of the U.S. fleet is older and less efficient than many foreign fleets. Therefore, replacement vessels will be needed.

18

CHAPTER II

RAILROADS

While the ship was a major factor in the birth of the United States, the railroad played a dominant role in its growth and development. It contributed to westward expansion and allowed access to the land's vast resources. California was bound to the Union as a result of the physical and commercial ties provided by the railroad that opened the continent from ocean to ocean.

Railways offered some distinct advantages over canals, which had previously provided the major routes for inland transportation. They were cheaper to construct, offered faster service, and did not freeze in winter. By no means were railroads problem-free: timetables reflected more wishful thinking than actual times of arrivals and departures, breakdowns were frequent, and the lack of standard-gauge tracks (gauge is the distance between the rails of a track) could mean numerous transfers from line to line. Moreover, trains were dangerous. Soft roadbeds, broken rails, collapsed bridges, and almost nonexistent brakes led to frequent and often serious wrecks. Nonetheless, the technology was well-suited to the pioneering spirit and economic needs of a young and growing nation.

UNITING THE COUNTRY

In 1830, only twenty-three miles of railroad track existed in the United States. The advantages of rail transport were becoming obvious, however, and the industry experienced rapid growth. Congress designated the nation's railways as postal routes in 1838, and the postmaster general ordered them to be used for all reasonable transportation of the mail. Track mileage increased to 30,000 miles by 1860, and Chicago was the terminal for 11 major railroads.

Railroads affected the relationship between the northern and southern states. Most lines ran east-west, connecting the major cities and the seacoasts to the Mississippi River. Virtually all southern railroads served southern riverport cities, with almost no ties to the North. Different size track gauges, a problem throughout a nation that still had 12 different track sizes in 1860, was most apparent in the South. The inability to run southern trains on northern tracks (and vice-versa) further separated the two segments of the country. The railroads contributed to the Union victory during the Civil War (1865) by providing the North with a formidable means of transporting millions of men, arms, and supplies to strategic locations.

It Pays to Go West

Even during the Civil War, the federal government was looking toward California and the western territories. The government wanted to make sure that this rich land remained a part of the Union, even though it was separated from the central government by an entire continent. The solution was to connect West to East with thousands of miles of railroad tracks. This not only created a physical link to the West but also provided a means of developing its vast commercial potential. As an incentive to build railroads in that largely unsettled and sometimes hostile expanse between the Mississippi River and California, the government offered financial support, as well as land grants, to those who would build the railroads.

In 1862, Congress passed legislation to promote a transcontinental railway. The legislation granted the Central Pacific and the Union Pacific Railroads direct subsidies of

- $16,000 for each mile of track laid on smooth ground.

- $32,000 per mile through uneven regions.

- $48,000 per mile through mountainous regions.

- A substantial right-of-way on lands on either side of the tracks.

A virtual explosion of railroad building followed the Civil War. The dream of uniting the country by rail was realized when the tracks laid by the Union Pacific, building from the east, and the Central Pacific, building from the west, met at Promontory Point, Utah. The momentous occasion was celebrated by driving the Gold Spike uniting the two tracks on May 10, 1869. For their efforts, the two companies received between 10 and 20 square miles of public land for every mile of track.

The 1880s saw 166,000 miles of track completed, and, by 1893, five transcontinental railroads were transporting huge quantities of agricultural, forestry, and mining products along with settlers, adventurers, and businessmen. The railroad companies owned 12 percent of all the land west of the Mississippi — 130 million acres — received in land grants from state and federal governments.

Time Zones

With the development of improved tracks and equipment, timetables began to reflect reality. This led to service complications, for the railways had to contend with almost 100 local times observed in different parts of the country. In order to provide scheduling uniformity, the railroad established, on November 18, 1883, the four time zones that are still used today — Eastern, Central, Mountain, and Pacific. While these time standards quickly came into general use, it was not until the Uniform Time Act of 1918 that they became national law.

GOVERNMENT REGULATION

As the railroad industry flourished, so did its abuses. Excessive rates, internal price wars, fraudulent investment schemes, and scandalous behavior became so widespread that eventually the government and the public reacted. In response to public pressure, many states formed commissions to control rates. But while states were granted the right to regulate businesses within their own state boundaries, the Supreme Court ruled that they could not control rates on interstate commerce. This set the stage for controls at the federal level. In 1887, Congress passed the Act to Regulate Commerce, which resulted in the formation of the Interstate Commerce Commission (ICC). The Elkins Act (1903) and the Hepburn Act (1906) gave the ICC further authority to regulate rates. On January 1, 1996, the Surface Transportation Board superseded the ICC.

STEAM TO DIESEL — BUT NOT ELECTRICITY

In 1895, the nation's first electrified train service began on the Nantasket Branch of the New York, New Haven, and Hartford Railroad. The first mainline electrification was through the 3.6-mile Baltimore Tunnel of the Baltimore and Ohio Railroad in 1895. However, despite early inroads, electric locomotives have played a minor role in the nation's railways, in contrast to European railroads, which are almost completely electrified.

Steam remained the major source of locomotive power into the 1950s. In 1925, a diesel switch locomotive went into service for the Central Railroad of New Jersey. In 1934, the Chicago, Burlington, and Quincy Railroad put the first diesel locomotive into mainline service, and in 1940, the Santa Fe Railroad began using diesels in regular freight service.

FADING GLORY

Like the shipping industry, railroads could not maintain their monopoly on moving the people and products of an entire nation and were themselves faced with new competitive forms of transportation: the car, the truck, and the airplane.

Several factors contributed to the decline of the railroads. As is often the case, success led to excess. In 1916, 254,000 miles of railway line crisscrossed the nation. The supply of tracks and equipment had outstripped the demand for their use. Multiple lines served the same routes, reducing the market share for each operator.

The nature of the market itself was beginning to change. By the end of World War II (1945), the U.S. economy was shifting from manufacturing toward services and technology, reducing the requirement for large quantities of bulk commodities, the mainstay of the railroad's freight business. Industrial centers sprang up all across the South, Southwest, and West, so that the need for long-haul transport of commodities from the Northeast to the rest of the country was diminished. The further movement of industry from the central city into the suburbs made many railroad routes obsolete, and financing for new tracks was often unavailable.

Rail passenger revenue also suffered from a changing economy and population distribution. Seventy years ago, 3 out of every 4 Americans traveling in the United States took the train. Railroads recorded almost 34 billion revenue passenger-miles (one paid passenger traveling one mile) in 1929.

In the early 1900s, however, America began a romance with the automobile that, to date, shows no sign of waning. As early as 1939, airplanes accounted for 2 percent of total revenue passenger-miles. By the 1990s, that percentage exceeded 90 percent. Unable to compete and burdened by price regulations, the fortunes of the nation's railways declined dramatically. Tracks, equipment, and facilities deteriorated. Many lines went bankrupt.

CONRAIL

In June 1969, the mighty Penn-Central Transportation Company, formed by the merger of two Eastern railroad giants, the New York Central and the Pennsylvania Railroad, collapsed. The bankruptcy of the nation's largest railway system shook the financial world and brought the catastrophic condition of the Northeast rail system to the nation's attention.

Consequently, in an effort to revitalize the rail system of the Midwest and Northeast, Congress established the United States Railroad Association (USRA) under the Regional Rail Reorganization Act of 1973 (PL 93-236) to plan and finance the restructuring of the Penn-Central and seven smaller bankrupt railways in the region. The 3R Act, as amended by the Railroad Revitalization and Regulatory Reform (4R) Act of 1976 (PL 94-210), also created the Consolidated Rail Corporation, known as Conrail, which was to eventually become a "for profit" railroad. Conrail carried only freight, not passengers.

Conrail began operating on April 1, 1976, with a $2.1 billion congressional authorization to repair, upgrade, and replace track, equipment, and facilities. Later legislation added more monies for a total of $3.3 billion in federal operating subsidies. Conrail slashed staff, phased out unprofitable routes, rebuilt much of the deteriorating roadbeds and tracks, and used modern technology to help run the railroad more efficiently. By the time the company was sold to the public in 1987, it was profitable. In 1993, Conrail had 11,831 miles of track, 64,834 rail cars, and 24,728 employees.

The (Ronald) Reagan Administration wanted to sell Conrail in 1981 because it considered the railroad a drain on the public treasury. In 1987, the government sold its 85 percent interest in Conrail to private investors for $1.65 billion, a figure many financial observers considered far too low. Conrail's present and former employees own the remaining 15 percent.

In late 1996, Conrail agreed to a corporate takeover by CSX Corporation for $8.4 billion. Within a week, the Norfolk Southern Corporation increased the offer by bidding $9.15 billion for Conrail. By early 1997, CSX and Norfolk Southern agreed to divide Conrail equitably in the East. In 1997, the Surface Transportation Board adopted a schedule to consider the transaction, and under the operating plan approved in July 1998, CSX and Norfolk Southern began operating most Conrail lines and facilities on June 1, 1999. However, in much of New Jersey and portions of the Philadelphia and Detroit metropolitan areas, Conrail continues to control and to manage and operate some lines and facilities.

RAILROAD DEREGULATION — THE STAGGERS RAIL ACT OF 1980

Railroads have bemoaned federal regulation for decades, but their major complaint was that the Interstate Commerce Commission (ICC) regulation kept rates too low to permit a reasonable profit or to attract enough capital investment to allow the repair or replacement of aging railroad equipment.

At the same time that deregulation was taking place in the airline and trucking industries, Congress passed the Staggers Rail Act (PL 96-448) in 1980. This legislation permitted the railroads greater freedom in setting their rates, although, in many cases, they have to justify rate hikes. The railways may also contract with other shippers to offer special services at special rates, a practice previously prohibited.

Rail deregulation, however, was not as comprehensive as air or trucking deregulation, and the Federal Railroad Administration (FRA) still plays a significant role in monitoring the railroads. It approves mergers and abandonment of rail lines, establishes standards for evaluating the financial condition of railroads, performs evaluations of a railroad's financial condition, and resolves rate and service disputes between railroads and shippers.

TODAY'S FREIGHT SYSTEM

America's railroads are currently categorized into three types: Class I, regional, and local. As of 1997, Class I railroads were those with a reported annual operating revenue of $256.4 million or

TABLE 2.1

Industry Totals, by Type of Railroad, 1997

Railroad	Number	Miles Operated	Employees	Freight Revenue ($000)
Class I	9	121,670	177,981	$32,322,291
Regional	34	21,466	10,995	1,611,435
Local	507	28,149	11,741	1,415,730
Total	550	171,285	200,717	$35,349,456

FIGURE 2.1

FREIGHT REVENUE

1988   1997

■ East   □ West

(Amounts shown in thousands)

Year	United States	East	West
1929	$ 4,825,622	$ 2,948,430	$ 1,877,192
1939	3,251,096	2,000,183	1,250,913
1944	6,998,615	3,991,867	3,006,748
1947	7,041,185	4,114,802	2,926,383
1955	8,538,286	4,828,871	3,709,415
1960	8,025,423	4,361,581	3,663,842
1965	8,835,958	4,797,206	4,038,752
1970	10,921,813	5,834,402	5,087,411
1975	15,389,809	7,804,519	7,585,290
1980	26,349,565	12,186,170	14,163,395
1985	26,687,652	12,444,633	14,243,019
1988	27,091,508	12,119,467	14,972,041
1989	27,058,765	11,997,588	15,061,177
1990	27,470,520	12,132,224	15,338,296
1991	26,949,280	11,701,307	15,247,973
1992	27,507,607	11,882,595	15,625,012
1993	27,990,562	11,986,218	16,004,344
1994	29,930,893	12,724,535	17,206,358
1995	31,355,593	12,973,711	18,381,882
1996	31,888,529	13,147,213	18,741,316
1997	32,322,291	13,407,206	18,915,085

Source of table and figure: *Railroad Facts, 1998 Edition*, Association of American Railroads, Washington, DC, 1998

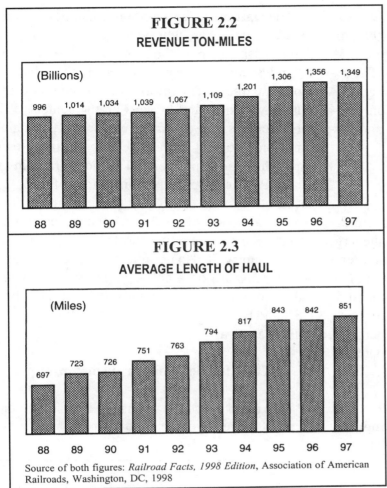

FIGURE 2.2
REVENUE TON-MILES

(Billions)

88	89	90	91	92	93	94	95	96	97
996	1,014	1,034	1,039	1,067	1,109	1,201	1,306	1,356	1,349

FIGURE 2.3
AVERAGE LENGTH OF HAUL

(Miles)

88	89	90	91	92	93	94	95	96	97
697	723	726	751	763	794	817	843	842	851

Source of both figures: *Railroad Facts, 1998 Edition*, Association of American Railroads, Washington, DC, 1998

since 1991, passing $32 billion in 1997. (See Figure 2.1 for the revenues from freight since 1929.)

American railroads handled an all-time high of 1.356 trillion-ton miles of freight traffic in 1996 and 1.349 trillion ton-miles in 1997. (Figure 2.2). The AAR attributes this gain to an increase in the average length of haul.

In 1997, the average length of haul hit an all-time high of over 850 miles (Figure 2.3), compared to 616 in 1980 and only 334 in 1929. Total tonnage shipped increased to 1.59 billion tons. Coal accounted for 44.5 percent of all railroad tonnage, chemicals and allied products (8.9 percent), and farm products (7.9 percent) made up much of the rest (Figure 2.4 and Table 2.2). The number of miles a train travels today is also much greater than 50 years ago.

Equipment

As anyone who has ever waited at a railroad crossing knows, a freight train can be very long. Those who amuse themselves by counting the number of cars on the train would have counted an average of 48 cars in 1929. The average number of cars grew steadily until 1985, when there were about 71 cars; in 1997, there was an average of 67 cars on a freight train. Today's average freight

above. Class I railroads (only) must report operating and financial data to the FRA. Table 2.1 shows that although the nine Class I railroads make up only 1.6 percent of the total number of railroads in the nation, in 1997 they accounted for the vast majority of miles operated (71 percent), railroad employees (89 percent), and freight revenue (91 percent).

The Association of American Railroads (AAR), the industry trade organization, pointed out that studies by both the General Accounting Office (GAO) and the FRA showed that freight rates fell significantly after the Staggers Rail Act was passed in 1980 (see above). In 1997, the railroads received 2.40 cents in revenue per ton-mile (the movement of one ton of freight the distance of one mile). Two particularly interesting points to note are the differences in revenue from freight over the years between the East and West sections of the country, and the steady increase in revenue

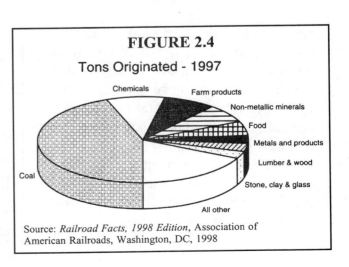

FIGURE 2.4
Tons Originated - 1997

Chemicals
Farm products
Non-metallic minerals
Food
Metals and products
Lumber & wood
Stone, clay & glass
Coal
All other

Source: *Railroad Facts, 1998 Edition*, Association of American Railroads, Washington, DC, 1998

car is longer, larger, and carries almost twice as much freight as the old railroad cars. In 1997, the average car capacity was 91.8 tons (Figure 2.5), nearly twice the tonnage of 70 years ago. The average train carries about 2,861 tons of freight today, compared to an average trainload of only 804 tons in 1929. Figure 2.6 shows the types and percentages of cars now in service

Operating Expenses

There are four basic categories of operating expenses for the railroad industry. By far the largest is transportation expenses (mainly train crews and fuel), which accounted for 45.1 percent of all operating costs in 1997. Other expenses include the maintenance of train equipment (25.3 percent), maintenance of tracks and rail yards (17.1 percent), and general and administrative costs (12.5 percent).

Financial Report

In 1997, the U.S. freight railroad industry posted one of its strongest financial results since World War II. Class I operating revenue rose 1.3 percent in 1997 to $33.1 billion, up from $32.7 billion in 1996. Operating expenses also rose at a rate of 3.6 percent to $27.3 billion from $26.3 in 1996, but this increase was due to special charges.

Innovation in
Freight Train Technology

The Union Pacific Railroad has pioneered one of the world's most advanced command-and-control systems for freight trains in its Harriman Dispatching Center in Omaha, Nebraska. Since opening in April 1989, the center has kept tabs on the movement of the 800 to 1,000 Union Pacific trains in transit each day on its 34,946-mile network. The company spent about $50 million on the control center itself and hundreds of millions more to upgrade communications along the tracks.

The Harriman Center is staffed 24 hours a day by 900 employees, who work three overlapping shifts. Dispatchers at the center are able to monitor trains through sensing devices in the rails laid along the tracks. The information is fed into computers, which create displays on the center's 172 video screens. The command center can also maintain voice contact with all Union Pacific crews through a radio network. The network allows Union Pacific to control the inventory of its 6,923 locomotives more efficiently, making sure that too many trains do not become concentrated in one geographic area, creating shortages in other parts of the country. It also permits dispatchers to know when trains are on a collision course even from half a continent away. Other railroads, including CSX and Burlington Northern, are putting together similar systems.

The Effect of Coal Transportation

The rapid growth in the use of low-sulfur coal to meet government-mandated regulations de-

TABLE 2.2
TONS ORIGINATED AND REVENUE BY COMMODITY - 1997

Commodity Group	Tons Originated		Revenue	
	(000)	% of Total	(millions)	% of Total
Coal	705,122	44.5 %	$7,698	22.0 %
Chemicals & allied products	141,497	8.9	4,815	13.8
Farm products	125,562	7.9	2,645	7.6
Non-metallic minerals	109,300	6.9	899	2.6
Food & kindred products	85,706	5.4	2,385	6.8
Metals & products	50,303	3.2	1,335	3.8
Lumber & wood products	48,138	3.0	1,471	4.2
Stone, clay & glass products	40,946	2.6	1,063	3.0
Petroleum & coke	37,539	2.4	978	2.8
Waste & scrap materials	36,977	2.3	711	2.0
Pulp, paper & allied products	32,123	2.0	1,507	4.3
Metallic ores	31,851	2.0	399	1.1
Motor vehicles & equip.	28,671	1.8	3,347	9.6
All other commodities	111,510	7.0	5,711	16.3
Total	**1,585,244**	**100.0 %**	**34,964**	**100.0 %**

Note: The total revenue shown here does not match freight revenue shown elsewhere in this publication. The commodity-specific revenue identified above is derived from a report based on traffic handled in 1997 and does not include adjustments for revenue absorption and corrections.

Source: *Railroad Facts, 1998 Edition*, Association of American Railroads, Washington, DC, 1998

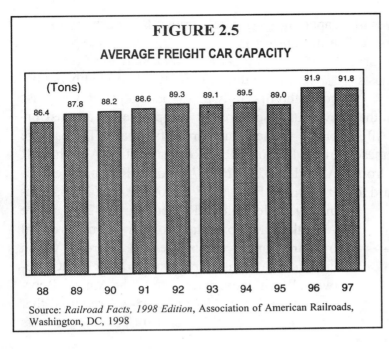

FIGURE 2.5

AVERAGE FREIGHT CAR CAPACITY

(Tons)

86.4	87.8	88.2	88.6	89.3	89.1	89.5	89.0	91.9	91.8
88	89	90	91	92	93	94	95	96	97

Source: *Railroad Facts, 1998 Edition*, Association of American Railroads, Washington, DC, 1998

and generate approximately 9 percent of all rail revenues. There are also about 34 regional railroads in the U.S. They are similar to, but significantly smaller than, Class I companies and operate about the same number of miles as short-line railroads. In 1997, regional railroads employed nearly 11,000 people and reported revenues of $1.6 billion. These carriers are divided into two categories — linehaul and switching/terminal. Linehaul railroads operate like Class I railroads but on a much smaller scale. Switching and terminal railroads operate in large cities and simplify the interchange of rail shipments among the railroads (usually Class I railroads) in their area. Frequently, carriers of this type are owned by Class I companies.

signed to lessen the amount of acid rain has benefited the nation's railroads. Most of the coal is produced in open-pit mines in the western United States. In order to haul the growing amount of coal, the railroads had to improve the condition of their track, equipment, and computerization to more efficiently move the coal around the country. This has contributed to the vast improvement of the nation's freight system over the past decade. In fact, European railroad officials are now seeking the advice of American railroad executives on how to improve their systems. While their passenger service may be far superior to America's, their freight system is aging and inefficient.

SHORT-LINE RAILROADS

A new segment of the railroad industry, short-line railroads, began to develop in 1980, when the Staggers Rail Act (PL 96-448) deregulated the railroads. With deregulation, large railroad companies could divest themselves of unwanted and unprofitable branch lines. New short-line railroad enterprises began to buy up the available properties.

Of the 550 U.S. railroads, 507, or nearly 92 percent, are short-line or regional carriers. Short-line railroads account for about one-third of all rail route miles, employ 11 percent of all rail workers,

The three top short-line railroad companies are RailTex, with 3,800 miles in North America, RailAmerica, with over 2,300 miles, and Genesee & Wyoming, Inc., with more than 1,500 miles. The companies buy old locomotives and maintain the tracks only at the speeds at which its trains travel — sometimes a mere 20 miles per hour. Short-line railroads move freight and pursue the small shipper.

Supporters of short-line railroads believe the large-railroad mergers should create new opportunities for the short-lines to keep on growing, as

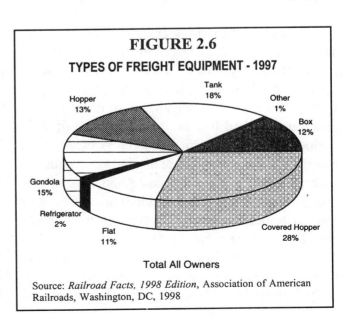

FIGURE 2.6

TYPES OF FREIGHT EQUIPMENT - 1997

Tank 18%
Other 1%
Box 12%
Covered Hopper 28%
Flat 11%
Refrigerator 2%
Gondola 15%
Hopper 13%

Total All Owners

Source: *Railroad Facts, 1998 Edition*, Association of American Railroads, Washington, DC, 1998

Class I railroads continue to divest themselves of unwanted lines. They see the smaller carriers being able to create profitable, more customer-oriented operations because of lower operating costs.

On the other hand, some opponents warn that short-line railroads are in a risky business. After all, the large railroad companies did not want these lines because they could not make money from them. They fear the short-lines may find it hard to be profitable.

TODAY'S PASSENGER SYSTEM — AMTRAK

A Shaky Beginning

As the railroad industry declined during the 1950s and 1960s, long-distance passenger service fell sharply. While rail passenger trains were the main mode of transportation prior to World War II, trains provided only 4 percent of intercity travel by 1958. Fearing increased automobile and airline competition, rail companies began eliminating unprofitable passenger lines until they almost disappeared. To fill the gap left by the decline in private passenger service, Congress passed the Railroad Passenger Service Act of 1970 (PL 91-518), creating the National Railroad Passenger Corporation, better known as Amtrak, a private/public corporation to operate on a "for-profit basis."

Amtrak's beginnings could be described as shaky at best. Amtrak began managing a national transportation system in May 1971 with a wide assortment of 20-year-old railway passenger cars from a variety of railroads. Many of its first intercity trains looked like rainbows because of their various colors. Ticketing and reservations were mostly handwritten. These limitations, coupled with poor on-time performance and lack of on-board amenities (no food service), did nothing to lure customers away from other forms of transportation, and the corporation steadily lost money. (It should be noted that even with the extensive, modern passenger systems in other countries, notably the high-speed lines in Germany, France, and Japan, no passenger service line in the world returns a profit.)

Realizing that Amtrak would probably not become the first railway to make a profit, Congress eventually ordered it to operate on an "as-for-profit" (rather than "for-profit") basis. The passage of the Regional Rail Reorganization Act (the 3-R Act, PL 93-236) in 1973 and the Railroad Revitalization and Regulatory Reform Act of 1976, commonly called the 4-R Act (PL 94-210), gave Amtrak the authority to take over 621 miles of rail from the bankrupt Penn-Central Railroad, which included the vital Northeast Corridor (NEC) between Washington and Boston. The Amtrak Reorganization Act of 1979 (PL 95-73) required that the company cover 50 percent of its annual costs by 1985.

Amtrak was given three mandates from Congress. First, to provide modern, efficient intercity rail passenger service; second, to help alleviate the overcrowding of airports, airways, and highways; and third, to give Americans an alternative to private automobiles and airplanes to meet their transportation needs.

Amtrak has struggled for survival on more than one occasion. In 1981, the incoming Reagan Administration included Amtrak among the government agencies that would be severely cut back, if not eliminated. In virtually every budget proposal, the administration tried to either sharply cut or completely eliminate Amtrak but ran into resistance from members of Congress representing the Northeast Corridor where Amtrak is most successful and popular. Still, many opponents of Amtrak feel that the expense of running the system cannot be justified during a time of government deficit, especially since some states receive very little benefit from the system while still having to support it.

Early Growth

By 1990, Amtrak looked very different from the fledgling passenger railroad started in the early 1970s. The system had progressed from "rainbow-

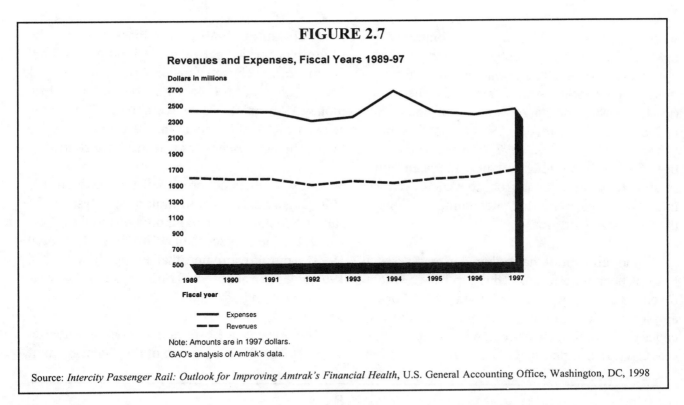

FIGURE 2.7

Revenues and Expenses, Fiscal Years 1989-97

Dollars in millions

Fiscal year

—— Expenses

- - - Revenues

Note: Amounts are in 1997 dollars.
GAO's analysis of Amtrak's data.

Source: *Intercity Passenger Rail: Outlook for Improving Amtrak's Financial Health*, U.S. General Accounting Office, Washington, DC, 1998

colored" trains heated by steam and purchased from 20 different bankrupt railroads, to a major transportation company with 24,037 employees operating about 220 intercity trains and 459 commuter trains each day over 25,000 miles and serving 535 destinations in 45 states.

Several factors contributed to these successes. Amtrak improved service, reduced costs, and implemented an aggressive marketing campaign pointing out the benefits and pleasures of train travel. The increased cost of air travel, coupled with the well-publicized stories of delays at the nation's airports, led some travelers to choose the train. While trains will never equal the speed of airplanes, some travelers with the time and desire to get better acquainted with America on the ground level, without the responsibilities inherent in car travel, will look to the rails.

Struggling Again

In 1992, for the first time in over a decade, Amtrak revenues and passenger miles declined in response to the national economic recession of the early 1990s. During those weak economic times, business and discretionary travel fell, hurting all

carriers. In addition, the airline industry responded with fare wars, further undermining Amtrak ridership.

However, several important events occurred during 1992. After years of negotiations, agreements were reached with nearly all of Amtrak's 14 labor organizations. The year also began the transition to a new generation of cars and locomotives that were delivered in 1993 and 1994. This allowed Amtrak to retire most of its original fleet of 40-year-old Heritage cars and worn-out locomotives.

Amtrak took steps to ensure its future as a viable carrier. The Department of Transportation and Related Agencies Appropriations Act (PL 102-388), approved in 1993, provided $700.1 million in federal funds to Amtrak for fiscal year 1993, of which $331 million was for operating purposes, and the balance for capital acquisitions and improvements. But it wasn't enough.

Like all major national intercity rail services in the world, Amtrak operates at a loss, and it has always needed government funding. Despite an improving economy, financial difficulties for Amtrak worsened to the point that, in 1995, Congress studied Amtrak's future and debated its long-term viability. In 1999, Amtrak's financial condition continues to deteriorate. Amtrak reduced its net losses (total expenses less total revenues) from about $892 million in fiscal year (FY) 1994 (in 1997 dollars) to about $762 million in 1997. The loss would have been $63 million higher had there not been a one-time increase in revenue from the sale of real estate and access rights for telecommunications in the Northeast Corridor.

Although Amtrak has reduced its net losses, it has not been able to close the gap between total revenues and expenses. (See Figure 2.7.) For example, in 1997, intercity passenger-related revenues grew by about 4 percent, while intercity passenger-related expenses grew by about 7 percent.

Each of Amtrak's 40 routes loses money. The Metroliner service between Washington, DC, and Boston, Massachusetts, makes a profit of about $5 per passenger. (All other trains on that route lose money.) Amtrak loses an average of $53 per passenger on each of its remaining 39 routes, and more than $100 per passenger on 14 of those routes.

Only 5 routes covered their train costs in FY 1997. Figure 2.8 shows Amtrak's route system. (In June 1999, Amtrak in Oklahoma restored service, which had been discontinued in 1979.) In March 1998, Amtrak estimated that its net loss for FY 1998 would be about $845 million, about $56 million more than budgeted.

The Amtrak Reform and Accountability Act of 1997 (PL 105-103) is part of the Department of

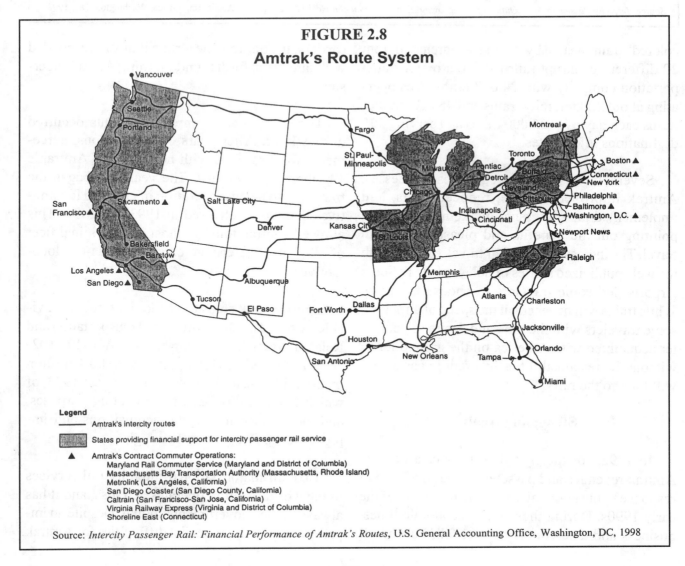

FIGURE 2.8

Amtrak's Route System

Legend

⎯⎯ Amtrak's intercity routes

▨ States providing financial support for intercity passenger rail service

▲ Amtrak's Contract Commuter Operations:
    Maryland Rail Commuter Service (Maryland and District of Columbia)
    Massachusetts Bay Transportation Authority (Massachusetts, Rhode Island)
    Metrolink (Los Angeles, California)
    San Diego Coaster (San Diego County, California)
    Caltrain (San Francisco-San Jose, California)
    Virginia Railway Express (Virginia and District of Columbia)
    Shoreline East (Connecticut)

Source: *Intercity Passenger Rail: Financial Performance of Amtrak's Routes*, U.S. General Accounting Office, Washington, DC, 1998

FIGURE 2.9
Plans for the Future — High-Speed Trains

Source: *National Railroad Passenger Corporation 1997 Annual Report*, National Railroad Passenger Corporation, Washington, DC, 1997

Transportation's (DOT) surface transportation reauthorization bill and approves $3.5 billion in federal funds for Amtrak's capital program over six years. Included in the act are incentives designed to encourage Amtrak to eliminate its dependence on federal operating subsidies. The act also established an Amtrak Reform Council to evaluate Amtrak's performance and make recommendations to Amtrak for financial reforms and further cost containment and productivity improvements. The DOT will increase Amtrak's funds if it concludes that Amtrak is cutting spending and raising enough revenue to become self-sufficient by 2002, when subsidies are due to end.

Looking to the future, Amtrak plans to expand mail and express freight service (delivery of higher-value, time-sensitive goods) and to institute high-speed rail service between New York City and Boston. The high-speed trains, called *Acela*, a combination of "acceleration" and "excellence," will cut travel time between the two cities from the current four-and-one-half hours to three hours by traveling at 150 miles-per-hour. (See Figure 2.9.) The time gains will be made possible through a $2 billion program that will include electrifying the entire 470-mile stretch between Washington and Boston and straightening curves in the tracks. Moreover, 20 new trains will have "tilt technology," enabling them to glide around corners by gently tilting into the bend. Service is scheduled to begin in November or December 1999.

Acela will have business-class seats with audio and power jacks, concierge service, dining cars with meeting tables, upgraded food, and beer on tap. All this comes with a price, however. The new one-way fare between New York and Boston or Washington will cost about $130 to $140, an increase from the current $114 fare, but still less than the $199 walk-up airplane fare.

Amtrak expects *Acela* to increase its market share in the Northeast Corridor from 12 to 15 percent annually — about 14.3 million passengers total. Amtrak believes *Acela* should generate $180 million in new profits in its first full year of service. If *Acela* is successful, similar high-speed Amtrak trains will enter service in the Great Lakes, Gulf Coast, California, and Pacific Northwest regions.

Amtrak and the federal government face difficult choices. The goal is for Amtrak to be free of federal operating support by 2002 by increasing revenues, controlling costs, and providing riders with quality service. Although Amtrak's business plans have helped to reduce net losses, significant challenges remain. It seems likely that Amtrak will continue to need federal assistance in terms of operations and capital well into the foreseeable future.

HIGH-SPEED TRAINS

The future of passenger rail will likely be in high-speed trains in an effort to reduce travel time, relieve congestion in increasingly crowded skies and cities, and win a portion of the air travel market. High-speed trains would be most practical for distances between 150 and 500 miles. For shorter distances, automobiles are preferred; for longer distances, airplanes would hold the advantage. Even at medium distances, trains would have to compete with airplanes, and, to keep fares low enough to compete, subsidies would be needed.

High-density corridors, where heavy passenger traffic occurs between several cities, are par-

FIGURE 2.10

TVG *Atlantique* en Route from Paris to Lemans, France

Source: *National Transportation Strategic Planning Study*, U.S. Department of Transportation, Washington, DC, 1990

ticularly well suited to high-speed train service. Currently, the fastest U.S. train in service is Amtrak's *Metroliner*, which reaches a maximum speed of about 125 miles an hour in its run between Washington and New York. Most Amtrak trains are much slower. Congress had expressed growing interest in programs to develop rapid rail lines like those in France and Japan, although current interest in such projects has since faded. The trains that are usually discussed for the American market could be either sophisticated wheeled vehicles that operate up to 200 miles per hour or futuristic trains driven on magnetic cushions at even higher speeds.

Most analysts agree that federal research grants would be needed to promote magnetic levitation, or maglev, technology for the fastest possible trains. (Maglev has powerful electromagnets that lift passenger cars about six inches above a guideway and then propel them at speeds up to 300 miles per hour.) But more conventional technologies are available that would require less research before being built. Amtrak already has embarked on the high-speed rail improvement program to reduce the travel time between New York and Boston by 90 minutes by electrification, "tilt technology," and straighter tracks.

European Fast Trains

Much of the technology and information about high-speed trains has come from Europe. Rail systems like the French TGV (*Train à Grand Vitesse*) have been in use for many years (Figure 2.10). The primary reason for the popularity of high-speed rail in Europe is the severe congestion on Europe's roads and in the skies, a situation that America is also facing in its busiest metropolitan hubs. In European cities, short-distance flights are extremely expensive. The train costs less, takes only slightly longer, and carries passengers from downtown to downtown.

The TGV holds the world speed record at over 320 miles per hour, and the trains average about 185 miles per hour in regular service. Italy, Sweden, and Germany also use high-speed trains. Each system is being supported to some degree by its government. Discussions are underway among the 12 European nations to link their high-speed systems into one network that will span the continent, expanding 1,800 miles of lines into 18,000 and enabling average speeds of over 150 miles an hour. The 250-mile trip from Paris to London, using the Channel Tunnel (Chunnel), has been in operation since the mid-1990s and takes about 4 hours and

TABLE 2.3

Scope, Approach, and Costs for 11 High-Speed Rail Corridors

Dollars in millions

Corridor	Scope	Approach	Estimated cost
California	Sacramento/San Francisco to San Diego (676 miles)	Considering new high-speed rail (220 mph) or maglev (310 mph)	$21,000-$29,000
Chicago-St. Louis	Chicago, Ill., to St. Louis, Mo. (282 miles)	Incremental (110 mph)	350
Chicago-Detroit	Chicago, Ill., to Detroit, Mich. (279 miles)	Incremental (110 mph)	800
Chicago-Milwaukee	Chicago, Ill., to Milwaukee, Wis. (85 miles)	Incremental (110 mph)	471
Wisconsin-Illinois-Minnesota	Chicago, Ill., to Minneapolis, Minn. (418 miles)	Incremental (speed unknown)	To be determined
Empire (N.Y.)	Buffalo to Albany to New York City (431 miles)	Incremental (125 mph)	315
Pacific Northwest	Vancouver, B.C., to Eugene, Oreg. (466 miles)	Incremental (125 mph)	1,865
Southeast	Washington, D.C., to Charlotte, N.C. (390 miles)	Incremental (110 mph)	To be determined
Keystone (Pa.)	Philadelphia to Harrisburg (104 miles)	Incremental (110 mph)	To be determined
Northeast corridor	Washington, D.C., to Boston, Mass. (457 miles)	Incremental (150 mph)	4,000
Gulf Coast	Houston, Tex., to Birmingham, Ala. (719 miles)	Incremental (speed unknown)	To be determined

Source: *Surface Infrastructure: High-Speed Rail Projects in the United States*, U.S. General Accounting Office, Washington, DC, 1999

15 minutes, roughly equal to that of an air flight if ground time for the traveler is included.

Unfortunately, many technical obstacles remain to delay the European plan for a rail network. The many nationalities, economic and political differences, diverse electrical systems, various languages, and different visual rail signals currently reflect the generalized lack of unity on the continent. Obtaining agreement among so many nations is an awesome obstacle.

Japan has had great success with its 34-year-old bullet-train system. Its newest bullet train, the *Shinkansen Asama 502*, travels the 141 miles between Nagano and Tokyo in just 104 minutes, cutting commuters' travel time in half. The Nagano to Tokyo train costs $65 one way, carries 630 passengers, and can reach speeds of 160 miles per hour.

The *Shinkansen*, which means "new trunk line," was begun in 1964 between Tokyo and Osaka and carried 100 million passengers in its first 1,016 days of operation. Today, the bullet trains generally run between 6 a.m. and midnight and are always crowded. In 1964, the train traveled at 125 miles per hour; in 1997, a prototype test train was clocked at 227 miles per hour. The *Shinkansen Asama 502* can span the length of the country in a day. It is important to remember that despite the success as a method of transportation, the Japanese rail system has had chronic, severe financial problems.

High-Speed Rail Projects in the United States

In 1999, there are 11 corridors in the United States in various stages of developing high-speed rail projects. (See Table 2.3.) (There were 12 corridors until January 1999, when Governor Jeb Bush of Florida halted plans for a high-speed train intended to link the cities of Orlando, Tampa, and Miami. Bush said the project posed too much financial risk for taxpayers.)

According to a 1999 General Accounting Office (GAO) study, *Surface Infrastructure: High-Speed Rail Projects in the United States,* most of the corridors are in the early stages of planning. Two exceptions are Amtrak's Northeast Corridor (see above) and the Pacific Northwest Corridor. Officials in the Northeast Corridor have been upgrading the system for several years, and officials in the Pacific Northwest Corridor, between Vancouver, British Columbia, and Eugene, Oregon, have bought high-speed rail trains and have obtained funding to upgrade its track.

Ten of the corridors would upgrade their systems gradually, by making a series of improvements to existing rail infrastructure (underlying foundation, such as tracks and communications systems) or equipment. The projects will improve track, signals, and safety systems along present rail lines by updating switches, replacing wooden railroad ties with concrete ties, and creating additional track capacity. New and improved signal and collision avoidance systems will also be needed to handle faster and increased traffic. California, on the other hand, is considering the development of a new high-speed rail system that would use new, more advanced technology able to reach speeds up to 310 miles per hour.

Federal funding for these projects may be obtained through various programs, including the High-Speed Rail program, the Magnetic Levitation Transportation Technology Deployment program, the Railroad Rehabilitation and Improvement Financing program, and the finance provisions under the Transportation Infrastructure Finance and Innovation Act of 1998 (TIFIA; PL 105-178) program. TIFIA helps large infrastructure projects costing at least $100 million (50 percent of a state's federal aid highway apportionment for the preceding fiscal year) by using federal funds to leverage significant private investment. To accomplish this, TIFIA authorizes the Secretary of Transportation to make secured loans, loan guarantees, and lines of credit available to eligible projects that will repay either all or part of the money from passenger fares.

A GLOBAL RAIL REVIVAL?

Some critics believe that rail is poised to make a comeback in much of the world. Rails are being revived and reinvented with new, sophisticated technologies and advances in comfort and speed. Airlines in Europe are now lobbying for more rail service to free overloaded terminals of short-trip passengers. The high-speed French TGV train has captured 80 percent of former air passengers on the Paris-Lyon route. In Japan, the bullet train has almost eliminated air travel between Nagoya and Tokyo. Germany, for the first time ever, is investing more in rail than in highways, and Sweden plans to invest as much in railways as roads over the next decade. The United States is a major exception in the industrialized world.

Trains offer a vital alternative to people who cannot afford a car or airline ticket or are physically unable to drive or fly. Only an estimated 10 percent of the world's people can afford a car.

Rail offers many advantages over highway or air transport according to Worldwatch Institute, an environmental activist group, including

- Greater energy efficiency.

- Less dependence on oil.

- Reduced air pollution.

- Lower emissions of greenhouse gases.

- Less air and road congestion.

- Fewer injuries and deaths.

- Less paved land area.

- Local economic development.

- Sustainable land use patterns.

- Greater social equity.

Despite these advantages, with the invention of the automobile, Americans began to use rail less. Western European countries, however, never abandoned their passenger rail systems when the automobile became popular — intercity trains, metros, and new light rail systems have been an established part of the landscape and lifestyle and formed an integral part of their transportation system. The national railways, the largest employers in several countries, represent some of the most comprehensive rail networks in the world. Japan is notable for maintaining high train ridership even as cars have become widespread.

Critics of federal and state subsidies for rail ask where the money will come from. Adequate funding is hard to find for all infrastructure, rail included. Supporters of rail contend that funding problems exist because national policy channeled billions of dollars into other transport modes, particularly highways. Contrary to popular belief, car and truck drivers do not pay their own way through user fees, but are heavily subsidized. According to the American Public Transit Association (APTA) in its *1999 Transit Fact Book* (Washington, DC), the public pays $2 to $3 trillion annually for highways and motor vehicle use, but only 53 percent to 68 percent of that amount is paid by users. The costs for building, maintaining, and operating highways are mostly paid by all citizens through taxes not directly related to use of an automobile.

TRANSPORTATION EQUITY ACT FOR THE TWENTY-FIRST CENTURY

In 1998, President Bill Clinton signed the Transportation Equity Act for the Twenty-first Century (TEA-21; PL 105-178). TEA-21 includes

several programs for the rail industry. A total of $60 million was authorized for fiscal years (FYs) 1999–2001 to fund projects to determine if that transportation systems using magnetic levitation (Maglev) are both possible and safe. Of this amount, $15 million will be used for research and development of low-speed superconductivity Maglev technology in urban areas.

High-speed rail development will receive $40 million for corridor planning and $100 million for technology improvements. As this capital will come out of the General Fund, appropriations from Congress will be needed to finance the program.

A new program was created to fund light density rail line pilot projects. It provides funding for capital improvements and rehabilitation of publicly and privately owned rail line structures. TEA-21 authorized $105 million for FYs 1998-2003, and the capital will come from the General Fund, requiring Congress to appropriate the finances.

The Alaska Railroad will receive $31.5 million for FYs 1998-2003 for grants for capital rehabilitation and improvements to passenger services from the General Fund. In addition, transit formula grant funding totaling $29.1 million for FYs 1998-2003 will be available for capital improvements to the Alaska Railroad's passenger operations. Most (80 percent) of this funding will come from the Mass Transit Account, and 20 percent will come from the General Fund.

TEA-21 also authorizes a new Railroad Rehabilitation and Improvement Financing program to provide credit assistance. This aid will consist of direct loans and loan guarantees to public or private sponsors of intermodal (using different modes of transportation in the shipment of goods from point of departure to final destination) and rail projects. TEA-21 does not provide a set amount of funds for this program but authorizes future appropriations to fund the credit assistance. The total amount of loans and guarantees that may be made under this program is $3.5 billion, with $1 billion reserved for projects primarily benefiting freight railroads other than Class I carriers.

CHAPTER III

HIGHWAYS

The transportation system in the United States provides U.S. residents with one of the highest levels of personal mobility in the world. Americans use roads and highways more often than any other mode of transport. U.S. passenger and freight travel is dominated by the automobile, the truck, and the highway system, which accounts for more than 90 percent of all travel and 75 percent of the value of all goods and services shipped. The nation's productivity and international competitiveness depend on fast and reliable transportation, making the status of highways and bridges of paramount importance to the vitality of the U.S. economy.

EARLY ROADS

Before the arrival of Europeans, eastern America was crisscrossed by thousands of Indian trails that cut through forests, connecting villages and natural waterways. Colonial settlers were very dependent on these waterways. While they did expand some of the existing overland trails, most of their road-building was aimed at carrying goods to and from rivers and seaports. A few hard-surfaced roads were constructed near the larger cities.

As the colonies grew, Americans found they needed land as well as water routes. By the early 1700s, the government had established a land postal service between the main cities along the eastern seaboard. Carriers on foot or horse-mounted riders, who averaged four miles an hour and did not work at night, carried the mail. In 1729, a letter took four weeks to travel the 600 miles from Boston, Massachusetts, to Williamsburg, Virginia, an average of about three miles per hour for an 8-hour work day.

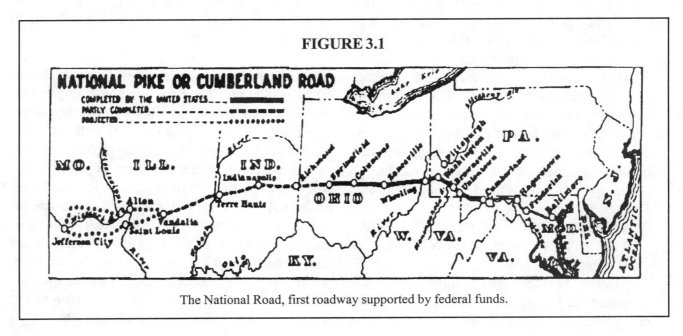

FIGURE 3.1

The National Road, first roadway supported by federal funds.

In 1750, a regular stage-wagon service was instituted between Philadelphia and New York City, and by the time of the American Revolution, a stagecoach could go from Philadelphia to Paulus Hook Ferry (now Jersey City), New Jersey, in two days. Traveling at today's speeds, the trip would take less than two hours.

NEW ROADS FOR A NEW NATION

The first intercity highway constructed in the newly independent United States connected Philadelphia and Lancaster, Pennsylvania. Built in 1793-94 with private funds, it was surfaced with stone and gravel, and travelers were required to pay a toll. Almost all road building during this period was a private enterprise, and the builders charged a toll for the use of their product, a practice that endured for the next 120 years.

FIGURE 3.2

Alfred Stieglitz, *Winter — Fifth Avenue*, 1893, carbon print, 1894

The one major road financed with federal funds during this period was the famous Cumberland Road, or National Pike. Opened in 1818, it connected Cumberland, Maryland, with Wheeling, West Virginia, and, later, Vandalia, Illinois. The road was heavily traveled by pioneers seeking to settle ever farther westward, stimulating trade and linking the Midwest with the central government. Initially a free-access road, the Pike became subject to tolls as successive portions of it came under the control of the various states through which it passed. (See Figure 3.1.)

Despite this activity, most of the roads in the young nation were undeveloped, rutted, winding tracks subject to damage by rain and snow. The new railroad industry and further development of local waterways and canals diverted attention away from road building and maintenance. Slow horse-drawn wagons and coaches, with their small capacity, could hardly compete economically with trains and barges.

INTEREST RENEWED

Ironically, the railroads were largely responsible for a renewed interest in road building. Because of

35

their ability to haul large quantities of goods for long distances, the railroads were instrumental in opening up the territories west of the Mississippi River. Towns sprang up all along the western-bound tracks. Many settlers used the vast expanses of land for farming. While the railroad could haul produce from the rural town to the big city, it was of little comfort to the farmer whose wagon, loaded with agricultural produce, was stuck in a mud-filled, rutted road on the way to the station.

During this same period, roads gained an unlikely ally—the bicyclist. Bicycling rapidly became a popular national fad, and Americans joined riding clubs for exercise and pleasure. Frustrated with the limited mileage and poor conditions of existing roads, these "wheelmen" banded together to establish "good roads." In fact, what became known as the Good Roads Movement was a major force in the development of our present-day system of roads and highways.

In 1891, the Good Roads Association was formed in Missouri, and by 1901, over 100 cycling organizations were vigorously campaigning for road expansion and improvement. These groups lobbied local and federal governments for financial aid, and their spokesmen traveled throughout the country, promoting not only the need for better roads but also the idea that road improvement and new road construction would inevitably require new taxes.

The need for government support and the expenditure of tax dollars was clearly dem-

onstrated by the Mecklenburg Road Law. In 1879, Mecklenburg County in North Carolina levied a road tax on all property in the county in an effort to improve the roads, which would aid the many farmers and rural residents of the area. Soon Mecklenburg County had the best roads in the entire state.

While the federal government had been eager to offer incentives for railroad development, it did not see the benefits of providing similar support for road building. Nonetheless, the need for better roads could not be ignored forever. In response to the combined clamor of farmers and bicyclists, the U.S. Department of Agriculture created the Office of Road Inquiry in 1893. The role of the office was to investigate, educate, and distribute information on road building.

TABLE 3.1
Functional Systems Mileage

Functional System	Rural	% Change 1986-1996	Urban	% Change 1986-1996	Total	% Change 1986-1996	% of Total Mileage
Interstate	32,920	0.2%	13,366	19.5%	46,286	5.1%	1.2%
Other Freeways/ Expressways	--	--	9,070	23.3%	9,070	23.3%	0.2%
Other Principal Arterial	98,232	17.2%	53,220	5.2%	151,452	14.8%	3.8%
Minor Arterial	137,652	-7.0%	89,523	19.6%	227,175	2.0%	5.8%
Major Collector	432,890	-0.1%	--	--	432,890	-0.1%	11.0%
Minor Collector	273,876	-7.5%	--	--	273,876	-7.5%	7.0%
Collector	--	--	88,509	17.4%	88,509	17.4%	2.2%
Local	2,124,792	-3.0%	579,935	19.3%	2,704,727	1.0%	68.8%
Total	3,100,362	-2.6%	833,623	18.1%	3,933,985	1.2%	100.0%

Source: *Our Nation's Highways*, Federal Highway Administration, Washington, DC, 1998

TABLE 3.2
Annual Vehicle-Miles of Travel
(Millions)

Functional System	Rural	% Change 1986-1996	Urban	% Change 1986-1996	Total	% Change 1986-1996	% of Total Mileage
Interstate	233,593	46.5%	355,196	53.1%	588,789	50.4%	23.6%
Other Freeways/ Expressways	--	--	158,233	50.0%	158,233	50.0%	6.3%
Other Principal Arterial	221,730	48.4%	380,320	32.2%	602,050	37.7%	24.1%
Minor Arterial	158,245	12.5%	300,658	44.0%	458,903	31.3%	18.4%
Major Collector	191,654	16.3%	--	--	191,654	16.3%	7.7%
Minor Collector	50,577	17.3%	--	--	50,577	17.3%	2.0%
Collector	--	--	129,972	44.5%	129,972	44.5%	5.2%
Local	108,156	19.9%	209,567	28.4%	317,723	25.4%	12.7%
Total	963,955	28.9%	1,533,946	41.1%	2,497,901	36.1%	100.0%

Source: *Our Nation's Highways*, Federal Highway Administration, Washington, DC, 1998

TABLE 3.3

Bridges by Jurisdiction

Jurisdiction	Number of Bridges
Federal	6,171
State	273,198
Local	299,078
Private	2,378
Unknown/ Unclassified	1,037
Total	**581,862**

Source: National Bridge Inventory, June 30, 1996

THE CAR IS BORN

It would be hard to overestimate the impact of the car on the development of our society as a whole and the field of transportation in particular (see Chapter

TABLE 3.4

Bridges by Functional System 1996

Functional System	Number of Bridges
Rural Bridge	
Interstate	28,638
Other Principal Arterial	34,445
Minor Arterial	38,525
Major Collector	96,576
Minor Collector	47,670
Local	211,059
Subtotal Rural	**456,913**
Urban Bridge	
Interstate	26,596
Other Fwy & Expwy	14,887
Other Principal Arterial	23,170
Minor Arterial	21,007
Collector	14,848
Local	24,441
Subtotal Urban	**124,949**
Unknown/ Unclassified	**0**
Total	**581,862**

Source: National Bridge Inventory, June 30, 1996

IV). At the turn of the century, horsepower provided the main form of transportation (Figure 3.2). Henry Ford introduced the Model T in 1908. Although it was not the first auto, it was the first to be mass-produced and was relatively inexpensive, making automobile ownership no longer limited to the wealthy, privileged few.

What had been a luxury quickly became a necessity. In 1910, 470,000 cars traveled the primitive American road system; by 1920, the number had swelled to over 9 million. The existing roads were woefully inadequate for this amount of traffic.

In 1904, only 9 percent of just under 2.4 million miles of roads in the United States were surfaced. What little control existed over their location, size, and maintenance was almost totally at the county or local level. A beautiful wide, paved road might end abruptly at a state line simply because the neighboring state had different budgeting priorities. However, due in large part to the efforts of the Good Roads Movement and other interested parties, the groundwork had already been laid for federal involvement, and local governments turned to Washington for financial assistance.

FEDERAL INVOLVEMENT AND FEDERAL AID

It was not until 1916 that federal funds for road development became uniformly available to all states. The Federal Aid Road Act of 1916 provided partial funding and technical assistance to build a network of new highways. All building projects had to be approved by the Federal Bureau of Public Roads. The states' responsibilities included project initiation, supplying the remaining funding, and the administration and maintenance of finished roads within their state boundaries. The roles and duties of the state and the federal government established in the 1916 act have remained basically the same in all later highway legislation.

In 1944, Congress passed the Federal Aid Highway Act (70 Stat. 838) to create the 40,000-mile National System of Interstate and Defense Highways, although major funding did not become available until the passage of the Federal Aid Highway Act of 1956

(70 Stat. 374). Although these two laws would eventually lead to one of the most complete interstate highway systems in the world, the original rationale for its development was to permit the rapid movement of troops and equipment around the country in case of war. From an original commitment of 50 percent, the federal government eventually provided up to 90 percent of construction and repair costs for roads in the Federal Aid System.

Revenue for this increased federal spending came from the Highway Trust Fund, established by the Highway Revenue Act of 1956 (70 Stat. 374, Title II), which got its money from taxes for highway use, equipment taxes (such as manufacturers' and car-sales taxes), and gasoline taxes. In 1987, Congress passed the Surface Transportation and Uniform Relocation Assistance Act (PL 100-17), which allocated another $87.9 billion over a five-year period to establish or continue federal highway and mass transit programs.

In 1991, the Intermodal Surface Transportation Efficiency Act (ISTEA; PL 102-240) became law. The act established the Bureau of Transportation Statistics (BTS). BTS collects data and studies freight activity and passenger travel throughout the country in order to improve the nation's highway system.

In June 1998, President Bill Clinton signed the largest public works program in U.S. history — the Transportation Equity Act for the Twenty-first Century (TEA-21; PL 105-178). TEA-21 reauthorizes ISTEA, which expired in 1997. TEA-21 will increase transportation spending in every state. The act commits $218 billion over the six-year period from 1998 to 2003 to transportation programs. The funds will be spent on highway and bridge projects ($175 billion), mass transit ($41 billion), and safety programs ($2 billion). TEA-21 builds on the programs undertaken in ISTEA and improves upon them. Significant features of TEA-21 include

- Assuring a guaranteed level of federal funds for surface transportation through 2003.

TABLE 3.5

Jurisdictional Control of U.S. Roads and Streets

Jurisdiction	Rural Mileage	Percent	Urban Mileage	Percent	Total Mileage	Percent
State	693,141	22.4	113,199	13.6	806,340	20.5
Local	2,238,308	72.2	718,950	86.2	2,957,258	75.2
Federal	168,913	5.4	1,474	0.2	170,387	4.3
Total	3,100,362	100.0	833,623	100.0	3,933,985	100 .0

Source: *Our Nation's Highways*, Federal Highway Administration, Washington, DC, 1998

- Extending the Disadvantaged Business Enterprises program by providing minority and women-owned businesses nationwide 10 percent participation in highway and transit contracting undertaken with federal funding.

- Strengthening safety programs by increasing the use of safety belts and encouraging the passage and enforcement of 0.08 percent blood alcohol level standards for drunk driving in every state.

- Continuing the program structure established for highways and transit under ISTEA and adding new programs.

- Investing in research and its applications to maximize the performance of the transportation system and emphasizing the development of Intelligent Transportation Systems to help improve operations and management of transportation systems and vehicle safety.

The National Highway System

The Intermodal Surface Transportation Efficiency Act (ISTEA; PL 102-240 — see above) changed the way the federal government classified roads by introducing the National Highway System, or NHS. (The term "highway," as used here, refers not only to major highways, but also rural roads and urban streets that lead to or connect major roads and that, collectively, make up the highway network or system.)

The National Highway System Designation Act of 1995 (PL 104-59) provided a framework for the NHS, which is made up of 157,000 miles of roads —

4 percent of all public roads. The NHS defines five different types of highways. *Interstate highways* crisscross the country (46,000 miles). Key *primary and urban arterials* carry the major portion of traffic entering and leaving the urban areas (89,000 miles). The *Strategic Highway Corridor Network* is 15,000 miles of 21 "corridors" linking major military installations and defense facilities designated by the Defense Department. Two thousand miles of *major connectors* and 5,000 miles of *high priority corridors* are highways that serve regional travel and connect with other modes of transportation, such as railway stations, harbors, and airports. (Remember, this is still named the National System of Interstate and Defense Highways.)

TODAY'S HIGHWAY SYSTEM

The nation's highway network consists of over 3.9 million miles of roads and streets, with most (79 percent) located in rural areas. (See Table 3.1.) This network accommodates 2.5 trillion vehicle miles of travel each year. (See Table 3.2.) Bridges are a critical link in the nation's infrastructure (basic facilities on which the growth of a community or state depends). In 1996, there were about 581,862 bridges on the highway network. (See Table 3.3.) Nearly 80 percent of these bridges were in rural areas. (See Table 3.4.) Also included in the network are almost 4,500 miles of toll roads, bridges, and tunnels.

Highway Classifications

The more than 3.9 million miles of roads in the United States are functionally classified as *arterials*, *collectors*, or *local roads*, depending on the type of service they provide. These categories are subdivided into rural and urban areas. (Table 3.1 shows highway mileage by function.)

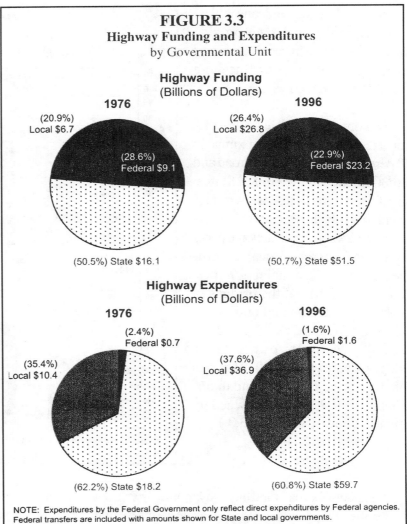

FIGURE 3.3
Highway Funding and Expenditures
by Governmental Unit

Highway Funding
(Billions of Dollars)

1976

(20.9%) Local $6.7
(28.6%) Federal $9.1
(50.5%) State $16.1

1996

(26.4%) Local $26.8
(22.9%) Federal $23.2
(50.7%) State $51.5

Highway Expenditures
(Billions of Dollars)

1976

(2.4%) Federal $0.7
(35.4%) Local $10.4
(62.2%) State $18.2

1996

(1.6%) Federal $1.6
(37.6%) Local $36.9
(60.8%) State $59.7

NOTE: Expenditures by the Federal Government only reflect direct expenditures by Federal agencies. Federal transfers are included with amounts shown for State and local governments.

Source: *Our Nation's Highways*, Federal Highway Administration, Washington, DC, 1998

Arterials, which are classified as principal or minor, provide connections to other roads. They usually have higher design standards, with wider or multiple lanes. In rural areas, principal arterials are subdivided into interstate and other principal arterials (OPAs). In urban areas, principal arterials are subdivided into interstate, other freeways and expressways (OF&Es), and OPAs.

Collectors are usually two-lane roads that serve shorter trips. They collect and distribute traffic to and from the arterial systems. They often provide the fastest and most convenient way to reach a local destination. In rural areas, collectors are subdivided into major and minor collectors.

Most public road mileage is classified as local. Local roads provide the access between residential and commercial properties and the more heavily traveled highways.

Nationwide, states have jurisdictional responsibility for approximately 20 percent of the total public road and street mileage in the United States. The federal government owns and maintains only those roads on federal Indian reservations and national parks — about 4 percent. Local governments control the remaining 75 percent (Table 3.5). Of the bridges in 1998, the states owned and maintained more than 273,000, and the federal government owned 6,171 bridges. There were 299,078 bridges that were locally owned and maintained, while 2,378 were owned by private entities. (See Table 3.3.)

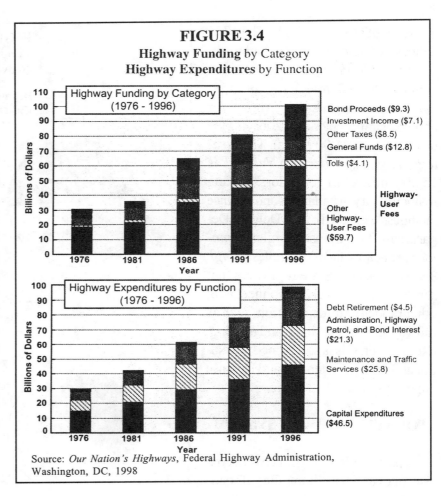

FIGURE 3.4
Highway Funding by Category
Highway Expenditures by Function

Source: *Our Nation's Highways*, Federal Highway Administration, Washington, DC, 1998

WHO PAYS WHAT?

Financing for roads and highways comes from both the public and private sectors. A variety of revenue sources finance the nation's highways: direct user fees (such as license fees, tolls, and taxes on both gasoline and vehicles), and indirect fees that come from income taxes and local property assessments. Federal, state, and local governments funded more than $101.5 billion in 1996, up from $31.9 billion in 1976 (Figure 3.3).

The largest share of money used to finance highways comes from highway-user fees, including tolls ($63.8 billion). General funds account for $12.8 billion, and other taxes, investment income, and bond proceeds pay for the remaining 24.9 percent. (See Figure 3.4.)

Highway construction, maintenance, and operating costs have risen dramatically, due primarily to inflation. Figure 3.3 shows the costs of keeping the nation's highways in shape, and Figure 3.4 illustrates the way capital is spent on improvements. Most con-

struction is for the improvement of existing highways and streets, such as resurfacing, widening pavements, minimizing curves, and improvements that generally provide safer, more efficient highways that accomodate the largest traffic and load-bearing capacities. Most new roads are built by local governments to serve residential users only.

PROBLEMS FACING
THE HIGHWAY SYSTEM

Highway Conditions

Although they differ on degree, most experts agree that U.S. roads and bridges are below standard. Table 3.6 illustrates the percentage of interstate highways that need improvement, according to the Federal Highway Administration (FHWA). The FHWA found that in 1995 about 7 percent of the interstate highways in the nation were in poor or mediocre condition, and, in 1996, 31 percent of its bridges were structurally deficient or functionally obsolete. (See Table 3.7.) *Struc-*

TABLE 3.6

Highway Condition by Functional System (Rural)
Annually 1990–1994
(Miles of pavement)

| | Rural | | | | | | | | | | | | | | |
| | Interstate | | | | | | | | | | | | | | |
Year	Not Reported	Poor	%	Mediocre	%	Fair	%	Good	%	Very Good	%	Unpaved	%	Total Reported	%
1990	–	2,904	8.7	*	*	10,694	31.9	*	*	19,949	59.5	–	–	33,547	100.0
1991	–	2,534	7.5	*	*	10,651	31.6	*	*	20,492	60.8	–	–	33,677	100.0
1992	–	1,733	5.2	4,670	14.1	5,754	17.4	9,105	27.6	11,765	35.6	–	–	33,027	100.0
1993	2,353	2,269	7.5	7,240	23.9	5,686	18.8	10,255	33.8	4,849	16.0	–	–	30,299	100.0
1994	621	2,045	6.4	8,356	26.2	7,537	23.7	10,401	32.7	3,497	11.0	–	–	31,836	100.0
1995	1,326	551	1.8	1,403	4.5	13,424	43.0	11,538	36.9	4,338	13.9	–	–	31,254	100.0

Highway Condition by Functional System (Urban)
Annually 1990–1995
(Miles of pavement)

| | Urban | | | | | | | | | | | | | | |
| | Interstate | | | | | | | | | | | | | | |
Year	Not Reported	Poor	%	Mediocre	%	Fair	%	Good	%	Very Good	%	Unpaved	%	Total Reported	%
1990	–	993	8.6	*	*	3,717	32.2	*	*	6,817	59.1	–	–	11,527	100.0
1991	–	881	7.6	*	*	3,744	32.3	*	*	6,978	60.1	–	–	11,603	100.0
1992	–	884	7.1	1,651	13.2	2,122	17.0	3,487	28.0	4,322	34.7	–	–	12,466	100.0
1993	1,454	1,228	10.7	2,830	24.8	2,315	20.3	3,000	26.3	2,051	18.0	–	–	11,424	100.0
1994	416	1,562	12.3	3,598	28.3	3,024	23.8	3,341	26.3	1,185	9.3	–	–	12,710	100.0
1995	857	222	1.8	1,057	8.6	6,237	50.7	3,389	27.5	1,402	11.4	–	–	12,307	100.0

Source: *National Transportation Statistics, 1997*, Bureau of Transportation Statistics, Washington, DC, 1996

turally inferior bridges need significant maintenance attention, rehabilitation or replacement. *Functionally defective* bridges are those that do not have the lane widths, shoulder widths, or vertical clearances adequate for the traffic demand, or the waterway of the bridge may be inadequate and allow occasional flooding of the roadway.

The FHWA reports that the percentage of roadways in good paved condition has improved over the past few years. Rural roads have improved more over recent years and are in better shape than urban roads. In 1996, 55 percent of rural interstates were in good or very good condition, up from 43 percent in 1994, compared to 38 percent of urban interstates that were in good or very good condition in 1996, up from 33 percent in 1994. (See Table 3.8.) The number of interstate bridges classified as deficient decreased, as did the number of faulty bridges on arterial and collector roads. Naturally, because of traffic loads and environmental conditions, all pavements will continue to deteriorate and will require ongoing rehabilitation programs to maintain the pavement structure in acceptable condition.

Traffic Congestion

Highway congestion continues to be a major concern for both urban and suburban areas of the nation. Population and business activities have increasingly become concentrated in metropolitan areas. Since 1980, about 86 percent of the country's population growth has been in metropolitan areas, with about 75 percent in the suburbs. This tremendous growth has greatly exceeded the nation's highway development. The Department of Transportation projects that this suburbanization will put an even greater demand on the already strained urban highway capacity.

Most peak-hour congestion in the United States occurs in the metropolitan areas with populations over one million. In 1996, the Federal Transit Administration (FTA) estimated that the annual economic loss to U.S. businesses caused by traffic congestion was $40 billion a year.

The measure of highway congestion severity is the ratio of the volume of traffic using a road in rush hour to the demand capacity of service flow of that road

TABLE 3.7

Bridge Conditions

(as of December 31, 1996)

	National Highway System [1]		Other Federal-Aid Highways [2]		Non-Federal-Aid Highways [3]		Total Highways	
	Number	Percent	Number	Percent	Number	Percent	Number	Percent
Structurally Deficient	9,690	7.6	22,597	13.2	69,231	24.4	101,518	17.4
Functionally Obsolete	23,230	18.2	24,025	14.1	33,953	12.0	81,208	14.0
All Other Bridges	94,816	74.2	124,334	72.7	179,987	63.6	399,137	68.6
Total Bridges in Inventory	127,736	100.0	170,956	100.0	283,171	100.0	581,863	100.0

[1] Includes all Interstate and other principal arterials.
[2] Includes all other highways except minor collectors and local roads and streets.
[3] Includes rural minor collectors and local roads and streets.

Source: *Our Nation's Highways*, Federal Highway Administration, Washington, DC, 1998

Highway fatality rates have declined significantly in both rural and urban areas over the past decade. This is partly due to changes in driving habits, such as increased use of seat belts, the decline in drunk driving, and the improvement in both highway and vehicle design. The Interstate System is the safest type of highway with the lowest fatality rates. Highway fatality rates have declined on both arterial and collector roads, especially in rural areas, but the rate of decline has been slower in urban areas.

(V/SF). The higher the value of the ratio, the more crowded the highway. For example, above 0.80, travelers on the road experience notable slowdowns. A ratio of more than 0.95 indicates serious congestion, and at 1.00 any incident will cause stop-and-go travel. Figure 3.5 shows that, by 1996, travel congestion on the urban Interstate System and urban National Highway System had stabilized at about 54 percent and 45 percent, respectively.

The first motor vehicle death in the United States occurred in New York City on September 13, 1899. In 1979, 53,524 people died in motor vehicle accidents. The number dropped to 40,982 in 1992, but

Highway Safety

Highway safety is one of the nation's most important concerns. The primary federal involvement in highway safety is the introduction of the most modern highway design and nationwide traffic control devices. Also, national programs discouraging alcohol and drug abuse, promoting proper use of seatbelts, and supporting various vehicle safety programs (such as defensive driving courses) contribute to improved highway safety.

TABLE 3.8

Pavement Condition on Highways: 1994 and 1996

(In percent)

	Year	Poor	Mediocre	Fair	Good	Very good	Total miles reported
Urban							
Interstates	1994	13.0	29.9	24.2	26.7	6.2	12,338
	1996	8.8	28.2	24.8	30.6	7.6	12,419
Other freeways and expressways	1994	5.3	12.7	58.1	20.9	2.9	7,618
	1996	3.4	8.8	55.1	26.0	6.7	8,403
Other principal arterials	1994	12.5	16.3	50.8	16.6	3.8	38,598
	1996	11.8	14.2	49.1	17.4	7.5	44,469
Rural							
Interstates	1994	6.5	26.5	23.9	33.2	9.9	31,502
	1996	3.9	19.4	21.8	38.4	16.4	31,298
Other principal arterials	1994	2.4	8.2	57.4	26.6	5.4	89,506
	1996	1.5	5.9	49.3	34.0	9.3	91,998
Minor arterials	1994	3.5	10.5	57.9	23.6	4.5	124,877
	1996	2.3	8.3	50.7	30.9	7.8	126,158

KEY: Poor = needs immediate improvement.
Mediocre = needs improvement in the near future to preserve usability.
Fair = will likely need improvement in the near future, but depends on traffic use.
Good = in decent condition; will not require improvement in the near future.
Very good = new or almost new pavement; will not require improvement for some time.

NOTE: Interstates are held to a higher standard than other roads, because of higher volume and speed. Percentages may differ from those in other published sources due to subsequent revision of data after publication of the cited source.

SOURCES: U.S. Department of Transportation, Federal Highway Administration, *Highway Statistics* (Washington, DC: 1995, 1996, and 1997), table HM-64.

Source: *Transportation Statistics, Annual Report, 1998*, Bureau of Transportation Statistics, Washington, DC, 1998

has been rising since. In 1997, there were 43,200 motor vehicle fatalities. By 1955, 3 million people had lost their lives in motor vehicle accidents; between 1966 and 1997, 1.5 million more people died in motor vehicle accidents. For all highway systems, there were 1.71 deaths per 100 million vehicle miles traveled (VMT) in 1997, the lowest rate on record. (See Figure 3.6.) Because total travel is growing, the *number* of persons killed and injured may increase, although the *rate* is declining.

Preserving the System: Growth and Maintenance of Roads and Bridges

While travel mileage has soared 1,000 percent since the mid-1940s, road mileage has grown only about 62.5 percent since the turn of the century. In 1960, there were 3.5 million miles of roads in the United States; in 1997, nearly 4 million miles. (See Tables 3.1 and 3.5.)

The increase in road travel naturally causes more wear and tear on the nation's road surfaces. Transportation experts agree that the nation's congested and decaying network of roads must be continually rebuilt and that the investment of billions of dollars would pay for itself by promoting economic growth and productivity.

To pay for this future need, the Federal Highway Administration (FHWA) has developed two investment requirement estimates — maintenance and new construction. The *Cost to Maintain Conditions and Performance* plan recommends funds to keep the system running at its current level; the *Cost to Improve Conditions and Performance* proposal recommends funds to bring the system to a higher level. The FHWA estimates the cost to maintain the 1995 level of highway and bridge conditions for the period 1996 to 2015 at $46.1 billion (Table 3.9), while the cost to improve the system is calculated to be $79.6 billion (Table 3.10).

Both scenarios include the costs of repairing pavements and bridges in poor or fair shape, eliminating

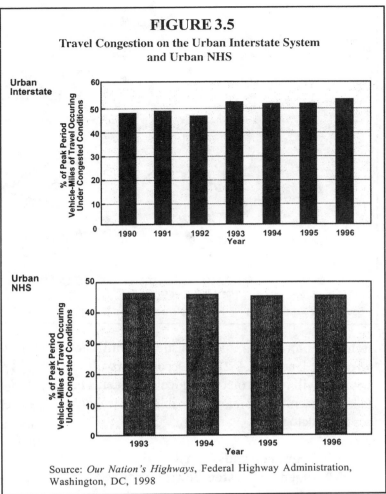

FIGURE 3.5

Travel Congestion on the Urban Interstate System and Urban NHS

Source: *Our Nation's Highways*, Federal Highway Administration, Washington, DC, 1998

unsafe conditions, and adding capacity. Under the *Cost to Maintain* plan, some facilities will improve and some will worsen, but overall, the system will stay as is. The estimates for *Cost to Maintain* are the lowest reasonable level of investment. Under the *Cost to Improve* scenario, all existing deficiencies will be improved. These estimates use figures from the upper limit of appropriate national investment based on either engineering or economic data.

INTELLIGENT TRANSPORTATION SYSTEMS

High-tech transportation, also known as intelligent transportation systems, combine automotive technology, computers, communications, and electronics to ease travel by reducing congestion and improving safety while remaining cost efficient. Some of the features of intelligent transportation systems are in-vehicle mapping systems, electronic message signs giving motor-

43

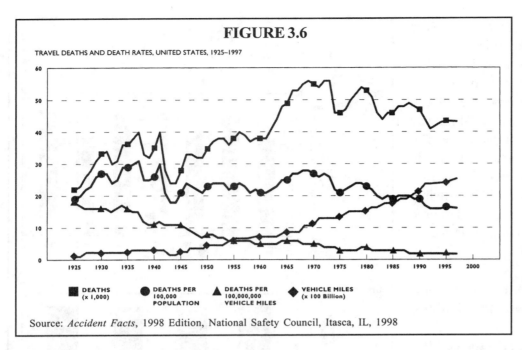

FIGURE 3.6

TRAVEL DEATHS AND DEATH RATES, UNITED STATES, 1925–1997

DEATHS (x 1,000)   DEATHS PER 100,000 POPULATION   DEATHS PER 100,000,000 VEHICLE MILES   VEHICLE MILES (x 100 Billion)

Source: *Accident Facts*, 1998 Edition, National Safety Council, Itasca, IL, 1998

rected the "smart cars." Other vehicles followed magnets embedded every four feet in a high-occupancy vehicle lane that they traveled. Although still in the developmental stage, these demonstrations show promise for the future.

A Minneapolis system uses highway video cameras, electronic road signs, and orchestrated traffic lights. Motorists receive updates from a special radio station. The experiment has helped to raise average speeds by 35 percent and reduce accidents by 27 percent on a three-mile stretch of Interstate 394. A Seattle concept, which involves electronic surveillance of entrance ramps and synchronization of traffic lights, has reduced travel time from 22 to 11.5 minutes on a 6.9-mile stretch of highway. Commuters on the Garden State Parkway between New Jersey and New York and on the Dallas Tollway are now using electronic toll-taking. The system involves the use of radio waves to identify cars and automatically deduct tolls from prepaid accounts. Motorists do not have to stop, but only slow down, as they go through tollbooths. In 1997, 77 U.S. toll facilities reported using electronic technology, up from 49 in 1995.

ists traffic information, and sophisticated traffic control centers. Under TEA-21, the Department of Transportation will fund projects to develop systems that "talk and listen" to one another, enabling the technologies to work together.

Smart Roads — A Traffic Management System for the Future?

Not surprisingly, during peak traffic periods, two-thirds of the cars on interstate highways are moving at less than 35 miles per hour. Around cities like New York, Los Angeles, Chicago, and Houston, many are barely moving at all. The National Highway System has reached its capacity. Limited space means that the historical remedy — building more roads — is not always an option. Seeking relief from the congestion, government, academic, and industry leaders are experimenting with automated highway and driver-information systems, known as Intelligent Vehicle-Highway Systems (IVHS), to route cars around bottlenecks, prevent tie-ups, and increase safety.

Two potential solutions to some of those problems were demonstrated in 1997. A combination of "smart cars," automated highways, and intelligent transportation systems displayed what they could do on a short test track at Miramar College in California. An onboard computer that contained radar, video, and laser sensors and followed radar-reflective tape di-

In California, a private company has opened a new toll road in the median of a heavily congested highway. The stretch of State Route 91 that runs through Yorba Linda has been known to be a 10-mile-long bottleneck. Now, commuters can cruise through this trouble spot at 65 miles per hour — for a fee. During rush hour, a one-way trip costs $2.50, which is collected electronically, like the method described above.

High-Occupancy Vehicle Lanes

High-occupancy vehicle (HOV) lanes are freeway lanes restricted during peak traffic hours to vehicles containing two or more passengers. They encourage car-pooling, relieve congestion, reduce gasoline consumption, and reduce air pollution.

There are more than 40 HOV projects in use in North America. They are dispersed among 25 metropolitan areas and cover roughly 400 miles, varying by hours of operation (from two to 24 hours per day) and occupancy requirements (two to three or more passengers, and bus-only lanes).

Critics feel that HOV lanes are underused and point out that the nine-to-five lifestyle for which they were planned is no longer valid, since work hours for many commuters are frequently unpredictable. They complain that HOV lanes are fully used only during a few hours per day. They note that a number of cities have found their HOV programs ineffective and have returned the lanes to the normal traffic flow.

TABLE 3.9

Maintain User Costs Scenario–Average Annual Investments Requirements: 1996 - 2015–Billions of Dollars (1995 Dollars)

	Capacity	System Preservation			Total
		Highway	Bridge	Subtotal	
Rural					
Interstate	$ 0.8	$ 1.9	$ 0.4	$ 2.4	$ 3.2
Other Principal Arterial	$ 0.7	$ 2.6	$ 0.3	$ 2.9	$ 3.5
Minor Arterial	$ 0.3	$ 2.0	$ 0.1	$ 2.0	$ 2.4
Major Collector	$ 0.2	$ 2.8	$ 0.1	$ 2.9	$ 3.0
Minor Collector	$ 0.0	$ 1.2	$ 0.2	$ 1.4	$ 1.4
Local	$ 0.0	$ 0.8	$ 0.5	$ 1.3	$ 1.3
Subtotal	**$ 2.0**	**$11.3**	**$ 1.6**	**$12.8**	**$14.8**
Urban					
Interstate	$ 4.5	$ 2.2	$ 2.3	$ 4.5	$ 8.9
Other Freeway & Expressway	$ 1.8	$ 1.0	$ 0.6	$ 1.7	$ 3.4
Other Principal Arterial	$ 2.0	$ 4.0	$ 0.7	$ 4.7	$ 6.8
Minor Arterial	$ 1.5	$ 2.9	$ 0.2	$ 3.1	$ 4.6
Collector	$ 0.6	$ 1.5	$ 0.0	$ 1.5	$ 2.2
Local	$ 4.5	$ 0.6	$ 0.2	$ 0.8	$ 5.3
Subtotal	**$15.0**	**$12.2**	**$ 4.0**	**$16.2**	**$31.2**
Total	**$17.0**	**$23.5**	**$ 5.6**	**$29.1**	**$46.1**

Source: *Condition and Performance: 1997 Status of the Nation's Surface Transportation System*, U.S. Department of Transportation, Washington, DC, 1998

San Diego County (CA) has turned some of its HOV lanes into HOT (high-occupancy toll) lanes. Under this plan, a vehicle with only one occupant in it may travel the HOV lanes for a fee of $50 per month. However, in other areas where this is not an option, frustrated commuters sometimes violate the two-occupant limit and travel in the high-occupancy lane alone in a car. Others buy lifelike dummies that the driver puts in the passenger seat, in an effort to make it appear that there are two persons in the vehicle. These drivers are subject to large fines if they are caught — in California, violators must pay a minimum fine of $270.

A spokesperson for the Department of Transportation admits that it is difficult to get people to give up the convenience of their own vehicles, but as traffic continues to increase, he predicts there will be more usage of high-occupancy lanes. Supporters of the HOV lanes call attention to the fact that HOV lanes, like highways, are designed for the present, as well as the future. When highways are built, they are planned for current traffic and the traffic that will exist 20 to 25 years in the future; HOV lanes will help ease today's rush hour congestion and will still be suitable 10 to 15 years from now.

TABLE 3.10

Maximum Economic Investment Scenario–Avg. Annual Investments Requirements: 1996 - 2015–Billions of Dollars (1995 Dollars)

	Capacity	System Preservation			Total
		Highway	Bridge	Subtotal	
Rural					
Interstate	$ 1.2	$ 2.6	$ 0.7	$ 3.3	$ 4.6
Other Principal Arterial	$ 1.0	$ 3.5	$ 0.6	$ 4.1	$ 5.1
Minor Arterial	$ 0.5	$ 3.2	$ 0.4	$ 3.7	$ 4.2
Major Collector	$ 0.3	$ 6.4	$ 0.6	$ 7.0	$ 7.3
Minor Collector	$ 0.0	$ 0.8	$ 0.6	$ 2.7	$ 2.8
Local	$ 0.0	$ 0.8	$ 0.6	$ 1.3	$ 1.3
Subtotal	**$ 3.0**	**$19.1**	**$ 3.1**	**$22.1**	**$25.2**
Urban					
Interstate	$10.3	$ 4.1	$ 3.0	$ 7.1	$17.4
Other Freeway & Expressway	$ 4.5	$ 1.7	$ 1.1	$ 2.7	$ 7.2
Other Principal Arterial	$ 4.2	$ 5.0	$ 1.2	$ 6.2	$10.4
Minor Arterial	$ 2.5	$ 5.7	$ 0.5	$ 6.2	$ 8.7
Collector	$ 1.0	$ 4.1	$ 0.2	$ 0.8	$ 5.4
Local	$ 4.5	$ 0.6	$ 0.2	$ 0.8	$ 5.4
Subtotal	**$27.0**	**$21.2**	**$ 6.2**	**$27.4**	**$54.4**
Total	**$30.0**	**$40.2**	**$ 9.3**	**$49.6**	**$79.6**

Source: *Condition and Performance: 1997 Status of the Nation's Surface Transportation System*, U.S. Department of Transportation, Washington, DC, 1998

CHAPTER IV

AUTOMOBILES

REVOLUTION ON THE ROAD

It would have taken a vivid imagination to envision the future potential of the first self-propelled land vehicle created by Nicholas Cugnot in 1769. Powered by a steam engine, it could reach a maximum speed of three miles per hour and travel 15 miles without refueling. In 1789, Oliver Evans patented a 42,000-pound, steam-powered carriage that could run on land or in the water.

The invention of the internal-combustion engine was a major development in automobile building. Gottlieb Daimler introduced the gasoline-powered car in Germany in 1887. The first successful American model was built by Charles and Frank Duryea in 1892-93, and by the turn of the century, 8,000 "horseless buggies" traveled the rough, unpaved roads of America.

The first factory devoted exclusively to the manufacture of automobiles was built by Ransom E. Olds in Detroit, Michigan, in 1899. Nine years later, Henry Ford's mass-produced, relatively inexpensive Model T transformed the automobile from a luxury into an affordable necessity. Americans' love of the freedom, mobility, and convenience of the car began and has never stopped.

TABLE 4.1

U.S. Car and Truck Production Summary

	Cars	% Tot.	Trucks	% Tot.	Total
1997	5,933,921	48.9	6,196,565	51.1	12,130,486
1996	6,082,835	51.4	5,749,410	48.6	11,832,245
1995	6,339,967	52.9	5,634,724	47.1	11,974,691
1994	6,601,220	53.9	5,648,767	46.1	12,249,987
1993	5,982,120	54.9	4,916,619	45.1	10,898,739
1992	5,666,891	58.3	4,054,563	41.7	9,721,454
1991	5,439,864	61.9	3,355,110	38.1	8,794,974
1990	6,077,885	62.1	3,705,548	37.9	9,783,433
1989	6,821,268	62.7	4,050,935	37.3	10,872,203
1988	7,137,397	63.5	4,100,557	36.5	11,237,954
1987	7,099,829	65.0	3,825,772	35.0	10,925,601

Source: *1998 Ward's Automotive Yearbook*, Ward's Communications, Southfield, MI, 1998

The automobile rapidly changed the nation's way of life. Workers no longer had to live near the factories where they worked, so they created and moved into the suburbs. Industry did not have to be built on waterways or railroad lines because trucks could go anywhere there were roads. Shopping centers, fast-food restaurants, and motels are all the result of increased mobility. Drive-in franchise restaurants meant that a hamburger bought at a fast-food chain in Detroit would taste the same as one purchased at a drive-in from the same chain in Des Moines or Denver. Drive-in movies, popular in the 1950s and 1960s, gave way to drive-through banks, cleaning establishments, and car washes.

Cars have also contributed to urban sprawl, a general decline in public transportation, air and noise pollution, and many injuries and deaths. Family life has changed since the younger generation

FIGURE 4.1

RETAIL SALES

Calendar 1997

Top-selling light trucks in 1997

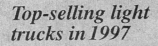

PICKUP

1 Ford F-series	710,156
2 Chevy C/K	527,842
3 Ram Pickup	350,257
4 Ford Ranger	298,796

SPORT-UTILITY

1 Ford Explorer	383,852
2 Jeep	Grand Cherokee 260,875
3 Chevy	Blazer 221,400
4 Ford	Expedition 214,524

VAN

1 Caravan	285,736
2 Windstar	205,356
3 Voyager	156,056
4	Econoline 150,135

Vans include commercial versions.

TOP 10 U.S. CAR SALES

			Market Share	Unit change from 1996
1	Toyota Camry	397,156	4.8%	+10.5%
2	Honda Accord	384,609	4.6%	+0.6%
3	Ford Taurus	357,162	4.3%	-10.9%
4	Honda Civic	315,546	3.8%	+10.2%
5	Chevy Cavalier	302,161	3.7%	+8.9%
6	Ford Escort	283,898	3.4%	0.0%
7	Saturn	250,810	3.0%	-10.0%
8	Chevy Lumina	228,451	2.8%	-4.0%
9	Toyota Corolla	218,461	2.6%	+4.5%
10	Pontiac Grand Am	204,078	2.5%	-8.2%

Top-selling cars by market segment in 1997

	Small	Middle	Large	Luxury
1st	Cavalier	Camry	LeSabre	DeVille
2nd	Escort	Accord	Intrepid	Town Car
3rd	Saturn	Taurus	Grand Marquis	Avalon

U.S. light vehicle market share
(Includes each company's total import and domestic volumes)

1997 Total volume: 15,121,690

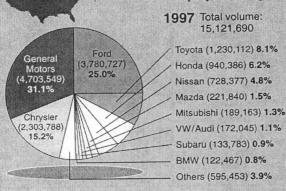

- General Motors (4,703,549) **31.1%**
- Ford (3,780,727) **25.0%**
- Chrysler (2,303,788) **15.2%**
- Toyota (1,230,112) **8.1%**
- Honda (940,386) **6.2%**
- Nissan (728,377) **4.8%**
- Mazda (221,840) **1.5%**
- Mitsubishi (189,163) **1.3%**
- VW/Audi (172,045) **1.1%**
- Subaru (133,783) **0.9%**
- BMW (122,467) **0.8%**
- Others (595,453) **3.9%**

1996 Total volume: 15,096,183

- General Motors (4,732,351) **31.3%**
- Ford (3,806,789) **25.2%**
- Chrysler (2,450,826) **16.2%**
- Toyota (1,159,718) **7.7%**
- Honda (843,928) **5.6%**
- Nissan (749,763) **5.0%**
- Mazda (238,285) **1.6%**
- Mitsubishi (186,127) **1.2%**
- VW/Audi (163,286) **1.1%**
- Subaru (120,748) **0.8%**
- Hyundai (108,468) **0.7%**
- Others (535,894) **3.6%**

Source: *1998 Ward's Automotive Yearbook*, Ward's Communications, Southfield, MI, 1998

can now come and go more freely. For most teen-agers, receiving a driver's license is an important rite of passage and a symbol of independence. For many people, the car is their second home. As they drive, they also eat breakfast, listen to a CD, and talk on a cellular phone. As with many inventions, the automobile has been a mixed blessing.

THE AUTO INDUSTRY TODAY

The transportation system in the United States provides U.S. residents with the highest level of personal mobility — in terms of trips made and miles traveled — in the world. The automobile dominates U.S. passenger travel.

In 1950, 23 major automotive companies made cars in the United States; today, there are only two American manufacturers — General Motors Corporation and the Ford Motor Company. The Chrysler Corporation merged with Daimler-Benz of Germany in 1998 and is now known as DaimlerChrysler AG. A number of foreign companies, such as Honda, Toyota, Volkswagen, and BMW, are also making cars in this country. The economic health of the former "Big Three" industry giants has roughly approximated that of the nation as a whole. The automobile market was weak during the early 1990s, but recovery started in 1992 and continues into 1999.

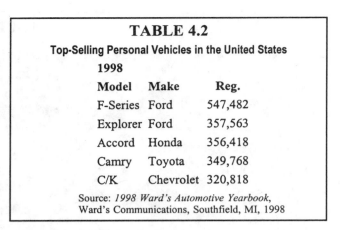

TABLE 4.2

Top-Selling Personal Vehicles in the United States

1998

Model	Make	Reg.
F-Series	Ford	547,482
Explorer	Ford	357,563
Accord	Honda	356,418
Camry	Toyota	349,768
C/K	Chevrolet	320,818

Source: *1998 Ward's Automotive Yearbook*, Ward's Communications, Southfield, MI, 1998

large, luxury Sport Utility Vehicles (SUVs) accounted for about three-fourths of the increase. (SUVs are considered to be light trucks.) SUVs have become the fastest growing sector of the motor vehicle market. More than 2 million SUVs were produced in 1997, an increase of 16 percent over 1996.

Retail sales dropped to 12.5 million new vehicles in 1991, the lowest level since 1983, another recession year in the United States. To lure consumers into dealer showrooms, the automobile industry launched a massive advertising campaign and offered rebates and discounts to buyers. With a recovering economy in 1993, U.S. retail sales rose to 14.2 million vehicles, 15.4 million units in 1994, dipped slightly to 15.1 million in 1995, and rose to 15.5 million in 1997. In 1997, the top sell-

PRODUCTION, SALES, AND REGISTRATIONS

The domestic production of automobiles and trucks dipped from 12.1 million units in 1997 to 11.2 million in 1998, but was still up sharply from 8.8 million units in 1991 and 9.7 million in 1992. Trucks accounted for 51.1 percent of the total production in 1997; cars for 48.9 percent. (See Table 4.1.) Production of the

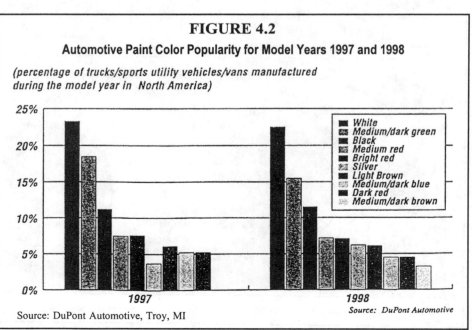

FIGURE 4.2

Automotive Paint Color Popularity for Model Years 1997 and 1998

(percentage of trucks/sports utility vehicles/vans manufactured during the model year in North America)

Legend: White, Medium/dark green, Black, Medium red, Bright red, Silver, Light Brown, Medium/dark blue, Dark red, Medium/dark brown

Source: DuPont Automotive, Troy, MI

Source: DuPont Automotive

ing cars were Toyota Camry, Honda Accord, and Ford Taurus. Most people who chose pickup trucks purchased Ford F-series, Chevrolet C/K, and Dodge Ram Pickup. The most popular SUVs were Ford Explorer, Jeep Grand Cherokee, and Chevrolet Blazer. In the van category, Dodge Caravan, Ford Windstar, and Plymouth Voyager were the top sellers. (See Figure 4.1.) Table 4.2 shows the five top-selling personal vehicles in 1998.

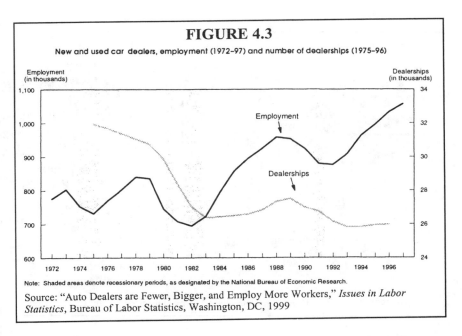

FIGURE 4.3

New and used car dealers, employment (1972–97) and number of dealerships (1975–96)

Note: Shaded areas denote recessionary periods, as designated by the National Bureau of Economic Research.

Source: "Auto Dealers are Fewer, Bigger, and Employ More Workers," *Issues in Labor Statistics*, Bureau of Labor Statistics, Washington, DC, 1999

White and dark green were the colors most car and light truck buyers chose in 1998. However, according to a survey conducted by DuPont Automotive, those colors were not quite as popular as they had been in the past. Earth tones, like medium brown, and colors perceived to be high-tech, like black, grew in popularity. Former favorites like red and teal (blue-green) slipped. (See Figure 4.2.) Color is important — research indicates that 40 percent of American consumers will switch vehicle brands if they cannot get their color of choice.

The number of new car dealerships peaked at 51,000 in 1950. By 1996, there were only about 26,000 automotive dealerships. The two factors responsible for this decrease are the increasing popularity of new car leasing and the arrival of the high-volume auto "superstore." (Superstores sell used and previously leased vehicles. They recondition the vehicles and include a warranty with the sale.) Most people who lease new cars lease them for two to three years. After that period of time, the high-quality, low-mileage, previously leased, late-model car becomes the stock for a superstore and is sold as a used car. The growing number of people purchasing their automobiles on the internet is also unlikely to benefit most car dealers.

In 1997, more used (19.2 million) cars than new (15.1 million) cars were sold, according to the National Automobile Dealers Association (NADA). There are three primary reasons for the used car

market growth. First, the average price of a new car in 1998 exceeded $23,000, up from the 1987 average of $13,000, while a used car cost an average of $12,422. The second reason is that the increased popularity of leasing vehicles has expanded the supply of used cars in good condition, often with many extras that the buyer could not afford in a new vehicle. Finally, the overall quality of cars has improved to the point that a used car offers good value for the money.

Although there are fewer new-car dealerships today, more people are employed by the dealerships. In 1950, there were fewer than 800,000 employees. By 1996, that number had grown to more than 1 million. This means that the average dealership in the late 1990s is bigger, has more employees, and sells more cars. Figure 4.3 shows the growth trends for dealerships and employees.

Even though the nation's economy is healthy, many potential new-car customers often choose either to drive their old cars longer or head for the used-car lot. The median age of cars on the road in 1998 was 8.1 years, up significantly from 6.5 years in 1990. The median age for trucks, including pickups, sport utility vehicles, and minivans, reached 7.7 years — the oldest ever. Americans are keeping their cars longer. The percentage of cars 14 years and older now account for more than 27 percent of all autos being driven, compared to only

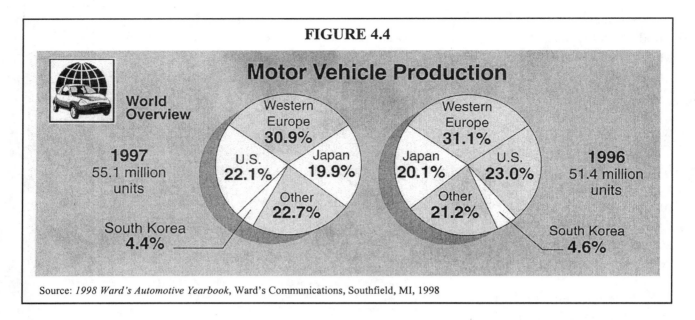

FIGURE 4.4

Motor Vehicle Production

World Overview

1997
55.1 million units

Western Europe **30.9%**

U.S. **22.1%**

Japan **19.9%**

Other **22.7%**

South Korea **4.4%**

1996
51.4 million units

Western Europe **31.1%**

Japan **20.1%**

U.S. **23.0%**

Other **21.2%**

South Korea **4.6%**

Source: *1998 Ward's Automotive Yearbook*, Ward's Communications, Southfield, MI, 1998

12 percent in 1980. In 1997, according to the Department of Transportation (DOT), 52.5 million cars on America's roads were at least 10 years old.

Car Registrations Continue to Increase

The number of cars on the roads continues to rise. In 1997, there were more cars, trucks, and buses registered in the United States than ever before. The Michigan-based Polk Company, which collects statistics for the motor vehicle industry, reported 202 million registered vehicles, up from 200 million in 1995 and 194 million in 1993. As the total number of vehicles registered in the United States continues to rise, so do the number of new car and truck registrations, which rose from 12.9 million in 1992 and almost 15 million in 1995 to 15.4 million in 1997.

WORLD PRODUCTION

In 1997, the worldwide production of 39 million cars and 16 million trucks and buses was the highest ever. (See Figure 4.4.) The United States' output was 12.1 million units, beating out Japan (11 million), previously the world's leader. Germany placed a distant third with 5 million units. North America (the United States, Mexico, and Canada), Asia, and Western Europe each manufactured one-third of the world's vehicles in 1997.

About 16 percent of the cars sold in the United States in 1997 came from foreign countries, mostly Japan. The proportion of imported cars sold in the United States has been dropping over the past decade; in 1987, almost one-third of all cars sold in America was made in another country.

Many Americans are recognizing that the quality of domestic cars has improved. Furthermore, many foreign-owned automakers, such as Honda, Toyota, and BMW, have opened up major manufacturing plants in the United States. Finally, some Americans prefer to purchase American cars to keep more Americans working.

Japanese Imports Remain Strong, But Slowing

Because many Japanese do not own private vehicles, preferring to use public transportation to get to and from work, most of the vehicles they make are sent abroad, especially to the United States. According to The Polk Company, in 1998, two Japanese automakers were represented in the five top-selling personal vehicles in the United States: Honda Accord in third place and Toyota Camry in fourth place (Table 4.2).

Since 1996, domestic manufacturers have produced more trucks than cars. On the other hand,

TABLE 4.3

MANUFACTURER CAR/LIGHT TRUCK SPLIT

LIGHT TRUCKS	1994	1995	1996	1997	1998	Change ('94-'98)
Domestic	47.1%	48.7%	51.4%	53.4%	56.8%	+9.7
Asian	23.3%	23.3%	24.3%	27.5%	29.2%	+5.9
European	3.7%	4.4%	4.7%	6.5%	8.9%	+5.2

CARS	1994	1995	1996	1997	1998	Change ('94-'98)
Domestic	52.9%	51.3%	48.6%	46.6%	43.2%	-9.7
Asian	76.7%	76.7%	75.7%	72.5%	70.8%	-5.9
European	96.3%	95.6%	95.3%	93.5%	91.1%	-5.2

Source: Polk

Source: Copyright © The Polk Company, Southfield, MI

Asian and European manufacturers produce far more cars than trucks. (See Table 4.3.)

American Car Sales in Japan

While Japanese imports account for a large segment of the U.S. vehicle fleet, relatively few American cars are sold in Japan. American automaker executives have expressed their frustration about the continuing failure of U.S. car manufacturers to make inroads into Japan's auto market. American automobile manufacturers feel that the Japanese market is closed to them because of the import duties on many American cars and the difficulties of establishing dealerships.

The Japanese, on the other hand, counter that the success of German auto manufacturers such as Mercedes-Benz, BMW, and Volkswagen in Japan is clear evidence that the American car manufacturers are not trying hard enough. According to a spokesperson for Nissan, not only does Detroit fail in its attempts to design cars specifically for the Japanese market, such as placing the steering wheel on the right instead of the left, but none of the American companies builds vehicles in Japan using Japanese workers.

Leaders of the American auto industry have pressed President Bill Clinton to limit Japanese auto imports into the United States. Executives of the auto industry want the president to limit imports of minivans and luxury cars by raising import tariffs, perhaps as high as 100 percent, which would make sticker prices higher and less competitive than in the past. The automakers are also asking for a change in regulations that would require Japanese cars made in the United States to contain more American-made parts.

THE COST OF OWNING AND MAINTAINING A VEHICLE

Driving Is Not Cheap

The average new car cost more than $23,000 in 1998. This figure included optional equipment, such as air conditioners and automatic transmissions, as well as state taxes and title costs.

In addition to the purchase price, the owner of a new car has considerable operating costs. The cost of driving a car in 1999 varied depending on the size of the car. Operating costs include gasoline and oil, maintenance, and tires. A small car owner paid 9.2 cents in operating costs per mile, a mid-size car owner paid 10.7 cents, a large car owner paid 12 cents, a sport utility vehicle (SUV) owner paid 11.6 cents, and a van owner paid 10.4 cents per mile in operating costs. (See Table 4.4.)

Ownership costs include insurance; license, registration, and taxes; depreciation; and finance charges. A small car owner paid $4,661 in ownership costs, a mid-size car owner paid $5,275, a large car owner paid $6,445, an SUV owner paid $6,332, and a van owner paid $5,722 in ownership costs in 1999. Total annual costs for a small car driven 20,000 miles in 1999 was $7,256; for a midsize car, $8,219; for a large car, $9,685; for an SUV, $9,297; and for a van, $8,628. (See Table 4.4.)

In 1927, Massachusetts became the first state to require drivers to carry auto liability insurance. Today, all states require drivers to show proof of financial ability to pay in case of an accident, and 44 states require every driver to carry insurance. Insuring a car is very expensive. In 1997, according to Dianna Gordon, in "The High Price of Auto Insurance" (*State Legislatures*, Denver, CO, March 1998), Americans paid an estimated $142 billion for auto insurance.

In 1996, drivers in New Jersey paid more for insurance than in any other state — an average of $1,013.74. Hawaii was next at $963.08, followed by the District of Columbia at $958.58. At the other end of the scale, Iowa drivers paid an annual average of $428.67, followed by South Dakota at $429.64, and Wyoming at $432.89.

THE BEST ACCORDING TO DRIVERS AND EXPERTS

According to a 1998 J.D. Power & Associates' survey of nearly 30,000 new car owners, Lexus owners are the happiest with their vehicles, followed by Infiniti, Saturn, and Jaguar owners. Mercury was in fifth place, up from seventeenth place the previous year. Improved Mercury quality was credited with the jump in customer satisfaction.

In 1999, *Consumer Reports* magazine selected the Volkswagen Passat as its top family sedan and Mazda Protégé ES model (well equipped) as its top small sedan. For driving fun, *Consumer Reports* chose the Mazda MX-5 Miata (well equipped), and for family fun, the Audi A6 was the favorite. In the SUV category, the Subaru Forester was the preferred small vehicle, and Lexus RX300 was the large vehicle choice.

The Ford F-150 was the favorite pickup truck, the Toyota Sienna was the best minivan, and the Honda Civic was the best green (environmentally friendly) vehicle. *Consumer Reports* judged the Mercedes-Benz E320 to be the best-tested vehicle over all, and a used 1993 Honda Accord for a best first car.

Many other sources can also provide valuable information when a person is purchasing a vehicle. A number of auto magazines give their readers thorough reviews of automobiles and light trucks. Other car buyers turn to the Internet, which has become particularly helpful in finding pricing, durability, and performance information.

TABLE 4.4

AUTOMOBILE DRIVING COSTS, 1999

Category	Small Car	Midsize Car	Large Car	Sport Utility Vehicle	Van
OPERATING COSTS (cents per mile)					
Gasoline & Oil	4.8	5.7	6.3	6.5	5.8
Maintenance	3.1	3.4	3.5	3.7	3.5
Tires	1.3	1.6	2.2	1.4	1.3
SUBTOTAL	9.2	10.7	12.0	11.6	10.4
OWNERSHIP COSTS (cost per year)					
Insurance	1,012	883	1,012	1,316	972
License, Registration, Taxes	175	223	279	410	392
Depreciation	2,871	3,355	4,084	3,648	3,468
Finance Charge	603	812	1,070	958	890
SUBTOTAL	4,661	5,275	6,445	6,332	5,722
DEPRECIATION FOR EXCESS MILEAGE (per 1,000 miles over 15,000 miles annually)					
	151	161	168	129	157
TOTAL ANNUAL COST					
10,000 miles per year	4,826	5,526	7,036	6,416	5,783
15,000 miles per year	6,041	6,880	8,245	8,072	7,313
20,000 miles per year	7,256	8,219	9,685	9,297	8,628

Source: American Automobile Association and Runzheimer International. Data for a popular model of each type listed with ownership costs based on 60,000 miles before replacement.

TABLE 4.5

Fuel Economy Standards for Passenger Cars and Light Trucks:
Model Years 1978 Through 1998
(in mpg)

Model year	Passenger cars	Light trucks[1]		
		Two-wheel drive	Four-wheel drive	Combined[2,3]
1978	[4]18.0	. . . .	. . . .	. . . .
1979	[4]19.0	17.2	15.8	
1980	[4]20.0	16.0	14.0	([5])
1981	2.0	[6]16.7	15.0	([5])
1982	24.0	18.0	16.0	17.5
1983	26.0	19.5	17.5	19.0
1984	27.0	20.3	18.5	20.0
1985	[4]27.5	[7]19.7	[7]18.9	[7]19.5
1986	[8]26.0	20.5	19.5	20.0
1987	[9]26.0	21.5	19.5	20.5
1988	26.0	21.0	19.5	20.5
1989	[10]26.5	21.5	19.0	20.0
1990	[4]27.5	20.5	19.0	20.2
1991	[4]27.5	20.7	19.1	20.2
1992	[4]27.5	. . . .	. . . .	20.2
1993	[4]27.5	. . . .	. . . .	20.4
1994	[4]27.5	. . . .	. . . .	20.5
1995	[4]27.5	. . . .	. . . .	20.6
1996	[4]27.5	. . . .	. . . .	20.7
1997	[4]27.5	. . . .	. . . .	20.7
1998	[4]27.5	. . . .	. . . .	20.7

[1]Standards for MY 1979 light trucks were established for vehicles with a gross vehicle weight rating (GVWR) of 6,000 pounds or less. Standards for MY 1980 and beyond are for light trucks with a GVWR of 8,500 pounds or less.

[2]For MY 1979, light trucks manufacturers could comply separately with standards for four-wheel drive, general utility vehicles and all other light trucks, or combine their trucks into a single fleet and comply with the standard of 17.2 mpg.

[3]For MYs 1982-1991, manufacturers could comply with the two-wheel and four-wheel drive standards or could combine all light trucks and comply with the combined standard.

[4]Established by Congress in Title V of the Act.

[5]A manufacturer who light truck fleet was powered exclusively by basic engines which were not also used in passenger cars could meet standards of 14 mpg and 14.5 mpg in MYs 1980 and 1981, respectively.

[6]Revised in June 1979 from 18.0 mpg.

[7]Revised in October 1984 from 21.6 mpg for two-wheel drive, 19.0 mpg for four-wheel drive, and 21.0 mpg for combined.

[8]Revised in October 1985 from 27.5 mpg.

[9]Revised in October 1986 from 27.5 mpg.

[10]Revised in September 1988 from 27.5 mpg.

Source: Automotive Fuel Economy Program, Twenty-First Annual Report to the Congress appearing in full in: U.S. Federal Register, Vol. 62, No. 107, Wednesday, June 4, 1997, p. 30656-30666.

TABLE 4.6

Domestic and Import Passenger Car and Light Truck Fuel Economy Averages for Model Years 1978-1996

(in MPG)

Model Year	Domestic			Import			All cars	All light trucks	Total fleet
	Car	Light Truck	Com-bined	Car	Light[1] truck	Com-bined			
1978 ...	18.7	....	....	27.3	....	....	19.9	....	....
1979 ...	19.3	17.7	19.1	26.1	20.8	25.5	20.3	18.2	20.1
1980 ...	22.6	16.8	21.4	29.6	24.3	28.6	24.3	18.5	23.1
1981 ...	24.2	18.3	22.9	31.5	27.4	30.7	25.9	20.1	24.6
1982 ...	25.0	19.2	23.5	31.1	27.0	30.4	26.6	20.5	25.1
1983 ...	24.4	19.6	23.0	32.4	27.1	31.5	26.4	20.7	24.8
1984 ...	25.5	19.3	23.6	32.0	26.7	30.6	26.9	20.6	25.0
1985 ...	26.3	19.6	24.0	31.5	26.5	30.3	27.6	20.7	25.4
1986 ...	26.9	20.0	24.4	31.6	25.9	29.8	28.2	21.5	25.9
1987 ...	27.0	20.5	24.6	31.2	25.2	29.6	28.5	21.7	26.2
1988 ...	27.4	20.6	24.5	31.5	24.6	30.0	28.8	21.3	26.0
1989 ...	27.2	20.4	24.2	30.8	23.5	29.2	28.4	20.9	25.6
1990 ...	26.9	20.3	23.9	29.9	23.0	28.5	28.0	20.8	25.4
1991 ...	27.3	20.9	24.4	30.1	23.0	28.4	28.4	21.3	25.6
1992 ...	27.0	20.5	23.8	29.2	22.7	27.9	27.9	20.8	25.1
1993 ...	27.8	20.7	24.2	29.6	22.8	28.1	28.4	21.0	25.2
1994 ...	27.5	20.5	23.5	29.6	22.0	27.8	28.3	20.7	24.7
1995 ...	27.7	20.3	23.8	30.3	21.5	27.9	28.6	20.5	24.9
1996 ...	28.3	20.5	24.1	29.7	22.1	27.7	28.7	20.7	24.9

[1]Light trucks from foreign-based manufacturers.

Source: *Automobile and Light Truck Fuel Economy: Is CAFE Up to Standards?*, Congressional Research Service, The Library of Congress, January 26, 1999

GOVERNMENT REGULATION

The Corporate Average Fuel Economy (CAFE) Standards

In 1973, the Organization of Petroleum Exporting Countries (OPEC) imposed an oil embargo that provided a painful reminder to America of how dependent it had become on foreign sources of fuel. Although the United States makes up only 5 percent of the world's population, it consumes 26 percent of the world's supply of oil, much of which is imported from the Middle East. The 1973 oil embargo prompted Congress to pass the 1975 Automobile Fuel Efficiency Act (PL 96-426), which set the initial Corporate Average Fuel Efficiency standards (commonly called the CAFE standards).

The CAFE standards required each domestic automaker, at the time Ford, General Motors, Chrysler (now DaimlerChrysler AG), and American Motors (which merged with Chrysler), to increase the average mileage of the new cars sold every year until achieving 27.5 miles per gallon (mpg) by 1985. Under the CAFE rules, car manufacturers could still sell the big, less efficient cars with powerful eight-cylinder engines, but to meet the *average* fuel efficiency rates, they also had to sell smaller, more efficient cars. Automakers that failed to meet each year's CAFE standards were required to pay fines. Those that managed to surpass the rates earned credits that they could use in years when they fell below the CAFE requirements.

Faced with the CAFE standards, the car companies became more inventive and managed to keep their cars relatively large and roomy with such innovations as electronic fuel injection and front-wheel drive. Ford's prestigious Lincoln Town Car achieved better mileage in 1985 than its smaller Pinto did in 1974.

TABLE 4.7

Alternative Transportation Fuels

Gasoline
A motor vehicle fuel that is a complex blend of hydrocarbons and additives, produced primarily from the products of petroleum and natural gas. Typical octane (R+M/2) level is 89.

Methanol
Commonly known as wood alcohol, CH_3OH, a light volatile flammable alcohol commonly made from natural gas. Energy content about half that of gasoline (implies range for the same fuel volume is about half that for gasoline, unless higher efficiency is obtained). Octane level of 101.5, allowing use in a high compression engine. Much lower vapor pressure than gasoline (low evaporative emissions, but poor starting at low temperatures).

Natural gas
A gas formed naturally from buried organic material, composed of a mixture of hydrocarbons, with methane (CH_4) being the dominant component. Octane level of 120 to 130. Energy content at 3,000 psi about one-quarter that of gasoline.

Liquid petroleum gas, LPG
A fuel consisting mostly of propane, derived from the liquid components of natural gas stripped out before the gas enters the pipeline, and the lightest hydrocarbons produced during petroleum refining.

Ethanol
Grain alcohol, C_2H_5OH, generally produced by fermenting starch and sugar crops. Energy content about two thirds of gasoline. Octane level of 101.5. Much lower vapor pressure than gasoline.

Hydrogen
H_2, the lightest gas. Very low energy content even as a cryogenic liquid, less than that of compressed natural gas. Combustion will produce no pollution except NO_x. Can be used in a fuel cell, as well as in an internal combustion engine.

Electricity
Would be used to run electric motors, with batteries as a storage medium. Available batteries do not attain high energy density, creating range problems. Fuel cells are an alternative to batteries. Fuel cells run on hydrogen, obtained either directly from hydrogen gas or from hydrogen "carriers" (methanol, natural gas) from which the hydrogen can be stripped.

Reformulated gasoline
Gasoline that has been reblended specifically to reduce exhaust and evaporative emissions and/or to reduce the photochemical reactivity of these emissions (to avoid smog formation). Lower vapor pressure than standard gasoline (which reduces evaporative emissions), obtained by reducing quantities of the more volatile hydrocarbon components of gasoline. Addition of oxygenates to reduce carbon monoxide levels.

SOURCE: U.S. Congress, Office of Technology Assessment, *Replacing Gasoline: Alternative Fuels for Light-Duty Vehicles*, OTA-E-364 (Washington, DC : U.S. Government Printing Office, September 1990).

Source: *Saving Energy in U.S. Transportation*, Office of Technology Assessment, Congress of the United States, Washington, DC, 1994

The Persian Gulf War in the early 1990s was another strong reminder to the United States of its continuing heavy dependence on foreign oil. In its aftermath, some members of Congress wanted to raise the CAFE standards to as high as 45 mpg for cars and 35 mpg for light trucks. Those in favor of raising CAFE standards by 40 percent claimed that this would save about 2.8 million barrels of oil a day. They also noted that if cars became even more fuel-efficient in the future, emissions of carbon dioxide would be significantly reduced. Carbon dioxide has been identified as the main "greenhouse" gas that contributes to global warming.

Moreover, with better mileage, the nation's millions of drivers would save money in gas costs. Despite some serious debate, these proposals gained little support, and they died a quiet death.

Table 4.5 shows the CAFE standards for 1978 through 1998 in miles per gallon (mpg). Table 4.6 gives CAFE averages for 1978 through 1996. In recent years, passenger cars have been losing market share to the larger, multi-purpose sport utility vehicles (SUVs), which are classified as light trucks. SUVs are subject to a less strict fuel economy standard of 20.7 mpg.

ALTERNATIVE FUELS

The use of alternative, nonpetroleum-based fuels in vehicles also offers opportunities to reduce overall energy use and emissions. Table 4.7 shows the variety of fuels that have been under consideration as alternative fuel sources in vehicles. According to the Department of Energy, there are about 386,000 alternative-fuel vehicles on the American roads.

Ethanol

To help reduce the nation's dependence on imported oil, Congress, in 1991, enacted the National Defense Authorization Act (PL 101-510), which includes a provision directing federal agencies to purchase gasohol (gasoline containing 10 percent ethanol) when it is available at prices equal to or lower than gasoline. Since 1991, federal agencies have taken a number of steps to encourage the use of gasohol. Executive Order 12759 of 1991 requires federal agencies operating more than 300 vehicles to reduce their gas consumption by 10 percent, an incentive to use gasohol. Despite these measures, however, use of gasohol has increased only slightly because of certain impediments — gasohol costs more than gasoline because it includes ethanol, and gasohol is sometimes unavailable due to the high cost of transporting and storing it. Most support for gasohol seems to come from farm states where the grains for gasohol are grown.

Natural Gas and Propane

One of the biggest problems for drivers who want to use alternative fuels like natural gas, ethanol, or propane is finding a pump. Experts believe that any fueling system needs a large customer base, and no one will buy cars that run on alternative fuel until a system has been set up. Natural gas requires less refinery work than gas and is already distributed around the continental United States. It also burns more cleanly than gasoline. However, as Amoco, which has the largest natural gas reserves among all major gas companies, found out, it does not sell.

Amoco built 37 fueling stations (basically compressors that would fill a tank to the necessary pressure) for $250,000 to $300,000 each. The company has closed all but four of the stations and will close the rest as the contracts expire. Each pump sold only about the equivalent of 20 gallons per day. None of the pumps made enough money to pay for the installation costs, and only one pump, located in Atlanta, Georgia, came close to covering its maintenance costs. That pump was built for the 1996 Olympics, when natural gas-powered vehicles were brought in for display.

In 1997, Chrysler was producing a natural gas version of its Dodge Ram pickup truck. Subsequently, its tank supplier went out of business, and since its merger with Daimler-Benz, further plans are on hold. Ford produced six natural gas vehicles in the 1998 model year. In August 1998, a natural gas Crown Victoria joined the New York City taxi fleet. Recently, some large cities have begun to use natural gas in their bus fleets.

Ethanol, made from corn, is also hard to find. According to the National Ethanol Vehicle Coalition in Jefferson City, Missouri, there are only 35 service stations that sell ethanol. Each station averages sales of 2,000 gallons per month, compared to big gasoline stations that sell hundreds of thousands of gallons each month. Nonetheless, Ford plans to build 250,000 cars, minivans, and pickup trucks that will run on ethanol mixtures by 2002.

Propane has been the most successful alternative fuel. According to the Department of Energy, about 71 percent of the approximately 386,000 alternative fuel vehicles in the country use propane.

Hydrogen

For decades, advocates of hydrogen have promoted it as the fuel of the future — abundant, clean, and cheap. Hydrogen researchers from universities, laboratories, and private companies claim their industry has already produced vehicles that could be ready to market if problems of fuel supply and distribution could be solved. Other experts contend that economics and safety concerns may limit hydrogen's wider use for decades.

Fuel Cell Vehicles

A fuel cell uses an electro-chemical process that converts the energy of a fuel into usable electricity. Some experts think that, in the future, vehicles driven by fuel cells could replace vehicles with combustion engines. Fuel cells produce very little sulfur and nitrogen dioxides and less than half the amount of the greenhouse gas carbon dioxide. Hydrogen, natural gas, methanol, and gasoline can all be used with a fuel cell. A New York-based firm, Plug Power, L.L.C., together with Arthur D. Little and the Department of Energy, has successfully tested fuel cell cars. Gary Mittleman, president of Plug Power, calls the breakthrough " ... a major step toward the advancement of zero-emission vehicles."

Electric Cars — Reality at Last?

Encouraged by government mandates and heavy smog caused by engines in urban areas, U.S. companies like General Motors and Ford are currently in various stages of production and development of electric and hybrid vehicles.

In 1997, 900 electric passenger vehicles, with a total value of $32 million, were sold in the United States, bringing the total number of electric vehicles on the American roads to 4,000. The average price of an electric vehicle in 1997 was $28,000. North America has 12 percent of all the electric vehicles in the world in use, and accounts for 10 percent of global sales.

EV1, a two-seater (Figure 4.5) by General Motors, was the first alternative fuel vehicle. It uses a battery pack of 44 nickel-metal hydride modules stored under the vehicle's floor and an electric motor, which move the EV1 160 miles on one charge. Currently, 480 customers in California and Arizona drive EV1s. EV1s can only be leased, and the monthly payment on the three-year lease is $399 — the same as the monthly payment for a Cadillac Catera. General Motors plans to introduce a hybrid production-ready model in 2001 and a fuel-cell production-ready vehicle in 2004.

Ford is working on an electric car that gets its power from a fuel cell rather than from batteries. The five-passenger, Taurus-size P2000 Diata is made of lightweight aluminum and weighs 2,000 pounds — 1,300 pounds less than the Taurus. The car carries compressed hydrogen gas and gets 63 miles per gallon. The fuel cell mixes the hydrogen gas with oxygen from the air to make water in a

FIGURE 4.5

EV1 Electric Car

Source: *Electric Vehicles: Likely Consequences of U.S. and Other Nations' Programs and Policies*, U.S. General Accounting Office, Washington, DC, 1994

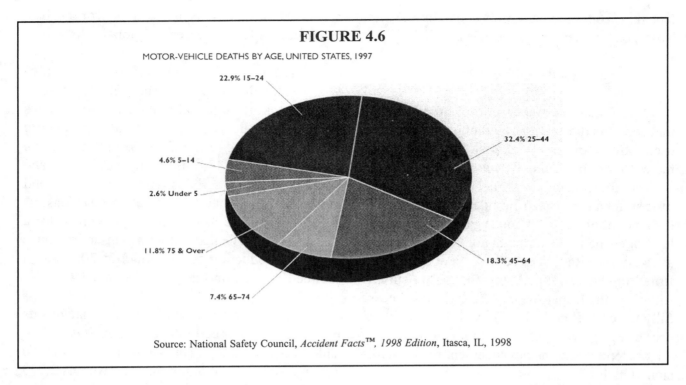

FIGURE 4.6

MOTOR-VEHICLE DEATHS BY AGE, UNITED STATES, 1997

22.9% 15–24

32.4% 25–44

4.6% 5–14

2.6% Under 5

11.8% 75 & Over

18.3% 45–64

7.4% 65–74

Source: National Safety Council, *Accident Facts™, 1998 Edition*, Itasca, IL, 1998

low-temperature chemical reaction that gives off electric current. This enables the car to run much farther than the totally electric car. The P2000 Diata is scheduled to go on sale in 2004.

Toyota has developed the RAV4-EV, a four-door, totally electric vehicle that seats five, can run 125 miles on a charge and can travel at 78 miles per hour. A permanent magnet motor is located under the hood, and a nickel-metal hydride battery is installed under the floor. More than 300 of the RAV4-EVs have been delivered to fleet customers. Consumer models may be available as early as 2000.

Honda has developed the EV Plus, a four-passenger zero-emissions vehicle. It was the first to use nickel-metal hydride batteries. The EV Plus has a city travel distance of 125 miles and a top speed of 80 miles per hour. The EV Plus has been available for lease in California since 1997. The cost to lease this car is $455 per month for 36 months. Overnight recharging costs $1.25.

Another zero-emission car, the NECAR3, has been developed by Mercedes-Benz. It is the first fuel-cell car to run on liquid methanol, made from natural gas. It travels 250 to 300 miles on a full 11-gallon tank. The prototype models are scheduled for 1999; consumers may be able to purchase this vehicle as early as 2004.

Tax breaks became available in 1993 for people who buy cars that run on alternative energy sources, especially for electric cars. Federal and state governments offer incentive payments of $7,000 to $8,000 to lower the purchase price, which can be about $35,000. The tax breaks are intended to compensate for the price difference between electric cars and the average gasoline-powered automobile, and to jump-start production of the vehicles. In 2003, 10 percent of all new cars offered for sale in California must be zero-emission vehicles. New York has a similar law.

SAFETY ON THE ROAD

The National Safety Council reports that deaths from motor vehicle accidents in 1997 (43,200) were down 11 percent from 48,290 in 1987. In 1997, more than 2.3 million persons suffered disabling injuries from motor vehicle accidents. Motor vehicle accident deaths made up 46 percent of all accidental deaths, with 30.1 percent of all motor vehicle fatalities occurring to persons age 24 and under. (See Figure 4.6.) About half (53 percent) of all transportation deaths involve automobiles; 41 percent, trucks; and 4 percent, motorcycles.

What Makes a Safe Car?

Today, as in the past, consumers are advised to buy the largest car they can afford, with as many airbags as they can afford. Experts advise buyers to look for safety features, such as height-adjustable seat belts, antilock brakes, traction control, all- or four-wheel drive, and daytime running lamps. Car buyers are advised to test drive the car to make sure they can sit comfortably 10 inches from the steering wheel and use the gas and brake pedals with ease. It is also important, after buying the car, to read the owner's manual to learn how to use the safety features.

Car manufacturers have sought to improve safety through a wide range of technological improvements. Today's cars are designed not only to help prevent an accident but to protect passengers if an accident should happen. Safety and car quality are uppermost in the minds of most new car buyers. The Insurance Institute for Highway Safety, which represents large national insurance firms and tests motor vehicles for safety, reports that 68 percent of car buyers claim safety as their most important criterion when making their choice about which car to buy.

The design of light trucks and sport utility vehicles (SUVs) has resulted in vehicles with handling and balance inferior to that of a standard car. Until recently, safety in the light truck segment of the automobile market received less attention than safety in cars. However, as a result of carmakers recognizing that "safety sells" and federal agencies responding to citizen input, by 2000, most new light trucks must meet the same standards as cars. Among the features already in use are automatic restraint systems, including air bags, side impact protection, rollover protection, head restraints, and antilock brake systems.

On the other hand, the height and stiff frames of SUVs, pickup trucks, and vans were responsible for an estimated 2,000 extra deaths in traffic accidents in 1996. The 2,000 deaths represent 5 percent of the approximately 40,000 Americans who die in fatal automobile crashes each year. Government regulators claim that the design of these vehicles and their weight pose dangers to cars. In a recent government test, a Chevrolet Lumina mid-size sedan, a Ford Explorer SUV, a Chevrolet S-10 pickup truck, and a Dodge Caravan minivan were each crashed at 35 mph into the front, driver-side corners of Honda Accord sedans traveling in the opposite direction at the same speed. The Explorer did the most damage; the Lumina, the least. The Explorer caused more than three times as much injury as the Lumina to the heads and twice as much injury to the chests and necks of the crash dummies in the driver's seat of the Accord. (The crash dummies were wearing seat belts, and the air bags deployed properly.)

Seat Belts

Seat belts have been standard equipment in cars for years. New York became the first state to enact

---

TABLE 4.8

Restraint Use Rates for Passenger Car Occupants in Fatal Crashes, 1987 and 1997

Type of Occupant	Restraint Use Rate (Percent)	
	1987	1997
Drivers	36	60
Passengers		
Front Seat	34	58
Rear Seat	25	40
5 Years Old and Over	28	49
4 Years Old and Under	49	68
All Passengers	30	50
All Occupants	33	56

Source: *Traffic Safety Facts, 1997: Overview*, National Highway Traffic Safety Administration, Washington, DC, n.d.

laws mandating their use in 1984. The old lap belt and shoulder restraints, however, have given way to newer, more effective devices. The "inertial reel" design favored by both safety experts and most European carmakers allows passengers to move around, but the reel pulls tight when the passenger sits upright.

By 1999, 49 states and the District of Columbia had adopted mandatory laws for the use of seat belts (New Hampshire being the lone exception), and all 50 states and the District of Columbia have child-restraint use laws in effect. The National Highway Traffic Safety Administration (NHTSA) estimates that more than 15,000 lives could be saved annually if car occupants wore seat belts. Mandatory seat-belt laws help encourage people to buckle up. If caught driving without a seat belt, the driver can be ticketed. The highest fine, $50, is imposed in three states — New Mexico, New York, and Texas. Table 4.8 compares the percentage of restraint use in 1987 and 1997.

In 1998 Congress passed, and President Clinton signed, the Transportation Equity Act for the Twenty-first Century (TEA-21; PL 105-178), re-authorizing the Intermodal Surface Transportation Efficiency Act (ISTEA; PL 102-240), which expired in 1997. Under TEA-21, states have many incentives to improve transportation safety, including grants to encourage programs that increase seat-belt use and reduce highway deaths. One part of the incentive program allows the transportation secretary to make grants to states that adopt primary safety belt laws allowing a law enforcement officer to pull a driver over for not wearing a seat belt. There are also grants for education in child protection.

Child Safety Seats

Although in recent years the increase in child safety-seat use has saved lives and prevented injuries to infants and toddlers, motor vehicle accidents remain the leading cause of death among U.S. children ages 1 to 4, according to the U.S. Department of Transportation. Researchers at the University of California, Irvine, found that adult drivers who fail to wear safety belts are only one-third as likely to use car restraints for their young children as drivers who use safety belts themselves. About 60 percent of children killed in car crashes are not buckled in, although there are often child safety seats in the cars.

In 1997, 604 children under age 5 were killed in motor vehicles crashes — more than half of those children were totally unrestrained. The number of fatalities among children younger than age 5 has increased steadily. The NHTSA claims the increase is because (1) the child population is growing and (2) children are being transported in automobiles more than in the past. The National Transportation Safety Board also points out that many parents do not install child safety seats correctly and often do not realize it until after a crash.

An estimated 80 percent of child seats in cars are not properly installed. The lack of correctly installed child car seats contributed to the deaths of about 50 preschool children in 1995. The NTSB supports a nationwide network of installation sites for child seats where parents and other caregivers can go to learn how to install the seats correctly.

Ergonomics

Ergonomics, in relation to cars, means that everything in the car is designed for easy viewing and driving. In the past, there was a trend toward unnecessary lights and controls on the dashboard. People spent too much time searching dashboard dials to find the gas gauge or the button to turn on the radio. In a car traveling 65 miles an hour, such distractions can cause major problems, including fatal accidents. Now, manufacturers are simplifying driving; for example, the controls and displays are not hidden by the steering wheel. The trend is toward a minimum number of dials and controls at the driver's fingertips.

Air Bags

Frontal collisions are the cause of almost half of all vehicle fatalities. The NHTSA believes that air bags may be the most important safety breakthrough in decades. As of 1995, every new car, domestic and imported, at a minimum, offered air bags as an option. Beginning with model year 1998, all new passenger cars were required to have driver and passenger air bags along with safety belts. These laws applied to light trucks beginning in model year 1999.

Air bags are designed to inflate when a car is involved in a collision when traveling more than 14 miles per hour. The device inflates in one-thirtieth of a second, about the same length of time as it takes to blink. Some companies are now introducing air bags in side panels, which would protect drivers and passengers from side-impact collisions. Federal regulators, however, point out that some of the side air bags on cars' rear seats could injure children riding too close to a door. The NHTSA has urged manufacturers to test side air bags thoroughly to protect children riding too close to them from injury. The NHTSA has concluded that air bags, together with lap/shoulder safety belts, offer the most effective safety protection available for passenger vehicle occupants.

This life-saving technology does have a drawback. The air bags inflate quickly to create a buffer between the upper body and the steering wheel, dashboard, and windshield. Ideally, the air bag is completely expanded before it comes in contact with the passenger. However, if the air bag is still inflating when it makes contact, injury and even death can occur. Passenger-side air bags have killed children and small adults by hitting them in the face. The force of the expanding air bag (about 200 miles per hour) causes the neck to break. For this reason, the NHTSA warns that children and infants should always be placed in the back seat of the vehicle. If a small adult or child must sit in the front seat of the car, experts advise that the seat should be adjusted as far back as possible. Air bags are useless in rear impact crashes or when a car rolls over.

In 1999, Ford Motor Company announced that it had found a way to make air bags inflate more safely. The new system is based on a computer that senses the car's speed, the weight and positions of the people inside, and the severity of the collision. Some parts of the new system will be installed in the 2000 Taurus. Within three years, the complete system should be on all new Fords sold in the United States. There will be no extra cost for the improved system. Although Ford was first to introduce the system, other automakers have similar systems in production.

The system will use a two-stage air bag that will expand at full force in higher-speed collisions and more slowly in lower-speed crashes. The bags will not inflate in minor fender-bender accidents. The bag will inflate more slowly if the driver or passenger is sitting closer to the air bag. It will also adjust to the weight of the rider, inflating with full force for a normal-size person, less force for a smaller person.

Anti-Lock Brake Systems

Next to seat belts and air bags, anti-lock brake systems (ABS) are probably the most important recent innovation in auto technology. Skids are caused when one or more tires lose the grip on the road and lock up (stop spinning). Anti-lock brakes help to prevent wheel lockup and help maintain steering control during sudden stops, evasive maneuvers, and on slippery surfaces. As with air bags, ABS is becoming a standard feature on most higher-priced cars and mid-priced models, and even some less expensive cars. ABS typically costs $500.

A December 1996 study by the Insurance Institute for Highway Safety found that cars with anti-lock brakes are more likely than cars without anti-lock brakes to be in fatal crashes, many of which involve only a single vehicle. Experts find this puzzling, but suggest that drivers may be taking more risks with anti-lock brakes or not using them properly. Anti-lock brakes need hard, continuous pressure to engage, rather than the pumping action many drivers have learned.

Front-Wheel, Rear-Wheel, and Four-Wheel Drive

In a car, not every wheel is created equal. Most cars are equipped to send power from the engine to either the wheels in the front (front-wheel drive) or to the ones in the back (rear-wheel drive). Some deliver power to all four wheels at once (four-wheel or all-wheel drive). All have different advantages.

Front-wheel drive vehicles have the weight of the engine pushing down on the tires, thus improving traction on slippery roads. Large car owners prefer rear-wheel drive. If a car is towing a boat or trailer, rear-wheel drive puts extra force on the rear axle, which creates extra traction. Also, rear-wheel drive is called the "driver-friendly" option. When the driver pushes down on the gas pedal, the weight is transferred to the rear wheels, causing faster starts, which makes this option popular with sports car owners and other high performance drivers. Spreading the power to all four wheels (four-wheel drive) provides a better grip on the road, an important safety feature for driving on snow, ice, or unpaved roads.

A new alternative is the so-called Traction Control System (TCS), which is a spin-off of the anti-lock brake system. When a wheel begins to spin while accelerating, the TCS gently brakes only the spinning wheel, thus slowing it down until it regains traction. The technology of TCS is simpler than that of four-wheel drive and uses less fuel. In the future, TCS will possibly become a popular, as well as cheaper, option for new car buyers.

Space-Age Technology — Smart Cars

With the help of new technology known as Intelligent Vehicle Highway Systems (IVHS), the cars of the future will largely be mobile computers and will provide safety features that not only reduce accidents (Figure 4.7), but also provide even more driver comfort. Ford is working on an infrared vision system that can see through the heaviest fog and has planned new head-up displays (HUD). The rear-view mirror can be replaced with a small video monitor that is not obstructed by back-seat passengers' heads. Located on the windshield (similar to the displays used in advanced military fighter aircraft), they offer a better view of the road, showing lanes, cars, and obstacles.

Safety officials are currently testing an electronic black box that automatically calls 911 for help after an auto accident. When the vehicle crashes, an electronic box beneath the back seat transmits the exact location to a satellite through the car's cellular telephone. The National Highway Traffic Safety Administration is developing the technology with Caltrans, a private company. The system is being tested in about 500 vehicles in Erie County (Buffalo), New York, and could be available nationwide by 2003.

Chrysler (DaimlerChrysler AG) has developed the Enhanced Accident Response System (EARS) that automatically unlocks the power door locks (if the car is equipped with an electrical system and if it is working) when an accident occurs. Then, 10 seconds after the vehicle comes to a complete stop, EARS turns on the interior lights. EARS is standard on all 1998 Dodge, Chrysler, and Plymouth minivans, and Dodge Durango, Dakota, and Ram pickup trucks.

The National Highway Traffic Safety Administration (NHTSA), in cooperation with industry and academia, is working to develop test-crash avoidance systems. These include

- Cruise control systems that will automatically maintain a safe distance from the vehicle ahead.

- Lane tracking systems that will help alert and prevent a driver from drifting into the next lane or off the highway.

- A cooperative intersection that will communicate data on traffic signals and oncoming vehicles, reducing the risk of intersection collisions.

- Automated collision notification systems that will guide emergency service personnel to the scene of an accident.

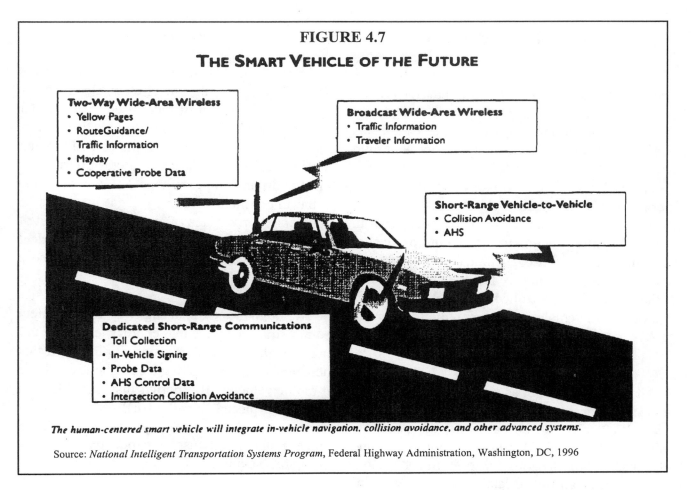

FIGURE 4.7

THE SMART VEHICLE OF THE FUTURE

Two-Way Wide-Area Wireless
- Yellow Pages
- RouteGuidance/ Traffic Information
- Mayday
- Cooperative Probe Data

Broadcast Wide-Area Wireless
- Traffic Information
- Traveler Information

Short-Range Vehicle-to-Vehicle
- Collision Avoidance
- AHS

Dedicated Short-Range Communications
- Toll Collection
- In-Vehicle Signing
- Probe Data
- AHS Control Data
- Intersection Collision Avoidance

The human-centered smart vehicle will integrate in-vehicle navigation, collision avoidance, and other advanced systems.

Source: *National Intelligent Transportation Systems Program*, Federal Highway Administration, Washington, DC, 1996

High-tech equipment is available in many luxury cars now. These "extras" include on-board navigational systems to guide drivers around traffic jams and bad weather. There are systems that use satellites to pinpoint the car's location and automatically call for help if an air bag deploys, tires that can run for 50 miles after they have gone flat, and sensors that detect rain on the windshield and automatically turn on the wipers. Today, road maps stored on compact disks are read by onboard computers and can be displayed on car dashboards.

Engineers in the United States, Europe, and Japan are developing "smart cars" capable of driving themselves. These cars enable a driver to enter a freeway, turn the driving responsibilities over to the car, and read the morning paper on the way to the office. In 1997, a combination of "smart cars," automated highways, and "intelligent" transportation systems was demonstrated in California. Cars followed along highway lanes, automatically slowing down and speeding up in response to the traffic flow. The vehicle was directed by a combination of radar, video, and laser sensors commanded by an onboard computer. The National Automated Highway System Consortium sponsored the demonstration.

At many car rental agencies throughout the United States, drivers can rent "smart cars" equipped with microcomputers, multiple antennas, a cellular phone, and a transponder that communicates with Global Positioning Satellites. The "TravTek" car provides the driver with information on traffic trouble spots and sightseeing attractions. In some cities in California, New Jersey, and Texas, drivers on certain toll roads do not have to stop and pay tolls. A scanner, which reads the bar codes on the car windshield sticker, identifies the car and automatically debits the driver's account. Oklahoma has electronic collections system-wide on all of the state's 10 toll roads. Electronic readers also operate overseas.

What Makes a Safe Driver?

According to NHTSA, approximately three-quarters of the more than 6 million motor vehicle collisions on U.S. highways annually are caused by drivers' attention being diverted in the moments before collision. Despite every device that auto manufacturers can provide to ensure car safety, it is primarily the vehicle's driver who ultimately determines whether or not a car or truck will be involved in an accident. Many factors play a part in traffic fatalities, including the amount of alcohol consumed before getting behind the wheel, the age of the driver, and the speed of the vehicle. When other factors are controlled, driver characteristics far outweigh vehicle factors in predicting a crash.

Alcohol Impairment

The use of alcohol as a contributing factor in fatal traffic accidents has been steadily decreasing since 1982, most likely because of tougher enforcement of liquor and DWI laws in most states and the raising of the drinking age to 21. In 1982, about 57 percent of all traffic fatalities involved an intoxicated driver (this includes motorcyclists). In 1997, NHTSA reported that 38.6 percent of all traffic deaths involved a legally intoxicated person (blood alcohol concentration of 0.10 or higher) — nearly 16,200 alcohol-related fatalities.

The highest rates of intoxication were for drivers in their early 20s. About 26 percent of all drivers ages 21 through 24 involved in a fatal accident were legally drunk. The rate of intoxication decreased steadily with age, and only about 5 percent of drivers on the road over age 65 involved in fatal accidents were drunk.

TEA-21 (see above) provides incentive grants from a $500 million fund to states that have enacted and are enforcing laws where blood alcohol concentration levels to determine legal intoxication have been lowered from levels of 0.10 to 0.08. Currently, 16 states have such laws. Grants are also available for programs that work to lower alcohol-related fatalities.

Telephones

In 1999, more than 60 million people in the United States subscribed to wireless telephone services, and 85 percent of them used their cellular telephones while driving. Experts warn that the distraction caused by using a telephone in a moving vehicle quadruples the risk of a crash during the time the driver is on the phone — about the same as the impairment caused by legal intoxication. Apparently, driver lack of attention, not the act of dialing, causes most of the accidents. The accident rate was the same even when the driver used a hands-free telephone.

Although the National Highway Traffic Safety Administration agrees that cellular telephone use increases the risk of a collision, it points out that there are benefits of having a cell phone available in motor vehicles. It reported that, in 1996, cell phone users placed 2.8 million calls for emergency assistance, and that, in many instances, cellular phones reduced response time to automobile accidents, thus saving lives.

Young Drivers and Accidents

The youngest drivers, those under age 20, are the most accident-prone. Thereafter, accident rates decrease, a notable exception being drivers over the age of 69 who are involved in traffic fatalities. (See Figure 4.8.) Young drivers between the ages of 16 and 24, particularly male, are disproportionately high contributors to traffic accidents and highway deaths. Young drivers also pose the greatest loss for insurers. According to the American Automobile Association (AAA) Foundation for Traffic Safety, about 75 percent of young driver citations are issued for speeding.

Young males consistently have more costly claims, and in addition to speeding, principal factors involved in young driver accidents are losing control of the vehicle and rear-ending the car in front. The AAA also reports that insurance companies are reducing the number of young policyholders covered under traditional coverage by sending them to more costly risk insurers.

64

FIGURE 4.8

Driver Involvement Rates per 100,000 Licensed Drivers by Crash Severity, Age, and Sex, 1996

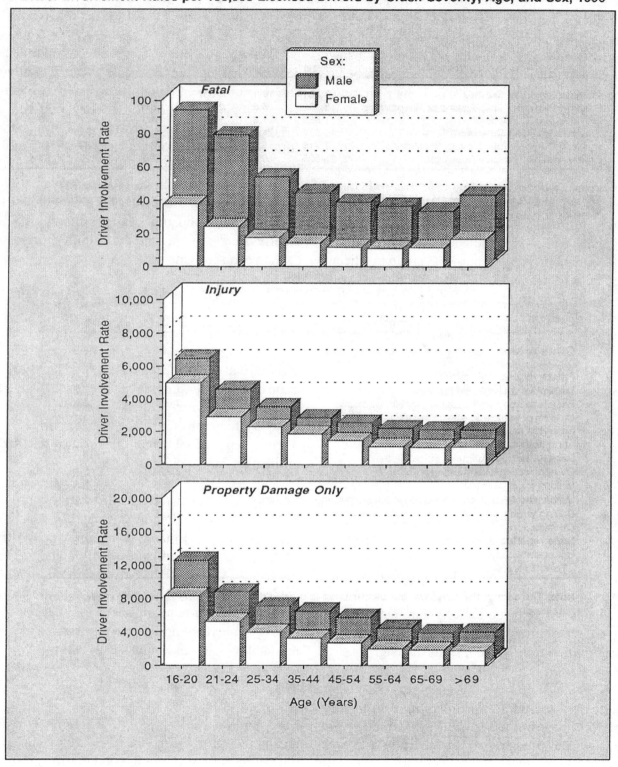

Source: *Traffic Safety Facts, 1997, Overview*, National Highway Traffic Safety Administration, Washington, DC, n.d.

Many young people object to being penalized with high insurance rates and are proposing "age-free" insurance policy programs. Under such policies, young beginning drivers would be required to pass rigorous driver education courses and sign contracts agreeing to abide by safety belt laws, drinking-and-driving laws, and other safety behaviors. In return, they would pay higher premiums for a specified time and then be eligible for refunds if they lived up to the contract terms.

Citing inadequate driver training as contributing toward teenage driving error, several organizations, such as the National Highway Traffic Safety Administration, the Insurance Institute for Highway Safety, and the National Association of Independent Insurers, propose a "graduated licensing" license. Under such a program, teens would not go directly from learner's permit to adult license. Rather, there would be an intermediate stage involving more restrictions and greater supervision during a teen's most dangerous driving years, from 16 to 18. The aim is to control and monitor their progress toward full driving privileges as restrictions are lifted when drivers gain added experience and maturity.

Older Drivers and Accidents

As the U.S. population matures, an increasing number of elderly drivers will be on the road. When the miles they drive are considered, elderly persons are disproportionately involved in collisions, particularly two-vehicle collisions. The National Safety Council has found that there are definite crash patterns among older drivers. They often fail to yield the right-of-way and sometimes do not pay attention to, or do not see, signs and signals.

Senior citizens' driving skills may diminish in other ways, including functional losses in vision, reaction time, and the speed of information processing. They often have more difficulty with backing and parking maneuvers. Older drivers have the most accidents making left turns across traffic. The American Automobile Association's Foundation for Traffic Safety notes, however, that it is not chro-

nological age but the driver's overall functional ability which predicts difficulties. This means that one cannot assume that a driver who is age 60 is necessarily more able to drive than one who is 75.

Older people enjoy the freedom and independence of driving their own cars as much as anyone else. Looking toward the future, when many more senior citizens will be on the road, the AAA has sponsored a study to develop guidelines for a "grade" licensing program — a license that carries some restrictions. Several states are already experimenting with these licenses, which attempt to balance the risks and safety needs of older drivers and others. The goal of the program is to help elderly drivers maintain their mobility for as long as they can safely do so.

Accidents and Driver Error

Most accidents on the road result from the interaction of three factors — the driver, the vehicle, and the road conditions. While motorists have little or no control over highway conditions and usually cannot predict whether their vehicles will perform correctly, they can control the way they drive. Table 4.9 lists types of improper driving that resulted in injuries or fatal accidents in 1997.

Right-of-way mistakes and speeding caused the most accidents and fatal injuries. The National Safety Council estimated that some type of driver error caused 66.1 percent of all accidents. (See Table 4.9.) Of collisions between motor vehicles, angle-collisions (collisions which are not head-on, rear-end, rear-to-rear, or sideswipe) caused most deaths, while rear-end collisions generated the most nonfatal injuries and injury accidents.

Road Rage

Aggressive driving, or "road rage," is erratic and dangerous driving characterized by speeding, tailgating, failing to yield, weaving in and out of traffic, passing on the right, making improper lane changes, running stop signs and lights, making hand and facial gestures, screaming, honking, and

TABLE 4.9

IMPROPER DRIVING REPORTED IN ACCIDENTS, 1997

Kind of Improper Driving	Fatal Accidents	Injury Accidents	All Accidents
Total	100.0	100.0	100.0
Improper Driving	64.6	73.8	66.1
Speed too fast or unsafe	16.8	13.2	11.0
Right of way	15.0	22.2	16.8
Failed to yield	*10.1*	*15.9*	*12.7*
Disregarded signal	*1.8*	*4.0*	*2.6*
Passed stop sign	*3.1*	*2.3*	*1.5*
Drove left of center	7.5	2.1	1.5
Made improper turn	3.7	3.6	4.0
Improper overtaking	1.1	0.8	1.1
Followed too closely	1.2	11.3	10.6
Other improper driving	19.3	20.6	21.1
No Improper Driving Stated	35.4	26.2	33.9

Source: Based on reports from 12 state traffic authorities.

Source: National Safety Council, *Accident Facts™, 1998 Edition*, Itasca, IL, 1998

flashing headlights. Dr. Arnold Nerenberg, a clinical psychologist, told the House Transportation Committee that he considers road rage to be a mental disorder. Dr. Ricardo Martinez, head of the National Highway Traffic Safety Administration, told the committee that NHTSA estimates that about one-third of highway crashes and about two-thirds of the resulting fatalities can be blamed on aggressive driving.

Reported incidents of "road rage" have soared 51 percent in the past five years, according to the American Automobile Association Foundation for Traffic Safety. AAA studied 10,037 aggressive driving incidents between 1990 and 1997 and found that the majority of aggressive drivers are men between the ages of 18 and 26. However, AAA also found that there were hundreds of cases involving older men and women who just "snapped" in traffic.

A recent AAA member survey showed that more motorists named aggressive drivers as their top concern on the roads. More drivers feared the aggressive driver (44 percent) than the drunk driver (31 percent). Growing concerns about these drivers and the problems they cause on the roads has led NHTSA to develop a number of programs to combat aggressive driving, including an education and awareness program and a demonstration project to study effective enforcement.

Arizona has passed an aggressive driving law, which creates the misdemeanor offense of aggressive driving. It is defined as an event where a driver speeds and commits two or more listed traffic offenses. Such offenses include failing to obey a traffic control device, driving recklessly, passing a vehicle on the right by traveling off the pavement, changing lanes erratically, following too closely, and failing to yield the right of way. The offender may receive a fine of up to $2,500, six months in jail, and have his driver's license suspended for 30 days. In addition, the driver must attend driver training and education classes. Arizona is the first state to create a specific offense of aggressive driving, although eight other states have introduced similar bills in their legislatures.

On the other hand, there are some who believe that there is no such thing as road rage and that it is a product of media hype. They point out that traffic injury and fatality rates are decreasing nationwide. According to Howard Fienberg, a research analyst at the Statistical Assessment Service in Washington, DC, "If you give people the term road rage, which is not defined anywhere, they react to it and associate it with just about anything." Certain people have always driven aggresively or taken their anger out on others while they were behind the wheel of an automobile.

AUTO CRIME

Thefts

Car theft increased by nearly two-thirds between the early 1980s and 1991, peaking at 1.66 million incidents. Since then, car theft has been decreasing, with 1.35 million vehicles valued at $7.5 billion stolen in 1997. Thanks to theft-prevention devices, there are fewer casual thieves, although there are still many professional thieves. When a professional auto thief steals a car, it is likely out of the country or stripped for parts within days or even hours. Recovery rates have fallen from about 70 percent to 50 percent in the past five years.

The National Insurance Crime Bureau, an Illinois-based nonprofit organization that studies vehicle theft and insurance fraud, estimates that about 200,000 stolen vehicles were shipped out of the country — nearly half of the 450,000 vehicles that were stolen but never recovered — in 1997. Many of the stolen vehicles leaving the country are hidden in big steel containers and loaded onto trucks and flatbed rail cars or cargo ships. Luxury sport utility vehicles, such as the Mercedes M-class and Lexus RX-300, are in the greatest demand overseas because they can handle bad roads in places like Russia, Colombia, and China.

In 1998, the three most-stolen automobiles were the 1989, 1988, and 1990 Toyota Camry. The 1994 and 1990 Honda Accord EX were in fourth and fifth places, respectively. In fact, the top 10 most-stolen vehicles were all Toyotas and Hondas. According to CCC Information Services, Inc., which tracks trends in theft and other vehicle damage claims for the insurance industry, Camrys and Accords were popular with car thieves because there were a large number of them sold.

Moreover, these cars usually last for many years, so their parts are in great demand. In addition, many of the parts for these vehicles are interchangeable over several model-years. The most-stolen American-made vehicles, in 1998, were the 1997 Ford F150 XL 4x2 pickup, followed by the 1995 Ford Mustang, the 1989 Chevrolet Caprice, and the Chevrolet C/K series 4x2 pickup. The most-stolen sport utility vehicle was the 1993 Jeep Grand Cherokee 4x4.

A vehicle stolen for its parts will earn a thief a lot more money than the whole vehicle would. According to the Texas Automobile Theft Prevention Authority, the estimated resale value of a 1993 GM Sierra is $7,000, while the estimated total value in stolen parts of the 1993 Sierra is $21,000. A breakdown of some of the major nonmechanical parts are camper top, $1,000; bumper assembly, $450; grille assembly, $865; hood, $410; radiator housing, $1,475; fenders $490; horn, $65; wheels $1,395; passenger compartment items (panels, air outlets, glove compartment, etc.), $2,200; doors and hinges, $3,410; bed (tailgates, fuel-tank shield, bumper steps), $2,870; and trailer hitch, $275.

TABLE 4.10

Places where carjackings occurred, 1992-96

Characteristic of incident	Percent of carjacking incidents		
	All	Completed	Attempted
Total	100%	100%	100%
Place of occurrence			
At or near victim's/friend's/neighbor's home	26%	25%	26%
Commercial place/parking lot[a]	20	16*	25
Open area/public transportation[b]	40	46	35
Other	13	13*	14
Distance from home			
At/near home	22%	25%	19%*
1 mile or less	22	27*	18*
5 miles or less	21	16*	26
50 miles or less	30	30	29
More than 50 miles	5*	3*	8*

*Based on fewer than 10 sample cases.
[a]Includes stores, gas stations, office buildings, restaurants, and other commercial places.
[b]Includes on the street (other than in front of victim's, neighbor's, or friend's home), in parks, and on public transportation, such as in a bus or train station or in an airport.

Source: *Carjackings in the United States, 1992-96*, Bureau of Justice Statistics, Washington, DC, 1999

Air Bags

Officials estimate that more than 50,000 air bags are stolen each year nationwide. As air bags have become more common in cars and light trucks, they have also become more popular with thieves. Police estimate that half of all recovered stolen vehicles are missing at least one air bag. Air bags, particularly on the driver side, are easy to steal because they are held in place with only a few nuts and bolts, according to the National Insurance Crime Bureau. Stolen air bags can be sold for $100 to $200, and are passed off as new, selling for up to $1,000 to an unsuspecting motorist.

Carjacking

Carjacking, a type of robbery, is a theft or an attempted theft of a motor vehicle by force or threat of force. Most carjackings (66 percent) occur in the evening or at night. Table 4.10 shows that 60 percent of carjackings take place in open, public places. Some commercial locations include stores, gas stations, office buildings, and restaurants. Other popular public locations might be on the street, in a park, or near public transportation, such as a bus or train station or at an airport. Most carjackings occur locally — 65 percent took place within five miles of a victim's home.

Between 1992 and 1996, according to the Bureau of Justice Statistics in *Carjackings in the United States, 1992-1996* (Washington, DC, March 1999), there were 48,787 carjackings, nearly half of which were completed. About 9 of 10 (92 percent) of all completed carjackings involved a weapon, while 75 percent of all attempted carjackings involved a weapon. About one-fourth (23 percent) of all completed carjackings involved injury to the victim, while 10 percent of all attempted carjackings resulted in injury. While all completed carjackings were reported to the police,

TABLE 4.11			
	Carjackings		
Annual average, 1992-96	Total	Completed	Attempted
Number of incidents	48,787	24,520	24,267
Number of victimizations	53,452	27,710	25,742
Rate per 10,000 persons	2.5	1.3	1.2
All carjackings	100%	100%	100%
No weapon	17	8*	25
Total with weapon	83	92	75
Firearm	47	72	22*
Knife, other, or unknown	36	20	52
Percent of carjackings			
With injury	16%	23%	10%
Reported to the police	79	100	57

*Based on fewer than 10 sample cases.

Source: *Carjackings in the United States, 1992-96*, Bureau of Justice Statistics, Washington, DC, 1999

only 57 percent of attempted carjackings were reported. (See Table 4.11.)

Often the carjacker is a young male who is after the vehicle or its expensive, flashy, customized accessories. The criminal may accost the person sitting in the vehicle, eject the victim, and then take off with the car. Some police officials believe that the new anti-theft devices make it too difficult for the vehicle to be stolen, so the thieves prefer to steal the cars at gunpoint.

Government Action

In October 1996, President Bill Clinton signed the Carjacking Correction Act of 1996 (PL 104-217), making carjacking a federal offense. If bodily injury has been inflicted, the maximum sentence may be increased from 15 to 25 years. When President Clinton signed the act, he said that he "hopes this legislation will increase the security of all Americans — particularly women."

In August 1997, Louisiana passed a state law called the "Shoot the Carjacker" law, giving motorists in that state who fear for their lives the authority to use deadly force against their assailants. Although there are laws that permit self-defense throughout the United States, this is the first law that specifically focuses on self-defense against carjacking.

CHAPTER V

BICYCLES, MOTORCYCLES, AND RECREATIONAL VEHICLES

BICYCLES

As noted in Chapter III, bicycles played an important role in the development of roads in America. In the early 1900s, the bicycle was a form of transportation as well as recreation. However, the growing number of cars (and the increasing hazards for cyclists) led to a decline in the use of bicycles as a serious mode of transportation. Bicycling has recently regained popularity as a form of exercise and sport.

Bicycle riding is one of the most popular recreational activities in the United States. In 1998, the Bicycle Market Research Institute reported that the bicycle industry was a $5 billion-per-year industry, up from $4.3 billion in 1993 and $3.6 billion in 1990. Because of government pressures to protect the environment, bicycles may likely become more important as a transportation option.

Who Rides Bikes?

According to the Bicycle Federation of America, approximately 47 million Americans age seven and older ride bicycles in a given year, and about 105 million people ride a bike at least one time in a year, up 10 percent from 1990. More than 8 million people used their bicycles to commute to work in 1998, double the 3.8 million in 1990.

For many years, the typical bicycle owner was a child or a teenager. Today, however, according to Richard Killingsworth, a health scientist for the Centers for Disease Control and Prevention (CDC) in Atlanta, Georgia, less than one percent of children between the ages of 7 and 15 rides a bike to school, and only 2.5 percent of youngsters who live within two miles of school ride their bikes there. These figures indicate a 60 to 70 percent decline from the 1970s. Analysts blame this drop on parental fears of crime and traffic, tight scheduling of organized play, television, computer games, and fewer sidewalks. Most of today's bicycle sales are to adult riders.

Men (53 percent) are somewhat more likely than women (47 percent) to ride bikes. Thirty-one million people ride their bicycles regularly (at least one time per week). Nearly 4 million riders participate in recreational bicycle events, and 250,000 race their bikes. Twenty-five million people ride mountain and hybrid (combination) bikes, and 1.7 million tour on their bicycles. According to Kevin Condit, marketing director for Adventure Cycling, a non-profit organization that offers tours and helps cyclists plan their own trips, interest in bicycle tours has grown at about 10 percent per year through the 1990s.

Commuters

Most bicycle commuters live in the Pacific states, where 10 out of 1,000 riders travel to school or to the workplace by bicycle. Most bicycle commuters (80 percent) are male, and 70 percent of those are between the ages of 15 and 34. These bicycle riders are, on average, less educated and earn less than other commuters. (Cyclists in this age group earn approximately $24,000 per year, while the median income for noncyclists in the 15- to-34 year age group is about $29,000 annually). On the other hand, middle-aged bike travelers, 45 to 54 years old, earn slightly more ($36,000) than other commuters of the same age group ($35,000).

Long Beach, California, has installed bikestations. Commuters who wish to bike to work ride to the bikestation, where a valet parks the cycle for the day. Bikestations also offer repairs, bike rentals, changing rooms, and outdoor cafés. They are part of a variety of new federally funded programs developed to encourage Americans to ride their bicycles.

Mountain Bikers

Mountain biking, as a sport, began in 1971. The mountain bike has upright seating, 26-inch wheels, and larger tires that are more shock-absorbent than traditional road bike tires, making the ride more comfortable. Its range of gears allows for more versatility. According to the Bicycle Federation of America, mountain bikes made up 55 percent of bicycles sold by dealers and specialty retailers in 1997, down from 63 percent in 1995. Mountain bikes are now considered to be a maturing segment of the industry.

Mountain biking became an Olympic event in 1996, with BMW and Montague Corporation donating red, white, and blue folding cycles. The 29-pound bike is now available through BMW dealers and sells for $795. Some of the features of the bike include cantilevered brakes and 21 speeds, which are adjusted by twisting the handgrip. The pedals are designed for special biking shoes that lock into the pedals in much the same way ski boots latch into skis.

The Mercedes-Benz High Performance Mountain Bike has 27 speeds and an all-aluminum silver frame. It folds into its own carrying case and sells for $3,495.

Recreational Cyclists

Over 33 million people ride their bicycles for fun. Bicycle enthusiasts and casual riders tend to be better educated and more affluent than the average American: 40 percent have college degrees, and 35 percent live in households with earnings of $50,000 or more. Thirty-nine percent of recreational riders are in professional or managerial jobs, and their median age (half are older, half are younger) is 35. Most riders (31 percent) live in the mid-West, 27 percent live in the South, and 20 percent each live in the Northeast and the West.

Pedalcyclists (riders of vehicles equipped with pedals) are classified into four categories by level of participation, from most to least active — enthusiasts, who represent 2.7 percent of the total; moving-up riders (those increasing their participation), 7.3 percent; casual riders, 21 percent; and infrequent riders, 69 percent of the total. Not surprisingly, most bike-riding occurs in the summer months.

Although enthusiasts and moving-up riders comprise the smallest segments of the market, they account for 30 percent of the money spent on bicycling equipment. A cycling enthusiast expects to pay $900 for a new bike, while a casual rider plans to spend $350, and an infrequent rider will pay little more than $200. Although only 16 percent of recreational riders own helmets, 69 percent of enthusiasts do.

A Positive Outlook for the Industry

Bicycle sales have experienced a series of ups and downs in the past several decades. A dramatic increase in gasoline prices in the 1970s and a growing concern over health and fitness combined to produce

TABLE 5.1	
Year	Million Bicycles Sold *
1998	11.1 (projected per The Bicycle Council)
1997	11.0 (projected per The Bicycle Council)
1996	10.9
1995	12.0
1994	12.5
1993	13.0
1992	11.6
1991	11.6
1990	10.8
1989	10.7
1988	9.9
1987	12.6
1986	12.3
1985	11.4
1984	10.1
1983	9.0
1982	6.8
1981	8.9
...1973	15.2 (record high year)

*Source: Bicycle Manufacturers Association, includes bicycle wheel sizes 20-in. and over

Source: "A Look At the Bicycle Industry's Vital Statistics," *1998-99 STATPAK*, National Bicycle Dealers Association, Newport Beach, CA, 1999

record overall sales of about 15.2 million bicycles in 1973. Sales then tumbled to 6.8 million in 1982, rose to 12.6 million in 1987, fell sharply to 9.9 million the following year, and reached 13 million in 1993. In 1998, an estimated 11 million bicycles were sold. Industry sales seem to be leveling off at approximately 11 million units annually. (See Table 5.1.)

Bicycle sales are generally linked to two factors: market saturation and changing demographics. To continue the growth that bicycle sales enjoyed at their peak, owners would have to replace their bikes every three years. Currently, however, the average bike is replaced only once every seven years.

More companies are making a wider variety of cycles. Constant improvements are being made in design and materials, including aerodynamic handlebars and disc wheels. Indoor fitness equipment has become an important part of the bicycle industry. Exercise bicycles and associated accessories have provided another path through which the bicycle industry can sell to people committed to physical fitness. Since cycling does not subject people to the pounding of some other sports, it can be a lifetime activity. About half the bicycle stores in the United States sell some indoor exercise equipment.

In recent years, the federal government has budgeted significant transportation money for construction of bicycle-specific facilities, such as bike paths and road improvements, which will make cycling more accessible.

The Imports

In 1979, American manufacturers heavily dominated the market: 9 million bikes were built in the United States that year, compared to only 1.8 million manufactured overseas. By the late 1980s, the situation had changed, with 5.4 million bicycles imported, primarily from Taiwan and Korea, and only 4.5 million domestic bikes being sold.

In 1995, imports accounted for 42 percent of American bicycle sales. Among these, 52 percent came from the People's Republic of China (Mainland) and 42 percent from the Republic of China (Taiwan). In 1998, the statistics remained about the same, with nearly 60 percent of mass merchant bicycles produced in the United States and the rest coming from East Asia, primarily China. On the other hand, approximately 80 percent of specialty bicycles purchased in America are imported.

Bikes and Accidents

Bicycle riding can be a hazardous activity. Every year more than 1 million bicycle injuries are serious enough to require medical treatment. The National Highway Traffic Safety Administration (NHTSA) reported that 813 pedalcyclists were killed in 1997, down somewhat from 833 in 1995 — about 2 percent of all traffic fatalities. (See Table 5.2.)

Fifty years ago, most of the bicyclists were children age 14 and under, and 48 percent of all deaths resulting from bicycle accidents came from this age group. In 1940, only 13 percent of those killed biking were age 25 and older, probably because riding a bike

---

TABLE 5.2
Nonoccupant Traffic Fatalities, 1987-1997

Year	Pedestrian	Pedalcyclist	Other	Total
1987	6,745	948	132	7,825
1988	6,870	911	136	7,917
1989	6,556	832	107	7,495
1990	6,482	859	124	7,465
1991	5,801	843	124	6,768
1992	5,549	723	98	6,370
1993	5,649	816	111	6,576
1994	5,489	802	107	6,398
1995	5,584	833	109	6,526
1996	5,449	765	154	6,368
1997	5,307	813	154	6,274

Source: *Traffic Safety Facts 1997 — Pedalcyclists*, National Highway Traffic Safety Administration, Washington, DC, 1998

was then considered a child's activity. By 1997, however, the situation was far different, with persons ages 25 to 64 accounting for 46 percent of all deaths from bicycle accidents. Although one-third of pedalcyclists killed in traffic crashes in 1997 were between 5 and 15 years of age, the average bicycle fatality in 1997 was 30.8 years old.

Males (53 percent) make up a little more than half of all bike riders, but they are much more likely to be involved in bicycle accidents. In 1997, males accounted for more than 87 percent of the bike deaths. Not surprisingly, most of these fatal injuries (about 90 percent) involved collisions with motor vehicles. For 65 percent of the pedalcyclists killed, police reported one or more errors related to the cyclists' behavior. Table 5.3 shows that failure to yield the right-of-way (22 percent) and riding, playing, and working in the roadway (21 percent) accounted for most of the deaths.

Two factors affect cycling and safety. First, unlike the car driver, bicyclists are not surrounded by two or three tons of metal to help protect them in a crash or a fall. Second, most bicyclists do not wear protective helmets while riding.

Bike Helmets Make Sense

Head injuries are the most common cause of death and serious disability in bicycling accidents. Riders who wear helmets reduce their risk of suffering brain damage in a biking accident by 85 percent. Twenty-four states require bicycle helmets be worn statewide and/or in major population centers. For example, in California, all riders under age 18 must wear a bicycle helmet. In 1998, Gallup International asked teens how often they wear a helmet when riding a bicycle, motorcycle, or moped (*YOUTHviews*, vol. 6, no. 7, March 1999). Gallup found that 37 percent of teen-

TABLE 5.3
Pedalcyclists Killed, by Related Factors

Factors	Number	Percent
Failure to yield right of way	178	21.9
Riding, playing, working, etc., in roadway	170	20.9
Improper crossing of roadway or intersection	103	12.7
Failure to obey (e.g., signs, control devices, officers)	71	8.7
Operating without required equipment	39	4.8
Inattentive (talking, eating, etc.)	34	4.2
Not visible	33	4.1
Failure to keep in proper lane or running off road	32	3.9
Making improper turn	27	3.3
Erratic, reckless, careless, or negligent operation	18	2.2
Improper lane changing	17	2.1
Driving on wrong side of road	14	1.7
Improper entry to or exit from trafficway	6	0.7
Failing to have lights on when required	4	0.5
Other factors	100	12.3
None reported	217	26.7
Unknown	21	2.6
Total	**813**	**100.0**

Note: The sum of the numbers and percentages is greater than total pedalcyclists killed as more than one factor may be present for the same pedalcyclist.

Source: *Traffic Safety Facts 1997 — A Compilation of Motor Vehicle Crash Data from the Fatality Analysis Reporting System and the General Estimates System*, National Highway Traffic Safety Administration, Washington, DC, 1998

agers claimed they never wore a helmet when riding and 13 percent use their helmets "rarely." A similar proportion wore their helmets all of the time (12 percent), most of the time (13 percent), or some of the time (11 percent). (See Table 5.4.) The NHTSA estimates that if all children ages 4 to 15 would wear helmets, 39,000 to 45,000 head injuries and 18,000 to

TABLE 5.4

TEENS AND HELMETS

How often do you wear a helmet when riding a bicycle, motorcycle, or moped?

	All Teens (503)
All of the time	12 %
Most of the time	13
Some of the time	11
Rarely	13
Never	37
Not applicable/don't ride these	14

Source: "Many Teens Have Cars Using Air Bags: Fewer Use Bike Helmets," *YOUTHviews*, Vol. 6, no. 7, March 1999

55,000 scalp and facial injuries would be prevented every year.

One of the biggest myths about bicycle riding is that lower speeds mean lower risk of injury. "Head injuries generally occur not because of the vehicle's speed, but because of vertical distance — how far your head travels to hit the pavement," observes Harry Hurt, director of the University of Southern California's Head Protection Research Laboratory and principal investigator in research involving motorcycle and bicycle accidents.

Most non-fatal bicyclist injuries do not involve a collision with a car; according to the NHTSA, more than 50 percent involve hitting the roadway surface. According to Hurt, the average height of a person on a bicycle seat is 5.3 feet. At that distance, the head can hit the pavement at 12.6 miles an hour, which can lead to death or irreversible injury to the brain. Other studies by Hurt show that a fall from slightly less than four feet at 11 miles per hour can cause fatal brain damage.

Governmental Support for Bicycles

Bicycle use may increase in the next few years due to recent federal legislation. Provisions of the 1990 Clean Air Act Amendments (PL 101-549), the 1991 Intermodal Surface Transportation Efficiency Act (ISTEA; PL 102-240), and the Transportation Equity Act for the Twenty-first Century (TEA-21; PL 105-178) encourage local communities to build bicycling into their transit plans. The Clean Air Act sets standards for air quality and requires some metropolitan areas to develop methods to reach compliance. These include taking steps to make bicycling a more viable transportation alternative. The ISTEA gives an even greater boost to bicycling by requiring states and communities to develop transportation facilities and plans that include nonmotorized travel. TEA-21 is intended to reduce air pollution from cars and cut back on traffic congestion by encouraging greater use of carpools, mass transit, and bicycles. TEA-21 also continues to support transportation enhancements like bicycle and pedestrian trails and scenic highways.

Under ISTEA and TEA-21, individual cities and counties may decide how to spend their funds. Seattle installed bike racks on the front of all its city buses, and Massachusetts is building 50 miles of paved bike paths north and west of Boston.

Rails-to-Trails

Rails-to-Trails is part of a government program, started in 1986, designed to make use of the hundreds of miles of unused, scenic railway corridors. The Department of Transportation's Surface Transportation Board approves the abandonment of a line after service has been discontinued. Then a voluntary agreement, called railbanking, may be entered into between the railroad company and a park agency, allowing the rail corridor to be used as a trail until the railroad company might need the corridor for service again. In 1997, at least 52 trails were included in the railbanking program. A former 321-mile-long Nebraska railroad track is being converted to a biking, hiking, and horseback riding trail, which, when completed, will account for 11 percent of a coast-to-coast trail of interconnected pathways.

Rails-to-Trails helps local organizations convert abandoned railroad corridors into bike and pedestrian paths. By 1998, Rails-to-Trails had turned more than 10,000 miles of tracks in every state into public recreation trails for bikers, hikers, and horseback riders. The organization hopes an additional 20,000 miles will be built by 2005.

Much of the funding for Rails-to-Trails conversions was provided by ISTEA. The preservation and conversion of abandoned railway corridors was one of 10 specific nonhighway projects for which ISTEA set aside $3.3 billion. TEA-21 will continue to dedicate funds to improving bicycle access through more Rails-to-Trails. The Department of Transportation also contributes money ($30 million annually) through its Recreation Trails Trust Fund.

International Bicycle Use

In countries with high automobile ownership, the extent of bicycle use has varied depending upon public policy and popular attitudes. During the past two decades, railway passengers in Japan and Europe have increasingly relied on bicycles as a convenient, affordable way to reach train stations. On a typical workday, nearly 3 million bicycles are parked at rail stations throughout Japan. In Denmark, 25 to 30 percent of commuter rail passengers set off from home on bikes.

China

Before 1979, the Chinese government rationed bicycles, and only one person in four or five had a bicycle. Following government reforms of 1979, rationing ended, and one-third of the road space was set aside for cyclists. By 1990, in Shanghai, there was one bicycle for every 2.2 residents — one of the highest densities in the world. By 1998, there were 9 million bicycles in Beijing, and one street, East Xisi, (pronounced shee-suh) was used by up to 6,000 cycles per hour during peak periods. In October 1998, in order to ease traffic jams, East Xisi Street was turned into a bicycle-free zone, with its bicycle lanes turned into car lanes. The government has not indicated whether other bike-free streets are planned.

Great Britain

About three-fourths (72 percent) of all passenger trips in Britain are less than five miles long, and half are less than two miles in length. In 1996, the British Department of Transport developed a national cycling strategy designed to double bicycle use by 2002 (over 1996 numbers) and double it again by 2012 by combining short bicycle trips with public transportation for longer trips. Improvements include better bicycle safety, additional road space for cycling, and new bicycle parking facilities at the local level. The Minister for Local Transport has established a National Cycling Forum to coordinate the project.

Finland

Finland's government wants to make cycling a part of national traffic policy, to double bicycle trips from 12 percent in 1986 to 25 percent in 2000, and to cut the number of fatal accidents by half. Finland estimates that doubling bicycle use would save about $125 to $250 million (in U.S. dollars) per year. A newly-created national bike touring network of 13,670 miles has raised cycling's status. Finnish cycling interests continue to work to obtain more government funding to support the program and encourage local efforts to increase bicycle use.

New Kinds of Cycles

Bicycle innovators are working on new developments for the industry. An electric-powered bicycle is for sale in Japan. In the United States, an electric-powered cycle is on the market and is currently being used by some police departments. Called the EV Warrior, it is similar to a moped. Built from molded plastics, the cycle is outfitted like a recreational bike, but has two 24-volt, 900-watt electric motors mounted on the rear wheel. (The vehicle can reportedly run for 20 miles before it needs a charge.)

The bike's manufacturers are targeting commuters, environmentalists, college students, messengers, and older riders, or anyone who enjoys riding a bike but would like a little help on the hills. The base model of the Warrior starts at $1,399. The higher-priced model, with directional signals, flashing hazard lights, brake lights, a hydraulic front disc brake and an anti-theft security system, sells for $1,899.

MOTORCYCLES

Motorcycling is both a popular recreational activity and a source of transportation. According to the Motorcycle Industry Council, Inc., a non-profit, na-

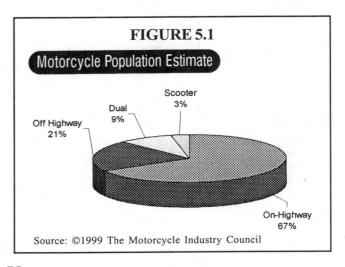

FIGURE 5.1

Motorcycle Population Estimate

Scooter 3%

Dual 9%

Off Highway 21%

On-Highway 67%

Source: ©1999 The Motorcycle Industry Council

75

TABLE 5.5

Value of the Retail Marketplace: 1997

State	Est. Economic Value of the Retail Marketplace ($000's)	Estimated Retail Sales of New Motorcycles Units	Estimated Retail Sales of New Motorcycles ($000's)
Alabama	$ 135,540	4,710	$ 33,750
Alaska	41,430	1,350	9,570
Arizona	190,700	6,320	49,010
Arkansas	82,250	2,890	19,000
California	1,129,850	40,140	319,780
Colorado	209,820	8,810	70,290
Connecticut	174,980	5,120	44,970
Delaware	34,330	960	7,930
Dist. of Columbia	13,330	470	3,080
Florida	569,820	20,030	161,260
Georgia	207,130	9,410	69,390
Hawaii	N/A	N/A	NA
Idaho	77,920	2,950	18,000
Illinois	488,220	15,780	142,560
Indiana	288,420	9,880	76,720
Iowa	150,200	4,290	37,400
Kansas	99,040	2,950	24,660
Kentucky	117,750	4,220	29,320
Louisiana	155,900	4,820	38,820
Maine	69,300	1,870	16,010
Maryland	186,420	5,760	47,910
Massachusetts	201,970	7,540	67,660
Michigan	421,130	15,550	122,970
Minnesota	193,490	7,330	64,820
Mississippi	70,520	2,330	16,290
Missouri	177,120	5,740	45,520
Montana	53,200	1,640	12,290
Nebraska	60,650	1,590	14,010
Nevada	104,420	3,570	26,000
New Hampshire	133,780	3,650	33,310
New Jersey	268,270	10,060	86,650
New Mexico	86,790	2,670	21,610
New York	493,220	16,510	144,020
North Carolina	307,240	12,360	99,240
North Dakota	34,500	900	7,970
Ohio	487,120	16,710	142,240
Oklahoma	136,950	4,380	34,100
Oregon	169,070	6,040	43,450
Pennsylvania	500,720	17,340	146,210
Rhode Island	37,230	950	8,600
South Carolina	161,280	5,660	41,450
South Dakota	48,610	1,230	11,230
Tennessee	191,170	6,340	49,130
Texas	535,190	18,510	151,490
Utah	107,910	3,930	26,870
Vermont	32,990	920	7,620
Virginia	200,120	8,040	67,040
Washington	188,120	8,700	63,020
West Virginia	77,320	2,430	17,860
Wisconsin	283,530	9,580	91,580
Wyoming	36,020	1,070	8,320
U.S. TOTAL	$ 10,222,000	356,000	$ 2,892,000

Note:
On-highway includes scooters and excludes mopeds. Off-highway includes competition motorcycles, and excludes ATVs.

Source:
1997 MIC Retail Sales Report,
Motorcycle Industry Council, Inc., Irvine, California, January, 1998.
1997 Motorcycle Retail Outlet Audit,
Motorcycle Industry Council, Inc., Irvine, California, August, 1997.
1996 Motorcycle Retail Outlet Profile Survey,
Motorcycle Industry Council, Inc., Irvine, California, September, 1997.

Source: ©1999 The Motorcycle Industry Council

tional trade association that represents the motorcycle industry, an estimated 27 million people rode motorcycles, scooters, or ATVs (all-terrain vehicles) in 1997. Industry and government agencies also use motorcycles in such varied activities as law enforcement, agriculture, and land resource management.

The Federal Motor Vehicle Safety Standards (FMVSS) define three categories or model types of motorcycles:

- On-highway — motorcycles designated for use on public roads. These machines must meet FMVSS standards. Generally, these vehicles have relatively large engines. Two-thirds (66 percent) of on-highway motorcycles have an engine displacement over 749 cubic centimeters (cc).

- Off-highway — motorcycles and all-terrain vehicles (ATVs) not meeting FMVSS standards. As a rule, these cycles have small engines. Nearly all (89 percent) off-highway cycles in use have an engine displacement less than 350cc.

- Dual Purpose — motorcycles designed with the capability for use on public roads and off-highway recreational use. They must also be certified by the manufacturer as being in compliance with FMVSS. Over half (56 percent) have an engine displacement of less than 350cc.

While the Federal Motor Vehicle Safety Standards regulate motorcycle manufacturing standards, the 50 states govern their operation, registration, and licensing.

Two-thirds (67 percent) of American motorcyclists ride on-highway bikes. About 1 of 5 (21 percent) ride off-highway motorcycles (this percentage does not includes ATVs, only motorcycles), 9 percent

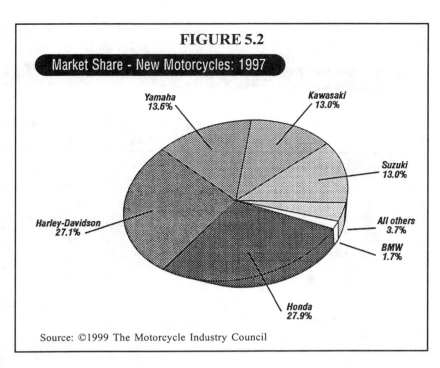

FIGURE 5.2

Market Share - New Motorcycles: 1997

Yamaha 13.6%
Kawasaki 13.0%
Suzuki 13.0%
All others 3.7%
BMW 1.7%
Harley-Davidson 27.1%
Honda 27.9%

Source: ©1999 The Motorcycle Industry Council

ride dual-purpose cycles, and 3 percent own scooters. (See Figure 5.1.)

Numbers

In 1998, there were 5.16 million motorcycle owners in the United States. Regionally, California has traditionally led the nation in motorcycle population. In 1997, the estimated motorcycle population in California totaled 913,400 bikes, followed distantly by Texas with 372,100. In 1997, 40,140 new units were sold in California and 20,030 were sold in Florida. The South had the highest motorcycle population in 1997, with 28 percent of all motorcycles in use. One-third (35 percent) of the nation's motorcycles, scooters, and ATVs were bought in the five states of California, Texas, New York, Florida, and Ohio. (See Table 5.5.)

Motorcycle sales peaked in 1970, when more than 1.1 million new units were sold. In 1980, 1 million were sold, and the number declined throughout the decade. The industry, however, recovered strongly during the 1990s with sales growing 66 percent from 1992 to 1998. In 1997, 356,000 new motorcycles (Table 5.5), both domestic and imported, were sold, up from 309,000 in 1995 and 330,000 in 1996. Meanwhile, retail sales of new motorcycles reached $2.9

TABLE 5.6

	% OF TOTAL OWNERS			
	1998	**1990**	**1985**	**1980**
Age				
Under 18	3.9%	8.3%	14.9%	24.6%
18 - 24	10.6%	15.5%	20.7%	24.3%
25 - 29	10.3%	17.1%	18.7%	14.2%
30 - 34	11.7%	16.4%	13.8%	10.2%
35 - 39	15.9%	14.3%	8.7%	8.8%
40 - 49	26.2%	16.3%	13.2%	9.4%
50 and over	18.4%	10.1%	8.1%	5.7%
Not Stated	3.0%	2.0%	1.9%	2.8%
Median Age	38.0 yrs.	32.0 yrs.	27.1 yrs.	24.0 yrs.
Mean Age	38.4 yrs.	33.1 yrs.	28.5 yrs.	26.9 yrs.
Household Income for Prior Year				
Under $10,000	2.5%	3.4%	10.9%	9.1%
$10,000 - $14,999	2.3%	4.4%	9.3%	13.0%
$15,000 - $19,999	4.6%	7.8%	11.6%	13.9%
$20,000 - $24,999	6.1%	10.8%	8.4%	12.9%
$25,000 - $34,999	13.3%	21.4%	18.3%	12.5%
$35,000 - $49,999	19.9%	19.6%	14.4%	5.9%
$50,000 and Over	33.0%	19.9%	6.1%	2.4%
Don't Know	18.3%	12.7%	21.0%	30.3%
Median	$44,100	$33,100	$25,600	$17,500
Marital Status				
Single	39.8%	41.1%	47.6%	51.7%
Married	59.2%	56.6%	50.3%	44.3%
Not Stated	1.0%	2.3%	2.1%	4.0%
Highest Level of Education				
Grade School	2.7%	5.9%	7.5%	13.5%
Some High School	8.7%	9.5%	15.3%	18.9%
High School Graduate	36.6%	39.4%	36.5%	34.6%
Some College	28.3%	25.2%	21.6%	17.6%
College Graduate	15.9%	12.4%	12.2%	9.2%
Post Graduate	6.2%	5.2%	5.2%	3.1%
Not Stated	1.6%	2.4%	1.7%	3.1%
Occupation of Owner				
Professional/Technical	29.4%	20.3%	19.0%	18.8%
Mechanic/Craftsman	16.4%	13.1%	15.1%	23.3%
Laborer/Semi-Skilled	12.3%	24.1%	23.2%	20.7%
Manager/Proprietor	7.6%	9.3%	8.9%	8.6%
Service Worker	7.3%	6.6%	6.4%	7.1%
Clerical/Sales	3.9%	6.8%	7.8%	9.3%
Farmer/Farm Laborer	2.8%	2.1%	5.1%	4.6%
Military	2.5%	1.5%	1.6%	1.9%
Other	14.7%	13.1%	4.6%	0.0%
Not Stated	3.1%	3.1%	8.3%	5.7%

Note: Percentages based on owners employed.

Source:
1980 Survey of Motorcycle Ownership and Usage, conducted for the Motorcycle Industry Council by Burke Marketing Research, Inc., Cincinnati, Ohio, April 1981.
1985 Survey of Motorcycle Ownership and Usage, conducted for the Motorcycle Industry Council by Burke Marketing Research, Inc., Cincinnati, Ohio, February 1986.
1990 Survey of Motorcycle Ownership and Usage, conducted for the Motorcycle Industry Council by Burke Marketing Research, Inc., Cincinnati, Ohio, February 1991.
1998 Motorcycle Owner Survey, conducted for the Motorcycle Industry Council, by Irwin Broh & Associates, Des Plaines, IL, October 1998 - (Based on 9 months preliminary data)

Source: ©1999 The Motorcycle Industry Council

billion in 1997 (Table 5.5), more than double the retail sales of $1.3 billion in 1990.

A Global Industry

Just like the automobile industry, the motorcycle industry is a global enterprise. In countries as far flung as Thailand, Italy, Indonesia, Germany, and China, the motorcycle is a method of transportation and a form of fun and sport. In 1997, in the United States, six major brands of motorcycles accounted for 96 percent of the nation's new registrations. Japanese brands accounted for 67.5 percent of the market, with Honda selling 27.9 percent of the motorcycles, followed by Yamaha (13.6 percent), and Kawasaki and Suzuki with 13 percent each. Harley-Davidson was the second most popular motorcycle with 27.1 percent market share, while BMW ranked sixth with 1.7 percent. (See Figure 5.2.)

The Motorcycle Owner — A Profile

In 1998, the average motorcycle owner, was 38 years old and married, with a high school diploma or more, and a median household income of $44,100. Of the motorcycle owners employed in 1998, nearly one-half (46 percent) held professional/technical or mechanic/craftsmen positions. Table 5.6 shows the motorcycle owner profiles for 1980, 1985, 1990, and 1998. In 1998, one-third (33 percent) of motorcycle enthusiasts had median

household incomes of $50,000 or more, up from 2.4 percent in 1980, 6.1 percent in 1985, and 19.9 percent in 1990.

Although the largest percentage of motorcycle riders were high school graduates all four years, an increasing proportion of cyclists attended college each of the four years. The proportions of college graduates and those who had a post-graduate education have steadily increased since 1980, while those who

TABLE 5.7

Motorcyclist Fatalities and Injuries and Fatality and Injury Rates, 1987-1997

Year	Fatalities	Registered Vehicles	Fatality Rate *	Vehicle Miles Traveled (millions)	Fatality Rate **
1987	4,036	4,885,772	8.3	9,506	42.5
1988	3,662	4,584,284	8.0	10,024	36.5
1989	3,141	4,420,420	7.1	10,371	30.3
1990	3,244	4,259,462	7.6	9,557	33.9
1991	2,806	4,177,365	6.7	9,178	30.6
1992	2,395	4,065,118	5.9	9,557	25.1
1993	2,449	3,977,856	6.2	9,906	24.7
1994	2,320	3,756,555	6.2	10,240	22.7
1995	2,227	3,767,029	5.9	9,797	22.7
1996	2,161	3,871,237	5.6	9,906	21.8
1997	2,106	--	--	--	--

Year	Injuries	Registered Vehicles	Injury Rate *	Vehicle Miles Traveled (millions)	Injury Rate **
1988	105,000	4,584,284	229	10,024	1,064
1989	83,000	4,420,420	188	10,371	1,049
1990	84,000	4,259,462	198	9,557	882
1991	80,000	4,177,365	192	9,178	876
1992	65,000	4,065,118	160	9,557	681
1993	59,000	3,977,856	148	9,906	596
1994	57,000	3,756,555	152	10,240	557
1995	57,000	3,767,029	151	9,797	582
1996	56,000	3,871,237	145	9,906	565
1997	54,000	--	--	--	--

* Rate per 10,000 registered vehicles.
** Rate per 100 million vehicle miles traveled.
-- = not available.
Sources: Vehicle miles traveled and registered vehicles — Federal Highway Administration. Traffic deaths — Fatality Analysis Reporting System (FARS), NHTSA. Traffic injuries — General Estimates System (GES), NHTSA.

Source: *Traffic Safety Facts 1997 — Motorcycles*, National Highway Traffic Safety Administration, Washington, DC, 1998

completed only grade school or some high school have declined. (See Table 5.6.) Motorcycle ownership has become attractive to growing numbers of middle-aged, often economically successful individuals who are seeking the perceived "freedom" of driving a motorcycle.

In 1998, according to the Motorcycle Industry Council, the greatest percentage of motorcycle owners were male (92 percent), but the percentage of female owners grew to 8 percent in 1998, up from 6 percent in 1990 and 1 percent in 1960. Women riders spent more (an average of $317) than men ($255) on riding apparel in 1998. Female riders had more education than male riders; 57 percent of women had attended college, compared to 44 percent of men. Women (37 percent) were more likely than men (32 percent) to hold white-collar positions.

In 1998, about three-fourths (76 percent) of motorcycle owners paid cash for their bikes. Eighty-two percent of on-highway motorcyclists rode for pleasure, and three-fourths (77 percent) rode in suburban or rural areas.

An Improving Safety Record

Over just one decade, the safety record for motorcycles has improved dramatically. In 1987, 4,036 people were killed on motorcycles. By 1997, this number had dropped to 2,106. At the

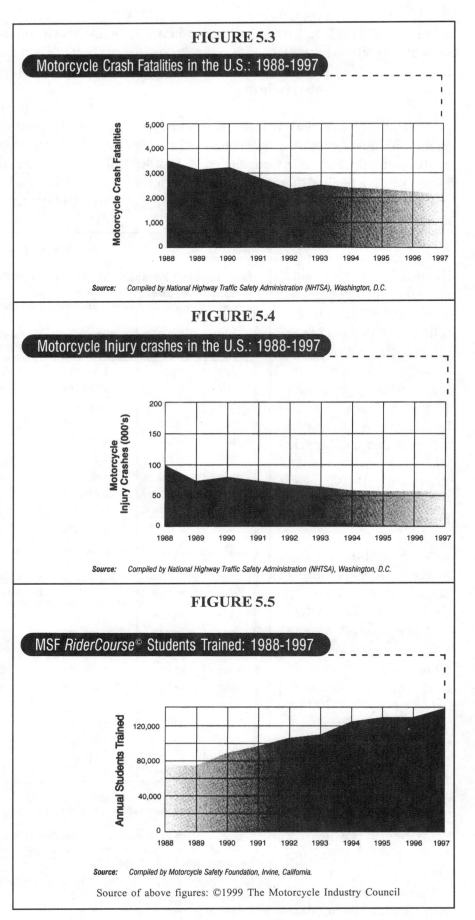

FIGURE 5.3

Motorcycle Crash Fatalities in the U.S.: 1988-1997

Source: Compiled by National Highway Traffic Safety Administration (NHTSA), Washington, D.C.

FIGURE 5.4

Motorcycle Injury crashes in the U.S.: 1988-1997

Source: Compiled by National Highway Traffic Safety Administration (NHTSA), Washington, D.C.

FIGURE 5.5

MSF *RiderCourse*© Students Trained: 1988-1997

Source: Compiled by Motorcycle Safety Foundation, Irvine, California.

Source of above figures: ©1999 The Motorcycle Industry Council

same time, while the number of miles traveled by motorcyclists hovered around 10 billion miles per year, the fatality rate was cut in half from 42.5 to 21.8 deaths per 100 million miles traveled during this period. (See Table 5.7 and Figure 5.3.)

Similarly, the number of injuries fell by half from 105,000 in 1988 to 54,000 in 1997. Meanwhile, the injury rate tumbled from 1,064 to 565 (1996) injuries per 100 million miles traveled. (See Table 5.7 and Figure 5.4.).

The Motorcycle Industry Council attributes part of the decline in fatalities and injuries to increased participation in *RiderCourse©* education and training programs developed by the Motorcycle Safety Foundation. These programs, designed for both beginning and experienced riders, are generally supported by state funding and administered by state agencies. Attendance at these programs rose from less than 80,000 in 1988 to almost 130,000 in 1997 (Figure 5.5). Safety helmet laws and a greater recognition of the dangers of drinking and driving, which has contributed to an overall decline in all forms of traffic fatalities, have also contributed to the decline.

When a motorcycle is involved in an accident, the rider's chances of being seriously hurt or killed are much higher than if he or she were riding in a vehicle that afforded more protection (car, truck, bus, etc.). Per registered vehicle, the mortality rate for motorcyclists is 3.1 times higher than the fatality rate for automobile occupants. The injury rate is 1.4 times higher than for auto riders. Motorcycles make up 2 percent of all registered vehicles in the United States and account for only 0.4 percent of all vehicle miles traveled. In 1997, motorcycles accounted for 5 percent of total traffic fatalities, 6 percent of all occupant fatalities, and 2 percent of all occupant injuries.

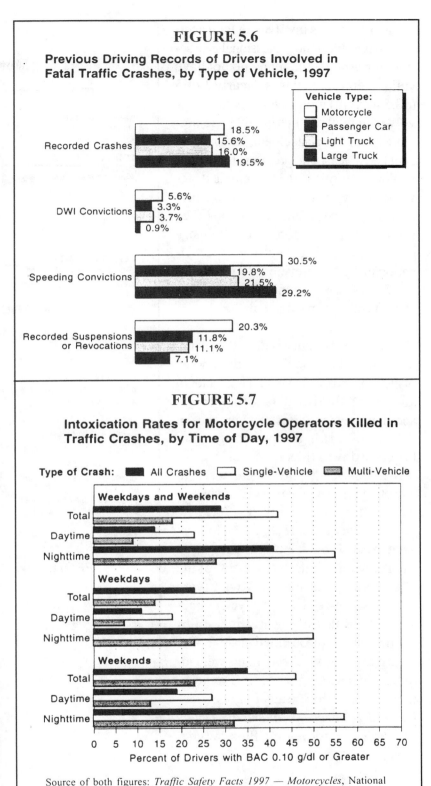

FIGURE 5.6

Previous Driving Records of Drivers Involved in Fatal Traffic Crashes, by Type of Vehicle, 1997

FIGURE 5.7

Intoxication Rates for Motorcycle Operators Killed in Traffic Crashes, by Time of Day, 1997

Source of both figures: *Traffic Safety Facts 1997 — Motorcycles*, National Highway Traffic Safety Administration, Washington, DC, 1998

Most cyclists involved in fatal accidents have little or no professional instruction or training, and many do not have valid operating licenses. Nearly 1 of 5 (18.5 percent) motorcycle operators involved in fatal crashes in 1997 had previously been in an accident, and 5.6 percent had at least one previous DWI conviction. One-fifth (20.3 percent) had previous license suspensions, and 30.5 percent had prior speeding convictions. (See Figure 5.6.) The Motorcycle Industry Council hopes that the growing participation in the Motorcycle Safety Foundation *RiderCourse©* training programs (see above) will improve this situation.

Severity of injury is directly related to speed, motorcycle size, and the amount of alcohol involved. Alcohol is a factor in almost one-third of all fatal motorcycle accidents. Fatal motorcycle crashes in 1997 involved a higher percentage of intoxicated drivers (blood alcohol levels of 0.10 grams per deciliter or greater) than any other type of fatal vehicle crashes — 27.9 percent for motorcycles, 20.2 percent for light trucks, 18.2 percent for passenger cars, and 1.1 percent for large trucks. Almost half (42 percent) of the 876 motorcycle operators who were killed in single-vehicle motorcycle crashes were intoxicated, and nearly three-fifths (57 percent) of those killed in single-vehicle crashes on weekend nights were intoxicated. (See Figure 5.7.) (For additional information on alcohol, see *Alcohol and Tobacco — America's Drugs of Choice*, Information Plus, Wylie, Texas, 1999.)

The Helmet Issue

One of the things that makes motorcycling attractive to some people is the freedom of riding in the open air, although this can have its drawbacks, such as driv-

FIGURE 5.8
Motorcycle Helmuts

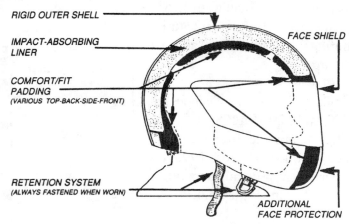

RIGID OUTER SHELL

IMPACT-ABSORBING LINER

COMFORT/FIT PADDING (VARIOUS TOP-BACK-SIDE-FRONT)

FACE SHIELD

RETENTION SYSTEM (ALWAYS FASTENED WHEN WORN)

ADDITIONAL FACE PROTECTION

BASIC CONSTRUCTION

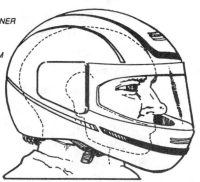

PROTECTS HEAD BY THE SHELL DISPERSING ENERGY AND THE LINER ABSORBING IMPACT

PROTECTS EYES AND FACE FROM DEBRIS AND WINDBLAST; PERMITS GOOD VISION

REFINES HEARING, CUTS WIND NOISE

PROVIDES COMFORT AGAINST ENVIRONMENTAL CONDITIONS

FASTENED RETENTION SYSTEM SECURES HELMET TO HEAD

PROTECTIVE/COMFORT ATTRIBUTES

SEE AND BE SEEN; BE PREPARED; ENJOY THE RIDE

Source: *What You Should Know About Motorcycle Helmets*, Motorcycle Safety Foundation, Irvine, CA, nd

TABLE 5.8

Status of State Motorcycle Helmet Use Requirements

State	Original Law	Subsequent Action, Date(s) and Current Status
AL	11/06/67	Helmet use required for all riders.
AK	01/01/71	Repealed effective 7-1-76 except for persons under 18 years of age, and all passengers.
AZ	01/01/69	Repealed effective 5-27-76 except for persons under 18 years of age.
AR	07/10/67	Helmet use required for all riders. Repealed effective 8/1/97 except for certain riders.
CA	01/01/85	Helmet use required by riders under 15 1/2 years of age.
		Effective 1-1-92 helmet use required for all riders.
CO	07/01/69	Repealed effective 5-20-77.
CT	10/01/67	Not enforced until 2-1-74. Repealed effective 6-1-76.
		Effective 1-1-90 adopted requirement for helmet use by persons under 18.
DE	10/01/68	Repealed effective 6-10-78 except for persons under 19 years of age.
		Also requires that a helmet be carried on the motorcycle for persons 19 and older.
DC	10/12/70	Helmet use required for all riders.
FL	09/05/67	Helmet use required for all riders.
GA	08/31/66	Helmet use required for all riders.
HI	05/01/68	Repealed effective 6-7-77 except for persons under 18 years of age.
ID	01/01/68	Repealed effective 3-29-78 except for persons under 18 years of age.
IL	01/01/68	Repealed effective 6-17-69 after being declared unconstitutional by the State Supreme Court on 5-28-69.
IN	07/01/67	Repealed effective 9-1-77. Effective 6-1-85 adopted requirement for helmet use by persons under 18.
IA	09/01/75	Repealed effective 7-1-76.
KS	07/01/67	7-1-67 to 3-17-70 for all cyclists. 3-17-70 to 7-1-72 only for cyclists under 21 years of age.
		7-1-72 to 7-1-76 for all cyclists. 7-1-76 to 7-1-82 applied only to persons under 16 years of age.
		After 7-1-82 applies only to persons under 18 years of age.
KY	07/01/68	Helmet use required for all riders.
LA	07/31/68	Repealed effective 10-1-76 except for persons under 18 years of age.
		Readopted for all cyclists effective 1-1-82. Helmet use required for all riders.
ME	10/07/67	Repealed effective 10-24-77. Amended effective 7-3-80 to require use by cyclists under 15 years of age.
MD	09/01/68	Repealed effective 5-29-79 except for persons under 18 years of age.
		Effective 10-1-92 helmet use required for all riders.
MA	02/27/67	Helmet use required for all riders.
MI	03/10/67	Repealed effective 6-12-68. New law adopted effective 9-1-69. Helmet use required for all riders.
MN	05/01/68	Repealed effective 4-6-77 except for persons under 18 years of age.
MS	03/28/74	Helmet use required for all riders.
MO	10/13/67	Helmet use required for all riders.
MT	07/01/73	Repealed effective 7-1-77 except for persons under 18 years of age.
NE	05/29/67	Never enforced. Declared unconstitutional by State Supreme Court and repealed effective 9-1-77.
		Effective 1-1-89 helmet use required for all riders.
NV	01/01/72	Helmet use required for all riders.
NH	09/03/67	Repealed effective 8-7-77 except for persons under 18 years of age.

(continued)

ing in bad weather, having insects fly into the driver's face, or having debris fly up from the road. As a result, motorcycle gear was invented to offer riders comfort and protection.

The most important piece of equipment for a motorcyclist is a helmet. Helmets protect the head in two ways. The outer shell resists penetration and abrasion, while the inner portion absorbs the shock by slowly collapsing on impact. Both the outer shell and the inner liner spread the force of an impact throughout the entire helmet. When a rider collides with the pavement while wearing a protective helmet, "it's sort of like falling head-first onto a foot-thick hard cushion," said Jim Fife, product development manager of Mountain Safety Research in Seattle.

In addition, a motorcycle helmet reduces wind noise and windblast and deflects insects and pebbles that fly into the rider's face. (See Figure 5.8.) The helmet with an ANSI or Snell sticker means that it conforms to the standards of the American National Standards Institute or the Snell Memorial Foundation.

Currently, 23 states, the District of Columbia, and Puerto Rico require helmet usage by all motorcycle operators and passengers. In another 24 states, only minors (drivers under 18 or 21) are required to wear

TABLE 5.8 (Continued)

Status of State Motorcycle Helmet Use Requirements (Continued)

State	Original Law	Subsequent Action, Date(s) and Current Status
NJ	01/01/68	Helmet use required for all riders.
NM	05/01/67	Initial law applied only to cyclists under 18 years of age and to all passengers. Law requiring helmet use by all cyclists adopted effective 7-1-73. Repealed effective 6-17-77 except for persons under 18 years of age.
NY	01/01/67	Helmet use required for all riders.
NC	01/01/68	Helmet use required for all riders.
ND	07/01/67	Repealed effective 7-1-77 except for persons under 18 years of age.
OH	04/02/68	Repealed effective 7-1-78 except for persons under 18 years and first year novices.
OK	04/27/67	4-27-67 to 4-7-69 helmet use required for all motorcyclists. From 4-7-69 to 5-3-76 for cyclists under 21 years of age. 5-3-76 for cyclists under 18 years of age.
OR	01/01/68	Repealed effective 10-4-77, except for persons under 18 years of age. Effective 6-16-89 helmet use required for all riders.
PA	09/13/68	Helmet use required for all riders.
RI	06/30/67	Repealed effective 5-21-76 except for passengers on motorcycles. Effective 7-01-92 helmet use required for operators under 21 years of age, all passengers, and first year novices.
SC	07/01/67	Repealed for ages 21 and over effective 6-16-80.
SD	07/01/67	Repealed effective 7-1-77 except for persons under 18 years of age.
TN	06/05/67	Helmet use required for all riders.
TX	01/01/68	Repealed effective 9-1-77 except for persons under 18 years of age. Effective 9-1-89 helmet use required for all riders. Effective 9-1-97 helmets required for riders under 21, those who have not completed a rider training course, and those without $10,000 medical insurance.
UT	05/13/69	Helmets required only on roads with speed limits of 35 mph or higher. Effective 5-8-77 law changed to require helmet use only by persons under 18 years of age.
VT	07/01/68	Helmet use required for all riders.
VA	01/01/71	Helmet use required for all riders.
WA	07/01/67	Repealed effective 7-1-77. 7-1-87 helmet use required for riders under 18. Effective 6-8-90 helmet use required for all riders.
WV	05/21/68	Helmet use required for all riders.
WI	07/01/68	Repealed effective 3-19-78 except for persons under 18 years of age, and for all holders of learner's permits.
WY	05/25/73	Repealed effective 5-27-83 except for persons under 18 years of age.
PR	07/20/60	Helmet use required for all riders.

- 23 states plus the District of Columbia and Puerto Rico require helmet use for all riders.

- 24 states require helmet use for certain riders.

- 3 states do not require helmet use for riders.

Source: *Traffic Safety Facts 1997 — A Compilation of Motor Vehicle Crash Data from the Fatality Analysis Reporting System and the General Estimates System*, National Highway Traffic Safety Administration, Washington, DC, 1998

helmets. Three states (Colorado, Illinois, and Iowa) have no laws requiring helmet use. (See Table 5.8.)

According to the National Highway Traffic Safety Administration (NHTSA), an unhelmeted motorcyclist involved in a crash is 40 percent more likely to incur a fatal head injury and 15 percent more likely to incur a non-fatal head injury than a helmeted motorcyclist. A Crash Outcome Data Evaluation System (CODES) study found that motorcycle helmets are 67 percent effective in preventing brain injuries and that unhelmeted motorcyclists involved in crashes were more than three times more likely to suffer brain injury than those using helmets.

Industry experts estimate that helmets are 29 percent effective in preventing fatal injuries to motorcyclists. The NHTSA estimated that helmets saved the lives of 486 in 1997. If all motorcyclists had worn helmets, 266 more lives could have been saved.

RECREATIONAL VEHICLES

Recreational vehicles (RVs) come in a variety of shapes and sizes, suited to the various needs of those

---

FIGURE 5.9

RV TYPES & TERMS

Recreation Vehicle/RV *(AR'-Vee)n.* — A recreation vehicle, or RV, is a motorized or towable vehicle that combines transportation and temporary living quarters for travel, recreation and camping. RVs do not include mobile homes, off-road vehicles or snowmobiles. Following are descriptions of specific types of RVs and their average retail price.

Towables

An RV designed to be towed by a motorized vehicle (auto, van, or pickup truck) and of such size and weight as not to require a special highway movement permit. It is designed to provide temporary living quarters for recreational, camping or travel use and does not require permanent on-site hook-up.

$13,878
Conventional Travel Trailer
Ranges typically from 12 feet to 35 feet in length, and is towed by means of a bumper or frame hitch attached to the towing vehicle.

$25,149
Fifth-Wheel Travel Trailer
This unit can be equipped the same as the conventional travel trailer but is constructed with a raised forward section that allows a bi-level floor plan. This style is designed to be towed by a vehicle equipped with a device known as a fifth-wheel hitch.

$5,643
Folding Camping Trailer
A recreational camping unit designed for temporary living quarters which is mounted on wheels and connected with collapsible sidewalls that fold for towing by a motorized vehicle.

$12,461
Truck Camper
A recreational camping unit designed to be loaded onto or affixed to the bed or chassis of a truck, constructed to provide temporary living quarters for recreational camping or travel use.

Motorized

A recreational camping and travel vehicle built on or as an integral part of a self-propelled motor vehicle chassis. It may provide kitchen, sleeping, and bathroom facilities and be equipped with the ability to store and carry fresh water and sewage.

$94,693
Motorhome (Type A)
The living unit has been entirely constructed on a bare, specially designed motor vehicle chassis.

$48,023
Van Camper (Type B)
A panel-type truck to which the RV manufacturer adds any of the two following conveniences: sleeping, kitchen and toilet facilities. Also 110/120-volt hook-up, fresh water storage, city water hook-up and a top extension to provide more head room.

$49,863
Motorhome (Type C)
This unit is built on an automotive manufactured van frame with an attached cab section. The RV manufacturer completes the body section containing the living area and attaches it to the cab section.

$31,765
Conversion Vehicles
Vans, pickup trucks and sport-utility vehicles manufactured by an automaker then modified for transportation and recreation use by a company specializing in customized vehicles. These changes may include windows, carpeting, paneling, seats, sofas, and accessories.

Source: Recreation Vehicle Industry Association, Reston, VA

who want to take the comforts of home with them when they travel. The Recreation Vehicle Industry Association (RVIA) recognizes five basic types of RVs: motor homes, travel trailers, folding camping trailers, truck campers, and van conversions. Motor homes and vans are motorized, while the rest must be towed or mounted to other vehicles.

Many RVs have comfortable beds, modern kitchens and bathrooms, and dining and living rooms. Many offer homelike luxuries, such as televisions, air conditioning, and microwave ovens. In 1998, some of the most popular electronic extra features included in RVs were surround-sound stereos, CD players, TVs, VCRs, and video game systems. New high-tech options include bedrooms that convert into offices featuring a dedicated spot for computer and internet jacks and moving walls that expand the interior living space for added comfort once the RV is parked. Known as a slideout, this feature allows the owner to electronically push a portion of the RV's exterior wall outward up to three and one-half feet to enlarge the living, dining, sleeping, or kitchen area. The only limitation on such amenities is cost. Costs range from an average of $5,600 for a folding camping trailer to $94,000 for a large motor home. (See Figure 5.9.)

"Liberty Lady," a luxury model RV, sells for $888,000 and features brass fixtures, etched glass, and paneling. There are two TVs (one in the front and another in the back), four "environment zones" for heating and air conditioning, a VCR and sound system, and a satellite dish. This RV also boasts a combination washer-dryer, full-size refrigerator, microwave and two-burner stove, closet with motorized carousel, and an outdoor entertainment center that includes another TV and stereo system. Other, more expensive models (up to $1.3 million) feature a 51-inch projection screen TV, global positioning equipment, air-operated pocket doors (similar to those seen on *Star Trek*), and a monitor that permits the owner to see who is at the front door.

Deliveries of new RVs, including conversion vehicles (CVs), peaked in 1972 at just over 583,000 units. A sharp increase in fuel prices due to the 1973 Mid-East oil embargo cut deliveries almost in half by 1974, but an expanding economy produced a rally during most of the remainder of the 1970s. Table 5.9 shows that, in 1980, a general recession dragged combined deliveries of recreation and conversion vehicles down to 178,500 units. Thereafter, deliveries climbed until 1989, when they dropped again.

The economic downturn of the early 1990s reversed the growth trend, and sales slipped 30 percent from 1988 to only 293,700 RVs (including CVs) purchased in 1991. By almost every measure, 1994 marked an exceptional year for the RV industry. Total RV deliveries grew to 518,800, the highest since 1978. Retail value of those shipments was $12.2 billion, the largest sales volume ever. In 1995, 475,200 RVs were delivered. Steel-intensive motor homes and towable recreational units accounted for 60 percent of 1995 shipments. Although shipments of RVs have climbed since 1995, shipments of CVs have dropped off. In 1998, 441,300 RVs and CVs, with a retail value of $12.8 billion, were shipped. (See Table 5.9.)

Who Owns RVs?

The Recreation Vehicle Industry Association (RVIA) reports that a recreation vehicle can be found in nearly 10 percent of all vehicle-owning households in the United States today — representing ownership of 9.3 million RVs in 8.6 million households. Almost half (45 percent) of today's RV owners are between 35 and 54 years old. About 40 percent are over age 55. In 1998, the typical RV owner was 48 years old, married, and had an income of $47,000.

Current owners have owned their present RVs for 5.7 years and intend to remain owners for another 10.6 years. RV owners report that they used their RVs from one to three weeks in the previous year. Forty percent of former RV owners plan to buy another recreational vehicle in the future. Among households that have never owned an RV, 50 percent reported an interest in purchasing an RV sometime in the future. Many of these potential buyers are 30 to 49 years old, indicating a strong sales potential for the industry.

A growing number of single people, especially women, are taking to the road alone in their RVs. Although most RV travelers are married, more single, divorced, and widowed women are becoming inter-

TABLE 5.9

Shipments History

	Year	Recreation Vehicles			Conversion Vehicles		
		RV Unit Shipments (In 000)	% Change From Prior Year	RV Retail Value (In Billions)	CV Unit Shipments (In 000)	%Change From Prior Year	CV Retail Value (In Billions)
	1978	389.9	- 5.8	4.077	136.4	+ 13.6	$1.606
*	1979	199.2	- 48.9	2.123	108.5	- 20.5	1.458
*	1980	107.2	- 46.2	1.168	71.3	- 34.3	.783
	1981	133.6	+ 24.6	1.253	99.8	+ 4.0	1.448
	1982	140.6	+ 5.2	1.879	111.3	+ 11.5	1.539
	1983	196.6	+ 39.8	3.485	104.2	- 6.4	2.837
	1984	215.7	+ 9.7	4.393	175.3	+ 68.2	3.340
	1985	186.9	- 13.4	3.936	164.8	- 6.0	3.093
	1986	189.8	+ 1.6	4.031	181.9	+ 10.4	3.533
	1987	211.7	+ 11.5	4.660	181.9	0.0	3.740
	1988	215.8	+ 1.9	4.955	204.2	+ 12.3	4.233
	1989	187.9	- 12.9	4.589	200.4	- 1.9	4.438
	1990	173.1	- 7.9	4.113	174.2	- 13.1	4.110
	1991	163.3	- 5.7	3.614	130.4	- 25.1	3.124
	1992	203.4	+ 24.6	4.411	179.3	+ 37.5	4.492
	1993	227.8	+ 12.0	4.713	192.4	+ 7.3	4.805
**	1994	259.2	+ 13.8	5.691	259.6	+ 35.0	6.505
*	1995	247.0	- 4.7	5.894	228.2	- 12.1	6.210
	1996	247.5	+ 0.2	6.328	219.3	- 3.9	6.038
	1997	254.5	+ 2.8	6.904	184.3	- 16.0	5.024
	1998	292.7	+15.0	8.364	148.6	-19.4	4.393

* *Gas & Credit Crunch*
** *Beginning in 1994, CV shipment figures include truck and sport-utility vehicle conversions.*

Source: Recreation Vehicle Industry Association, Reston, VA, 1999

ested in RV travel. RVing Women, a club based in Arizona, has a membership of 4,000 in the United States and Canada.

Wooing the "Mature" Consumer

The number of Americans age 55 and older is expected to increase by 27 percent from 2000 to 2010, as the early baby boomers reach their "mature" years. This age group will represent about 26 percent of all Americans, reaching 74.8 million citizens by 2010.

The RVIA hopes to capitalize on this increase in older Americans, who traditionally have not only more leisure time but also a larger net worth and higher disposable incomes. Studies indicate that RV ownership has increased 50 percent among householders age 55 and up since 1980. Forty percent of the 9.3 million RVs on the road in 1998 were owned by people over 55. Many in this older age group will enjoy early retirement and a more flexible schedule, which permits more leisure activity.

CHAPTER VI

THE TRUCKING INDUSTRY

Unlike boats, which must stay in the water and follow rivers, lakes, or oceans, and railroads, which must follow steel tracks, a truck can go anywhere there is a highway or a road. While trucks may not be able to carry as much freight as a barge or a railway car, trucks are limited only to the millions of miles of highways that crisscross the country, connecting coast to coast and border to border.

TONS HAULED AND FREIGHT REVENUE

In 1997, trucks transported 81 percent of the nation's general freight business, accounting for nearly 5 percent of the gross domestic product. Trucks hauled 60 percent (by weight — 6.7 billion tons) of the nation's intercity freight. The trucking industry earned 81.3 percent, or $371.9 billion, of total gross freight revenues for the year.

FUTURE GROWTH FOR
THE TRUCKING INDUSTRY

According to *Ward's Automotive Yearbook 1998* (Ward's Communications, Southfield, Michigan, 1998), the demand for freight transportation will continue to grow well into the next century. Trade between the U.S. and Canada and Mexico will be responsible for a large portion of the increasing demand, since trucks dominate cross-border freight movement. Projections indicate that trucking's share of the nation's freight bill will continue at about 82 percent through 2006, accounting for about $446 billion in gross revenues. Freight volume is expected to grow to 8.2 billion tons (up from 6.7 billion tons in 1997) over the next 10 years.

TYPES OF CARRIERS

The American Trucking Association (ATA) identifies three broad categories of motor carriers: 1) Class I, II, and III intercity carriers, 2) owner-operators, and 3) private motor carriers. Class I carriers are those with annual gross operating revenues of $5 million or more; Class IIs have revenues between $1 million and $5 million; and Class IIIs, which make up the majority of carriers, have revenues of less than $1 million.

Owner-operator carriers are independent truckers who own their trucks and operate for hire. These operators enter and exit the market at will, making it difficult to obtain data on their operations. Private carriers are owned and operated by companies for the purpose of hauling only their own materials and products.

TYPES OF TRUCKS

The trucking industry includes all trucks hired to transport goods from one point to another. A truck can be one of hundreds or thousands owned and operated by a major freight-hauling company, or it may be the single tractor-trailer of an independent operator. These include straight trucks, 3-, 4-, and 5-axle semitrailers, flatbed trailers, Rocky Mountain doubles, and mammoth turnpike doubles. (See Figure 6.1 for typical types and dimensions.)

Every truck, trucker, and trucking company plays a vital role in the nation's economy and lifestyle. Trucks connect raw materials to factories, factories to stores, and stores to homes. Oklahomans eat California let-

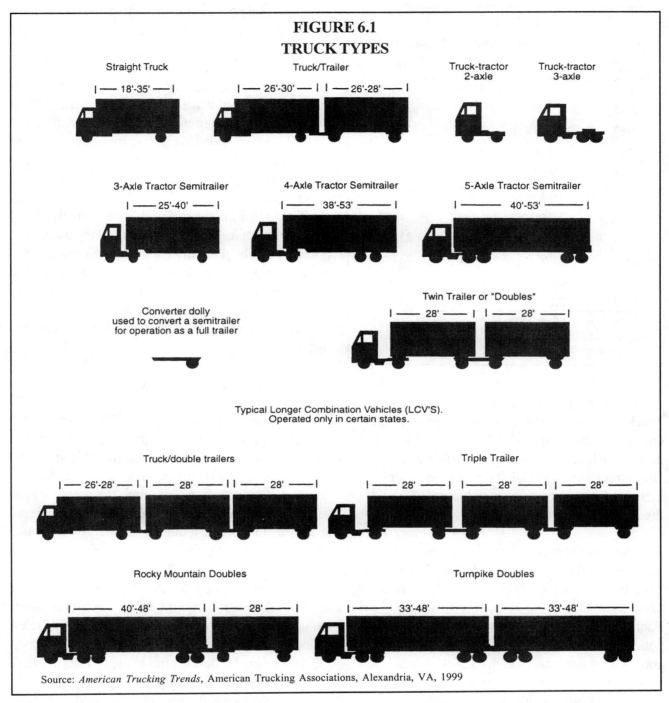

FIGURE 6.1
TRUCK TYPES

Source: *American Trucking Trends*, American Trucking Associations, Alexandria, VA, 1999

tuce, Nebraskans dine on Gulf shrimp, and Texans consume Florida corn. Works of art are enjoyed by millions of people as exhibits travel by truck from city to city. Cars manufactured in Detroit are brought by truck to the dealer's lot in Maine.

Big Rigs: Blessing or Curse

Any decision to allow the use of LCVs (longer-combination vehicles) involves safety concerns as well as economic factors. While LCVs may require some additional public investment in the highway infrastructure, these costs appear to be exceeded by the recurring annual benefits in the form of lower transportation costs. The safety issues are less easily answered. — Kenneth Mead, Director of Transportation Issues, before the U.S. Senate Subcommittee on Commerce, Science, and Transportation, 1994

TABLE 6.1
Number of Truck Drivers (Thousands)

Year	Total Drivers	Women	Minority
1987	2,543	4.1%	21.0%
1988	2,608	4.3%	20.3%
1989	2,616	3.9%	20.9%
1990	2,607	3.9%	21.9%
1991	2,666	4.1%	22.8%
1992	2,694	4.6%	22.1%
1993	2,786	4.5%	21.1%
1994	2,815	4.5%	23.1%
1995	2,861	4.5%	23.0%
1996	3,019	5.3%	22.7%
1997	3,075	5.7%	24.5%

US Department of Labor, Bureau of Labor Statistics.

Source: *American Trucking Trends*, American Trucking Associations, Alexandria, VA, 1999

The largest trucks on the highways are often called "truck trains" or "monster trucks." They are triple trailers, measuring just under 100 feet, and turnpike doubles, which are twin 45- to 48-foot trailers. The larger trucks are also called longer-combination vehicles (LCVs) or extra-long vehicles (ELVs). (See Figure 6.1.)

These trucks are much bigger, longer, and heavier than the standard 5-axle 18-wheeler that motorists have become accustomed to. A triple-trailer rig stretches about one-third the length of a football field. Each type of large truck weighs about 125,000 pounds. By comparison, the average family sedan is about 16 feet long and weighs 3,500 pounds.

Those in Favor of Big Rigs

Those who favor the use of these large freight haulers claim that big trucks provide a more efficient way to move goods, cutting fuel consumption and pollution. The trucking industry believes that the bigger rigs make sense — not only for their companies, but also for their customers. "We're moving more freight with less power and on a timely basis. The whole thing comes down to supply and demand. And the demand

is so great, we're shipping material across the country bumper to bumper," said an industry spokesman.

Truckers claim that the more even distribution of extra weight over more length means little added wear and tear to the highways. However, according to the Federal Highway Administration (FHWA), unless additional axles are added to trucks carrying extra weight, the lifetime of bridges and overpasses will be cut from 50 years to 29 years.

Trucking company officials also claim that they take very strict measures to ensure that the trucks are operated safely, that only the most qualified drivers are allowed to operate the LCVs, and that the drivers must submit to regular drug and alcohol tests. In addition, drivers are not allowed to drive more than 10 hours a day, and in bad weather, they must park the rigs.

Those Who Dislike the LCVs

Organizations opposing LCVs are concerned about the danger they represent to other drivers. A brochure prepared by Citizens for Reliable and Safe Highways (CRASH) included a photo of a school bus crushed like a soda can. Although the accident rate for LCVs is lower than that of other freight carriers, an accident involving a monster truck is often worse because of the size and weight of the vehicle.

The railroads oppose LCVs because they consider trucks their major competitor. The Association of American Railroads has released printed and television material opposing LCVs. If more shippers begin depending on double and triple trucks, it could cost the railroad industry up to $2 billion a year. "It may not mean the death of railroads, but it could cripple us," said George Whaley, a spokesman for the Association of American Railroads.

LAWS REGULATING SIZE AND WEIGHT

Since 1991, when the Intermodal Surface Transportation Efficiency Act (ISTEA; PL 102-240) became law, there has been a ceiling on truck sizes and weights. ISTEA expired on September 30, 1997, and

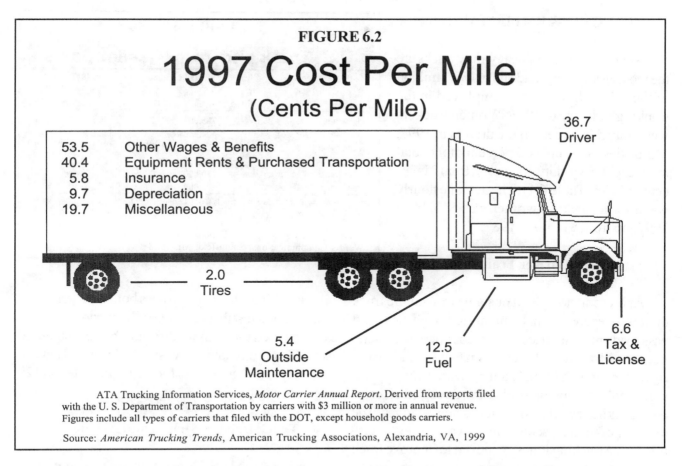

FIGURE 6.2
1997 Cost Per Mile
(Cents Per Mile)

53.5	Other Wages & Benefits
40.4	Equipment Rents & Purchased Transportation
5.8	Insurance
9.7	Depreciation
19.7	Miscellaneous

36.7
Driver

2.0
Tires

5.4
Outside
Maintenance

12.5
Fuel

6.6
Tax &
License

ATA Trucking Information Services, *Motor Carrier Annual Report*. Derived from reports filed with the U. S. Department of Transportation by carriers with $3 million or more in annual revenue. Figures include all types of carriers that filed with the DOT, except household goods carriers.

Source: *American Trucking Trends*, American Trucking Associations, Alexandria, VA, 1999

a new bill reauthorizing ISTEA was passed in May 1998. It will run for six years. The Transportation Equity Act for the Twenty-first Century (TEA-21; PL 105-178) continues the same provisions of ISTEA, but does require the Transportation Research Board to conduct a broad study of the impacts of federal size and weight laws for trucks.

Supporters of the bigger trucks want to raise the limits on truck size and are pushing for more triple-trailer trucks (three 26-29 foot trailers). These "triples," as they are called, currently make up less than one-tenth of 1 percent of the U.S. commercial fleet. At present, they may operate on only 17,923 miles of state and federal highways, or 1.6 percent of the nation's roads.

Proponents of larger trucks are also urging that the federal limit of 80,000 pounds gross weight on large trucks be increased to 97,000 pounds gross weight. They argue that a truck carrying heavy cargo, like automobile tires or steel products, is traveling partially empty, which is inefficient and nonproductive.

Furthermore, if the trucks were permitted to carry 97,000 gross pounds, backers say, four trucks could carry the weight now being carried by five trucks, lessening highway congestion.

Opponents argue that reconfiguring the trucks rather than enlarging them or allowing them to carry more weight makes more sense. They cite the dangers of increased accidents, when more trucks with heavier loads are traveling at high speeds on more highways.

PAYING THEIR SHARE

Trucks cause considerable damage to road surfaces because they are very heavy and travel a great number of miles. Trucks are taxed to help pay their share of road repair and maintenance. In 1997, according to the American Trucking Associations, trucks paid $28 billion in federal and state highway-user taxes, of which $12.3 billion was in federal taxes and $15.7 billion was in state highway user taxes. The average total annual state highway user fee for a typical 5-axle tractor-trailer was $4,976 as of January 1999.

91

TRUCKING EMPLOYMENT

Although drivers of heavy-duty trucks are the most visible, they made up only 3.1 million of the 9.5 million persons employed in the trucking industry in 1996. Women truckers were only 5.7 percent of the drivers in 1997. Minorities made up 24.5 percent of the total number of heavy-duty drivers, up from 21 percent in 1987 (Table 6.1). The average hourly wage for a trucking worker was $13.34 in 1997, up from $11.00 in 1987.

Truck Driver Training

At present, no federal or state laws require truck drivers to receive formal training, although they must pass road and written tests to get commercial drivers' licenses. Most truck drivers learn to drive their large rigs either through formal training in truck driver training schools or community colleges, through their companies, or informally from friends and relatives. The majority of training schools are not accredited or certified. The trucking industry moved to improve truck driver training by developing a training school certification program, and in 1989, the program certified the first eight training schools.

Yellow Freight Systems, Inc., one of the largest trucking companies, mandates that all drivers of their triple-trailer trucks take part in an eight-hour training program, consisting of four hours of video tape and classroom instruction and a four-hour road test. (Yellow Freight operates more triples than any other trucking company.)

Truck Driver Testing

Disturbed by the studies that cited driver error as a major cause of truck accidents, Congress passed the Commercial Motor Vehicle Safety Act of 1986 (PL 99-570). The act's goals were to improve driving ability, remove problem truck drivers from the road, and establish a uniform, standardized licensing system. In 1988, the Federal Highway Administration (FHWA) issued a final ruling establishing minimum federal standards for states to implement in testing commercial drivers, including all truck drivers. Since 1992,

TABLE 6.2

U.S. Truck and Truck-Trailer Sales

Market Segment	GVW Class	1998 Projected Units	% Chg. vs. 1997	1997 Actual Units	% Chg. vs. 1996
Light-Duty	1-2	795,000	0.5	790,700	5.1
Mid-Range	3-5	130,000	9.6	118,600	0.7
Medium-Duty	6-7	135,000	2.4	131,800	7.2
Heavy-Duty	8	190,000	6.4	178,600	5.0
Total Trucks	—	1,250,000	0.8	1,217,700	NA
Truck-Trailers	—	275,000	1.3	271,500	33.8

Note: Truck sales are those for commercial use only. Light trucks for personal use are excluded.

Source: *Ward's Automotive Yearbook*, Sixtieth Edition, Ward's Communications, Southfield, MI, 1998

all truck drivers have had to pass both a written exam and a driving test that meet federal standards. The test is considered much more difficult than the standard exam for an automobile license. The federal manual to help prepare truck drivers for the required test is 120 pages in length.

Truck Drivers, Drugs, and Accidents

In 1988, the U.S. Department of Transportation (DOT) issued regulations on drug testing policies for safety-sensitive airline, railroad, motor carrier (trucking), and shipping employees. Since 1989, tests have been given before employment, after accidents, periodically, when there is reasonable suspicion, and randomly. Employers must conduct unannounced drug tests on 50 percent of their employees each year. Approximately 3 million workers in the trucking industry are covered by the regulations. The random testing rule initially caused considerable controversy, mainly over the irregular testing schedule of independent truckers, which is somewhat difficult to enforce and expensive for the industry.

FHWA also issued regulations under the 1986 Commercial Motor Vehicle Safety Act (see above) that prohibit truck drivers from driving under the influence of alcohol or any illegal drug. The first violation results in a one-year suspension from driving a commercial motor vehicle; the second infraction is justification for permanent disqualification as a driver. Truck drivers are also required to undergo a medical checkup every two years for both mental and physical fitness.

TRUCK COSTS

The average tractor-semitrailer is very expensive to operate. The typical "big rig" gets only five to eight miles per gallon and travels 80,000 to 100,000 miles per year. According to the American Trucking Association, operating a truck cost the typical trucking company about $1.92 per mile. The major expenditures were wages and employee benefits (not including the driver), 53.5 cents per mile; purchasing or renting the trucks, 40.4 cents; and driver's salary, 36.7 cents. (See Figure 6.2.)

TABLE 6.3
Number of Total Business Failures vs. Trucking Failures

Year	All Business	Total Trucking	Local Trucking w/o Storage	Trucking except Local	Local Trucking with Storage
1987	61,111	1,345	668	621	56
1988	57,097	1,242	602	578	62
1989	50,361	1,263	690	501	72
1990	60,747	1,593	795	682	116
1991	88,140	2,297	1,345	787	165
1992	97,069	2,223	1,335	749	139
1993	86,133	1,650	1,002	526	122
1994	71,558	1,259	757	385	117
1995	71,194	1,403	817	475	111
1996	71,931	2,024	1,197	619	117
1997	83,384	2,708	1,609	920	120

Source: Dun & Bradstreet, a company of The Dun & Bradstreet Corporation, 1998

TRUCK SALES

Just as the 1990-1991 recession led to a temporary drop in the sale of cars, the economic downturn slowed sales of large trucks. In 1988, 186,500 trucks were sold; by 1991, only 122,400 were bought. Heavy-duty truck sales increased with the improving economy. Between 1994 and 1997, an average 208,500 heavy-duty trucks were sold annually. In 1998, however, only an estimated 190,000 heavy-duty trucks were purchased (Table 6.2). There are over 2 million heavy-duty trucks on American roads — twice the 1988 number.

THE EFFECTS OF DEREGULATION

Following years of government controls, Congress passed the Airline Deregulation Act of 1978 (PL 95-504), the Staggers Act of 1980 (railroads; PL 96-448), and the Motor Carrier Act of 1980 (PL 96-296), which lifted many restrictions on market entry and exit, pricing, scheduling, and routing in the transportation industry.

The arguments for and against deregulation followed a similar pattern in all areas of transportation.

Supporters argued that deregulation would benefit both the industry and the consumer by stimulating competition. Competition would, in turn, result in lower rates and better service for the consumer, eliminate poorly managed companies, and increase industry profits.

On the other hand, there was concern that a lack of controls would allow the major players with the most resources to gain the bulk of the consumer market, forcing even well-managed smaller companies out of business. Another fear was that the small or out-of-the-way consumer might be left out as companies concentrated on high-volume, highly profitable market segments.

Number of Carriers Entering the Market

After the trucking industry was deregulated, thousands of new companies sprang up, hoping to take advantage of the new ease of entry into the market and the ability to set their own prices. In addition, many existing companies quickly expanded and entered new markets. According to Russell B. Capelle, Jr., director of statistical analysis at the American Trucking Associations, "Many disappear within months. [New companies] find out the hard way that it is not easy."

Peaking in 1986, truck company failures have substantially outpaced those in other industries. The American Trucking Associations reported that 2,708 trucking companies failed in 1997, more than double the 1,345 that went out of business in 1987. (See Table

93

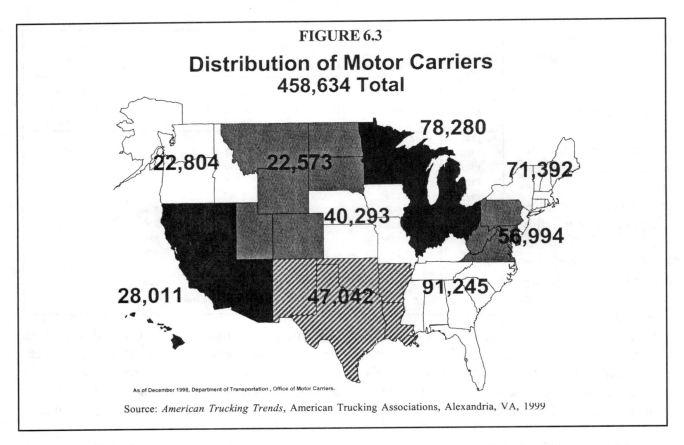

FIGURE 6.3

Distribution of Motor Carriers
458,634 Total

78,280

22,804

22,573

71,392

40,293

56,994

28,011

47,042

91,245

As of December 1998, Department of Transportation , Office of Motor Carriers.

Source: *American Trucking Trends*, American Trucking Associations, Alexandria, VA, 1999

6.3.) Competition is so tough that truckers often find it hard to make a living without being constantly on the road.

As of December 1998, 458,634 interstate motor carriers were on file with the Office of Motor Carriers. Most of these (78.5 percent) ran 20 or fewer trucks. Of those, 70 percent operated six or fewer trucks. Figure 6.3 shows the distribution of motor carriers across the country.

The most successful companies in the new world of deregulation have been the four trucking "giants"— United Parcel Service (UPS), Consolidated Freightways, Roadway Express, and Yellow Freight Systems, Inc. When other companies went out of business, the larger corporations were able to buy terminals and equipment at bargain prices. They also hired the best of their bankrupt competitors' drivers and acquired the failed enterprises' customers. This helped consolidate their dominance in the industry. Most transportation analysts believe that the giants of the industry will likely become stronger as new companies find it more difficult to acquire the capital they need to grow,

and the major companies take advantage of the cost savings that size can provide.

SAFETY OF TRUCKS

The National Highway Traffic Safety Administration reported that, in 1997, 4,871 large trucks (over 10,000 pounds in weight) were involved in fatal accidents in the United States. Truck tractors pulling semitrailers made up 63 percent of trucks involved in fatal crashes and approximately 50 percent of trucks involved in nonfatal crashes. Doubles accounted for only 3 percent of trucks involved in crashes, and triples for less than 1 percent. (See Figure 6.1 for illustrations of doubles and triples.)

A total of 5,355 people, 13 percent of all traffic fatalities reported in 1997, died in truck crashes. One of 8 traffic deaths resulted from a collision involving a large truck. The vehicle involvement rate (the rate per 100,000 registered vehicles) declined significantly from 96.3 in 1987 to 67.9 in 1996. Of truck-related fatalities, 78 percent of persons killed were occupants of another vehicle, 8 percent were nonoccupants, and

13 percent were occupants of a large truck (Table 6.4). Table 6.5 shows the numbers of people killed and injured in crashes involving at least one large truck for each year between 1988 and 1997.

Large trucks were much more likely to be involved in a fatal multi-vehicle crash than were passenger cars. Most of the collisions involving large trucks occurred in rural areas (67 percent), during the daytime (66 percent), and on weekdays (79 percent).

The National Center for Statistics and Analysis, part of the National Highway Traffic Safety Administration, reported that in half of the two-vehicle fatal crashes involving a large truck and another type of vehicle, both vehicles were proceeding straight at the time of the crash. In 10 percent of the accidents, the other vehicle was turning. In 9 percent, either the truck or the other vehicle was negotiating a curve. In 8 percent, either the truck (6 percent) or the other vehicle (2 percent) was stopped or parked in a traffic lane.

Drivers of large trucks were less likely to have a previous license suspension or revocation than were passenger car drivers. Almost 1 of every 3 truck drivers involved in fatal accidents had at least one prior speeding conviction, compared to 1 of 5 passenger car drivers involved in fatal crashes. (See Figure 6.4.)

In 1997, only 1.1 percent of drivers of large trucks involved in fatal crashes were intoxicated (blood alcohol levels of 0.10 grams per deciliter or greater). Drivers of these large trucks have shown the highest drop in intoxication rates since 1987 (59 percent). In 1997, the intoxication rate for drivers of passenger cars in fatal collisions was 18.2 percent; for light trucks, 20.2 percent; and 27.9 percent for motorcycles.

Driver Fatigue

The National Transportation Safety Board estimates that truck drivers who fall asleep at the wheel are a factor in 750 to 1,500 deaths on roads each year, and that fatigue contributes to as many as 40 percent of all heavy-truck accidents. In the United States, drivers are not supposed to drive longer than 10 hours at a time, and then they must have eight hours to rest.

Nonetheless, the 1997 "Commercial Motor Vehicles Driver Fatigue and Alertness Study," an eight-year, $4.45 million examination of 80 American and Canadian truck drivers, sponsored by the Department of Transportation, reported that nighttime truck drivers averaged about four-and-one-half hours of sleep daily. Daytime drivers got fewer than six hours of sleep.

Future Help for Drowsy Drivers

Some truck drivers turn to coffee, short periods of exercise, naps in the back of their cabs, or even amphetamines to wake themselves up when they start to feel tired. Others do nothing and may finally fall asleep at the wheel. In an effort to remedy this situation, the Department of Transportation (DOT) is testing some moderately priced devices that can keep track

TABLE 6.4

Fatalities and Injuries in Crashes Involving Large Trucks, 1997

Type of Fatality	Number	Percentage of Total
Occupants of Large Trucks	717	13
Single-Vehicle Crashes	*496*	*9*
Multiple-Vehicle Crashes	*221*	*4*
Occupants of Other Vehicles in Crashes Involving Large Trucks	4,189	78
Nonoccupants (Pedestrians, Pedalcyclists, etc.)	449	8
Total	**5,355**	**100**

Type of Injury	Number	Percentage of Total
Occupants of Large Trucks	31,000	24
Single-Vehicle Crashes	*14,000*	*11*
Multiple-Vehicle Crashes	*17,000*	*13*
Occupants of Other Vehicles in Crashes Involving Large Trucks	99,000	75
Nonoccupants (Pedestrians, Pedalcyclists, etc.)	2,000	2
Total	**133,000**	**100**

Source: *Traffic Safety Facts, 1997*, National Highway Traffic Safety Administration, Washington, DC, n.d.

TABLE 6.5

Fatalities and Injuries in Large Truck Crashes, 1988-1997

Year	Fatalities	Injuries
1988	5,679	130,000
1989	5,490	156,000
1990	5,272	150,000
1991	4,821	110,000
1992	4,462	138,000
1993	4,849	133,000
1994	5,144	133,000
1995	4,918	117,000
1996	5,142	130,000
1997	5,355	133,000

Source: *Large Truck Crash Profile: The 1997 National Picture*, Office of Motor Carriers, Federal Highway Administration, Washington, DC, 1998

There is no indication as to when significant amounts of spent fuel will be transported by road, but the thought of nuclear waste being trucked great distances alarms many people. Although there have already been more than 2,500 shipments, with no death or injury due to the radioactive nature of the cargo, many people are fearful of nuclear transportation.

The transportation of spent nuclear fuel is chiefly a federal responsibility, but the states are also involved. The U.S. Department of Transportation and the Nuclear Regulatory Commission are responsible for packaging regulations, certifications of container safety, regulations governing sabotage, escorts, routing, and employee training. The states are responsible for regulatory mechanisms, such as permits, liability rules, inspections, notification, and emergency training, to ensure safe transportation of spent fuel and other hazardous materials.

A pilot program developed under a 1990 congressional mandate is in effect in five states: Minnesota, Nevada, Ohio, West Virginia, and, as of 1998, Illinois. Under the program, the same forms for registrations and permits for carrying hazardous materials

of a driver's sharpness and give a warning before weariness overcomes the driver.

One such device is a pen-sized infrared camera mounted on the dashboard that would shine infrared light into the driver's eyes. People cannot see the light, but it can measure the amount of light reflected off the retina of the eye. If the light level becomes too low (because of closing eyelids), the camera would emit a sound, or shake the seat, or release a peppermint spray into the cab and rouse the driver. This device would work only at night, because daylight makes the measurement unreliable.

The lane tracker is another mechanism currently being evaluated that could alert drivers if they are weaving between lanes. The lane tracker watches the road and beeps if the driver is not steering a relatively straight course. Such devices must, of necessity, be able to warn drivers subtly, since a loud, distracting alarm could cause an accident on its own.

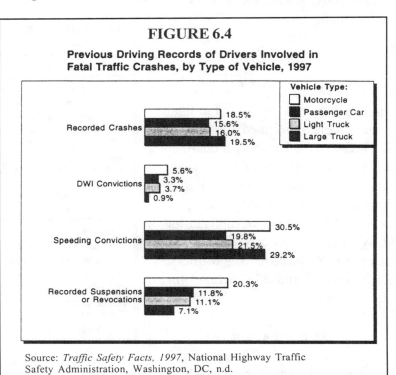

FIGURE 6.4

Previous Driving Records of Drivers Involved in Fatal Traffic Crashes, by Type of Vehicle, 1997

Vehicle Type:
☐ Motorcycle
■ Passenger Car
▨ Light Truck
■ Large Truck

Recorded Crashes: 18.5%, 15.6%, 16.0%, 19.5%

DWI Convictions: 5.6%, 3.3%, 3.7%, 0.9%

Speeding Convictions: 30.5%, 19.8%, 21.5%, 29.2%

Recorded Suspensions or Revocations: 20.3%, 11.8%, 11.1%, 7.1%

Source: *Traffic Safety Facts, 1997*, National Highway Traffic Safety Administration, Washington, DC, n.d.

are available in each state and are accepted in all five states. Several other states — Colorado, Missouri, New York, Wisconsin, and Wyoming — have expressed interest in the program, but are waiting to see what action the federal government takes. As of 1998, the federal government had still not decided whether or not the program should become a federal rule. Many states do not want to adopt the program as it exists today and then have to change if the federal rule is different.

After some congressional prodding to speed up the process, the Federal Highway Administration (FHWA) sent a letter, in March 1998, to all state governors and any other interested parties requesting comments on the program. FHWA received over 100 comments, the majority of which were favorable. Since then, a new director of the Office Motor Carriers, part of the Federal Highway Association (FHWA), has taken office, who seems to be more open to a unified program. FHWA needs at least 26 states to endorse the program before it moves ahead and establishes a federal program.

Safety Measures

All states are part of the Commercial Vehicle Safety Alliance, an organization of truck inspectors that has developed rigid safety rules for trucks carrying nuclear cargo. In addition, 10 states have stipulated certain routes that can be used for nuclear shipments; according to federal guidelines, these are the safest highways. Eighteen states require truckers to get permits before they are allowed to haul spent fuel. Prior to issuance, the trucking company's operations are analyzed, and its past conformance with safety regulations must be approved.

In 1997, 4 percent of trucks involved in fatal crashes and trucks involved in nonfatal crashes were carrying hazardous materials (HM). HM was released from the cargo compartment in about one-third of these crashes.

TRUCKS AND THE ENVIRONMENT

The Clean Air Act of 1970 (CAA; PL 91-604) and the Clean Air Act Amendments of 1990 (CAAA;

TABLE 6.6

Nitrogen Oxide Emissions from Mobile Sources

cars & light-duty trucks	49.0%
off-highway equipment -- diesel	27.7%
heavy-duty trucks/buses -- diesel	**18.5%**
heavy-duty trucks/buses -- gasoline	3.1%
off-highway equipment -- gasoline	1.3%

Particulate Oxide Emissions from Mobile Sources

off-highway equipment -- diesel	50.3%
heavy-duty trucks/buses -- diesel	**27.2%**
cars & light-duty trucks	14.6%
off-highway equipment -- gasoline	6.5%
heavy-duty trucks/buses -- gasoline	1.4%

Source: *Trucks and Clean Air: Meeting the Challenges of the Future*, American Trucking Associations, Alexandria, VA 1997

Trucks and Clean Air: Meeting the Challenges of the Future is produced under a cooperative effort between the American Trucking Associations and the Engine Manufacturers Association. No part may be reproduced without written permission of the ATA Department of Environmental Affairs, 2200 Mill Rd., Alexandria, VA 22314

PL 101-549) called for reduction in air pollutants from truck engines. Since then, the heavy-duty diesel truck engine has become far less threatening to the environment. Engine manufacturers have totally redesigned their motors to reduce emissions of the six major pollutants — carbon monoxide, lead, oxides of nitrogen, hydrocarbons, particulates, and sulfur dioxide. A truck engine manufactured in 1997 gave off nearly 70 percent fewer nitrogen oxides and 90 percent fewer particulates than a truck engine manufactured in 1987.

In 1997, diesel trucks accounted for less than 2 percent of hydrocarbon emissions in the United States and only about 5 percent of carbon monoxide emissions. On the other hand, heavy-duty diesel trucks and buses gave off 18.5 percent of all nitrogen oxide emissions and 27.2 percent of all particulate oxides from mobile sources. (See Table 6.6.)

CHAPTER VII

THE AIRLINES — MASTERS OF THE SKY

AIR FLIGHT IS BORN

From ancient times, people have dreamed of flying. Greek mythology tells the story of Icarus, who strapped on primitive wings and tried to fly to Sicily. However, so pleased was he with his initial flying attempt that he flew too close to the sun. His wings melted, and he plummeted to his death.

Not until 1783, when the Montgolfier brothers rose above the earth in the first manned balloon, did man actually fly. Benjamin Franklin, then ambassador to France, saw the flight. When asked what good it was, he replied, "What good is a newborn baby?" meaning that the eventual success of manned flight could not then be foretold.

The prototype of today's airplanes finally rose into the air on December 17, 1903, when Orville Wright took off from a beach near the town of Kitty Hawk, North Carolina, flew 59 seconds, and landed half a mile away from the take-off point. Only 66 years later, in 1969, the first spaceship landed on the moon, a trip of over 230,000 miles.

Advances in air travel and space technology have been more spectacular than those in any other form of transportation. Less than a century after the Wright brothers' flight, air transportation has become routine. The fast-paced technological advances in aviation are mostly taken for granted.

TYPES OF CARRIERS

Traffic at an airport falls broadly into three categories: (1) large commercial airlines and cargo haulers, (2) commuter, or regional, airlines and air taxis, and (3) general aviation. In general, *commercial* airlines are very large operations that fly between the major "hub" cities and have fleets consisting mainly of large jets. *Regional*, or *commuter,* airlines provide regularly scheduled service from the hubs to smaller, outlying communities and have fleets predominantly composed of aircraft with 60 or fewer seats. *General aviation* refers to airplanes owned and operated by individuals or companies for their private use.

Due to the dramatic growth of the regional airlines and the scramble to claim a share of the different market segments following deregulation (removal of governing rules) in 1978, these categories have become somewhat confusing. The Federal Aviation Administration (FAA), which regulates airlines, refers to the

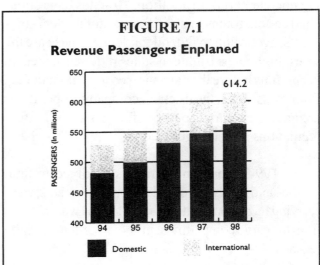

FIGURE 7.1

Revenue Passengers Enplaned

Source: Reprinted from the *Air Transport Association 1999 Annual Report* with permission of the Air Transport Association of America, Inc., 1301 Pennsylvania Avenue, NW, Washington DC, 20004. Complete copies of the annual report are available by calling 800-497-3326 (US & Canada) or 301-490-7951. For more information, go to www.air-transport.org

larger airlines as "commercial air carriers" and to the smaller airlines as "regionals" or "commuters," even though the regionals are, in fact, commercial airlines that operate for profit.

Large commercial airlines are sometimes referred to as scheduled airlines because they usually fly only on regular, fixed schedules. Again, regional airlines also offer scheduled services. In some cases, the term "scheduled" refers to both types of carriers. In addition, both types of carriers may provide charter, or "unscheduled," services.

THE INDUSTRY TODAY

Most Americans have flown in an airplane. A 1997 Gallup survey found that more than 80 percent of adults in the United States had traveled by air, and 45 percent of Americans had flown in the previous 12 months.

In 1998, 614.2 million passengers flew on more than 8.3 million flights on the nation's airlines. (See Figure 7.1 and Table 7.1.)

The FAA reported that 1998 was the fifth consecutive year of strong growth for the commercial aviation industry. Increases in both domestic and international markets continue to be driven by a generally strong U.S. economy. The 1997-1998 financial crises in Southeast Asia, Latin America, and Eastern Europe did not generally seriously harm U.S. commercial airlines' financial performance, although orders for new planes were down, and enplanements (airplane boardings) to both Southeast Asia and Latin America decreased.

Between 1991 and 1998, U.S. commercial air carrier passenger enplanements rose 36 percent, and U.S. commercial air carrier revenue passenger miles

TABLE 7.1

1988-1998 Summary

U.S. Scheduled Airlines

(In millions, except when noted)

	1988	1989	1990	1991	1992	1993	1994	1995	1996	1997	1998
Traffic — Scheduled Service											
Revenue Passengers Enplaned	454.6	453.7	465.6	452.3	475.1	488.5	528.8	547.8	581.2	599.1	**614.2**
Revenue Passenger Miles	423,302	432,714	457,926	447,955	478,554	489,684	519,382	540,656	578,663	605,574	**619,456**
Available Seat Miles	676,802	684,376	733,375	715,199	752,772	771,641	784,331	807,078	835,071	860,803	**874,170**
Passenger Load Factor (%)	62.5	63.2	62.4	62.6	63.6	63.5	66.2	67.0	69.3	70.3	**70.9**
Average Passenger Trip Length (in miles)	931	954	984	990	1,007	1,002	982	987	996	1,011	**1,009**
Freight & Express Revenue Ton Miles	9,632	10,275	10,546	10,225	11,130	11,944	13,792	14,578	15,301	17,959	**18,116**
Aircraft Departures (in thousands)	6,700	6,622	6,924	6,783	7,051	7,245	7,531	8,062	8,230	8,192	**8,309**
Financial											
Passenger Revenues	$50,296	$53,802	$58,453	$57,092	$59,828	$63,945	$65,422	$69,594	$75,286	$79,471	**$80,986**
Freight & Express Revenues	7,478	6,893	5,432	5,509	5,916	6,662	7,284	8,616	9,679	10,477	**10,651**
Mail Revenues	972	955	970	957	1,184	1,212	1,183	1,266	1,279	1,362	**1,690**
Charter Revenues	1,698	2,052	2,877	3,717	2,801	3,082	3,548	3,485	3,447	3,575	**3,811**
Total Operating Revenues	63,749	69,316	76,142	75,158	78,140	84,559	88,313	94,578	101,938	109,568	**113,346**
Total Operating Expenses	60,312	67,505	78,054	76,943	80,585	83,121	85,600	88,718	95,729	100,982	**104,034**
Operating Profit (Loss)	3,437	1,811	(1,912)	(1,785)	(2,444)	1,438	2,713	5,860	6,209	8,586	**9,312**
Interest Expense	1,846	1,944	1,978	1,777	1,743	2,027	2,347	2,424	1,981	1,733	**1,826**
Net Profit (Loss)*	$1,686	$128	($3,921)	($1,940)	($4,791)	($2,136)	($344)	$2,314	$2,804	$5,170	**$4,894**
Revenue per Passenger Mile (in cents)	11.9	12.4	12.8	12.7	12.5	13.1	12.6	12.9	13.0	13.1	**13.1**
Rate of Return on Investment (%)	10.8	6.3	(6.0)	(0.5)	(9.3)	(0.4)	5.2	11.9	11.5	14.7	**12.0**
Operating Profit Margin (%)	5.4	2.6	(2.5)	(2.4)	(3.1)	1.7	3.1	6.2	6.1	7.8	**8.2**
Net Profit Margin (%)	2.6	0.2	(5.1)	(2.6)	(6.1)	(2.5)	(0.4)	2.4	2.8	4.7	**4.3**
Employees (Average full-time equivalent)	480,553	506,728	545,809	533,565	540,413	537,111	539,759	546,987	564,425	586,509	**621,058**

* Excludes fresh-start accounting extraordinary gains of Continental and Trans World in 1993.

Source: Reprinted from the *Air Transport Association 1999 Annual Report* with permission of the Air Transport Association of America, Inc., 1301 Pennsylvania Avenue, NW, Washington DC, 20004

TABLE 7.2

THE WORLD'S TOP 25 AIRLINES

In RPKs

Rank	Airline	No. of RPKs (000,000)
1	United	200,496
2	American	175,309
3	Delta	166,271
4	British Airways	112,029
5	Northwest	107,381
6	Continental	86,741
7	Japan Airlines	78,813
8	Air France	74,542
9	Lufthansa	71,897
10	US Airways	66,564
11	Qantas	58,619
12	Singapore	57,737
13	KLM	57,304
14	All Nippon	53,825
15	Southwest	50,553
16	Cathay Pacific	40,679
17	TWA	39,401
18	Air Canada	37,346
19	Alitalia	35,527
20	Thai Int'l	34,448
21	Iberia	32,521
22	Korean	32,277
23	Swissair	30,283
24	Varig	27,056
25	Malaysia	27,022

In operating revenue

Rank	Airline	Op. revenue (000)
1	UAL Corp.	$17,561,000
2	American (Airline Group)	17,449,000
3	Delta	14,400,000
4	British Airways	14,360,000
5	FedEx	13,666,319
6	Lufthansa Group	12,686,100
7	Air France Group	9,695,000
8	Japan Airlines	9,647,108
9	Northwest	9,044,800
10	US Airways Group	8,688,000
11	Continental	7,951,000
12	Swissair (SAirGroup)	7,749,000
13	All Nippon	7,525,000
14	KLM	6,323,000
15	Qantas	5,367,000
16	Alitalia	4,998,105
17	SAS Group	4,860,000
18	Southwest	4,163,980
19	Singapore	4,131,917
20	Iberia	4,046,000
21	Air Canada	4,008,000
22	Korean	3,796,518
23	Cathay Pacific	3,422,000
24	TWA	3,259,147
25	Airborne Express	3,074,525

In operating profit

Rank	Airline	Op. profit (000)
1	American (Airline Group)	$1,951,000
2	Delta	1,793,140
3	Lufthansa Group	1,593,123
4	UAL Corp.	1,478,000
5	US Airways Group	1,014,000
6	Air France	993,666
7	FedEx	907,297
8	British Airways	712,190
9	Continental	701,000
10	Southwest	683,611
11	SAS Group	488,185
12	Swissair (SAirGroup)	480,200
13	Singapore	320,500
14	Qantas	315,480
15	Iberia	304,000
16	Alitalia	298,852
17	Korean	253,699
18	Airborne Express	234,467
19	Japan Airlines	206,833
20	Comair	204,089
21	KLM	201,663
22	America West	197,846
23	Alaska Airlines	194,000
24	Aeromexico /Mexicana	140,148
25	Atlas	136,568

In net profit

Rank	Airline	Net profit (000)
1	American (Airline Group)	'$1,791,000
2	Delta	1,077,552
3	UAL Corp.	821,000
4	Lufthansa Group	801,190
5	US Airways Group	538,000
6	Singapore	475,201
7	FedEx	435,445
8	Southwest	433,431
9	Continental	383,000
10	SAS Group	335,786
11	British Airways	332,000
12	Iberia	265,714
13	Air France	328,300
14	Swissair (SAirGroup)	247,600
15	Korean	245,546
16	Alitalia	221,483
17	Japan Airlines	219,017
18	KLM	216,372
19	Qantas	201,300
20	Alaska Airlines	190,500
21	Airborne Express	137,285
22	Comair	132,935
23	America West	103,016
24	Cargolux	92,000
25	Austrian	91,000

In passengers

Rank	Airline	Pass. (000)
1	Delta	105,390
2	United	86,867
3	American	81,477
4	US Airways	57,990
5	Southwest	52,586
6	Northwest	50,500
7	Continental	43,625
8	All Nippon	41,491
9	Lufthansa	36,059
10	Air France	33,169
11	Japan Airlines	31,363
12	British Airways	31,325
13	Alitalia	24,103
14	TWA	23,920
15	Iberia	21,753
16	SAS	21,688
17	Korean	19,714
18	Japan Air System	19,518
19	Qantas	18,865
20	America West	17,792
21	Thai Int'l	15,613
22	KLM	15,077
23	China Southern	15,052
24	Air Canada	14,800
25	Alaska	13,056

In FTKs

Rank	Airline	FTKS (000)
1	FedEx	9,925,906
2	Lufthansa Cargo	6,696,000
3	UPS	5,571,613
4	Korean	5,224,016
5	Singapore	4,828,248
6	Air France	4,595,040
7	Japan Airlines	4,049,722
8	British Airways	3,884,420
9	KLM	3,719,056
10	United	3,422,332
11	Cathay Pacific	3,339,000
12	China Airlines	2,796,000
13	Cargolux	2,687,893
14	EVA	2,538,930
15	Northwest	2,484,460
16	American	2,346,186
17	Swissair	1,965,561
18	Nippon Cargo	1,962,601
19	Delta	1,922,116
20	Martinair	1,817,700
21	Asiana	1,805,757
22	Thai Int'l	1,524,972
23	Alitalia	1,521,708
24	Polar	1,466,500
25	Emery	1,406,675

In employees

Rank	Airline	No. of employees
1	FedEx	145,000
2	American	92,000
3	United	91,000
4	Delta	71,300
5	British Airways	64,000
6	Air France	55,747
7	Lufthansa	54,695
8	Northwest	50,565
9	Continental	43,900
10	Swissair	43,696
11	US Airways	38,210
12	Qantas	28,169
13	Singapore	28,000
14	Southwest	25,844
15	KLM	25,800
16	TWA	25,000
17	Saudia	24,843
18	Thai Int'l	24,186
19	SAS	23,992
20	Air Canada	23,326
21	Malaysia	23,309
22	Iberia	22,065
23	Indian	21,943
24	Japan Airlines	19,811
25	Alitalia	18,465

In fleet size

Rank	Airline	No. of aircraft
1	American	648
2	FedEx	625
3	Delta	605
4	United	577
5	Northwest	409
6	US Airways	381
7	Continental	353
8	Southwest	280
9	British Airways	271
10	Air France	227
11	Lufthansa	224
12	UPS	217
13	TWA	206
14	SAS	185
15	Air Canada	152
15	Alitalia	152
17	All Nippon	143
17	Qantas	143
19	Japan Airlines	138
20	Continental Express	135
21	Iberia	129
22	Aeroflot Russian	120
23	Mesa Air Group	115
24	Korean	113
25	Saudi Arabian	110
25	America West	110

SOURCE: Direct airline reports. Year ended December 31, 1998 or most recent fiscal year.
1) Pre-tax

Source: "The World Airline Report," *Air Transport World*, Penton Media, Inc., Cleveland, OH, July 1999

TABLE 7.3

Passenger Yield

Revenue per Passenger Mile (In cents)

	1988	1997	1998
Domestic	12.3	13.9	14.0
International	10.4	11.0	10.4
Total	11.9	13.1	13.1

Freight & Express Yield

Revenue per Freight & Express Ton Mile (In cents)

	1988	1997	1998
Domestic	114.9	79.8	82.5
International	41.3	44.0	43.9
Total	78.4	58.3	58.8

Source of both tables: Reprinted from the *Air Transport Association 1999 Annual Report* with permission of the Air Transport Association of America, Inc., 1301 Pennsylvania Avenue, NW, Washington DC, 20004

TABLE 7.4

Employment

U.S. Scheduled Airlines

	1988	1997	1998
Pilots & Copilots	43,795	60,434	64,099
Other Flight Personnel	7,807	10,713	11,060
Flight Attendants	76,297	96,198	97,574
Mechanics	55,001	65,500	69,927
Aircraft & Traffic Service Personnel	211,795	269,581	290,109
Office Employees	40,611	38,354	40,944
All Other	45,247	45,729	47,345
Total Employment	480,553	586,509	621,058

Average Compensation per Employee

	1988	1997	1998
Salaries & Wages	$35,877	$50,008	$50,420
Benefits & Pensions	5,774	9,714	9,819
Payroll Taxes	2,684	3,543	3,558
Total Compensation	$44,335	$63,265	$63,797

(RPMs) grew 38 percent. (A revenue passenger mile is one fare-paying passenger transported one mile.) The financial performance of commercial airlines has shown considerable improvement over the past five years. The industry has reported net profits of over $14.7 billion. In 1998, U.S. carriers reported operating profits of $9.3 billion and net profits of $4.9 billion for the year. See Table 7.1 for a general statistics on the nation's scheduled airlines.

The large commercial airlines continue to restructure (develop a new organization plan) and cut costs to facilitate future growth and finance new aircraft. It is vital for the airlines to set fares that will attract enough passengers and still provide a profit. In addition, the major airlines are under pressure from start-ups with lower expenses, such as Western Pacific and Frontier, and expanding regional operators, like Southwest, with efficient operations and lower overhead. Major airlines have asked for concessions from the pilots' and flight attendants' unions in order to cut costs.

Debate over the Big Jets

Many experts are debating the future of jumbo jets. Major international carriers are building hubs in cities that do not generate enough traffic to fill giant, 600-passenger, four-engine aircraft. Instead, smaller two-engine jumbo planes, such as the 767, are increasingly being used because their 176 to 230 seats are more easily filled. While overseas flights, particularly to Asia, still use the larger aircraft, the fragmentation of air routes (dividing fewer long routes into more short ones) has created demand for smaller planes carrying between 300 and 400 passengers. In 1995, Boeing introduced its two-engine giant, the 777 (350 to 475 seats). Boeing also builds the MD-11 that carries 231 to 350 passengers. (The MD-11 was originally built by McDonnell Douglas, now part of Boeing.) Airbus Industries, a European consortium, offers two competitors for the market, the A330 and the A340 (253 to 485 seats). In June 1998, the FAA awarded the Russian Ilyushin IL-96T cargo plane an air-worthiness certificate. A passenger version, the Ilyushin IL-96M, which carries 436 passengers, will be introduced soon, although it is debatable whether this aircraft will find a market in the United States.

Nonetheless, the opening China market, which could attract numerous overseas Chinese for homeland visits, still motivates Airbus and the now-merged Boeing and McDonnell Douglas to propose 600-800 passenger craft. Forecasts show that, as we get closer to 2010, the demand for widebody jets will steadily increase and will eventually account for as much as 70.7 percent of equipment expenditures. Asia/Pacificheadquartered airlines will account for most of the larger airplane purchases.

The Crowded Skies

In 1997, the privately owned fixed-wing (wings fastened to the fuselage, as distinguished from a helicopter) fleet numbered 166,800, with turbine-powered engines accounting for about 9,000 of that number. The rest of the fleet had piston engines turning propellers, rather than jet engines. Individuals or companies privately own almost all of these aircraft. The 4,822 commercial airline planes are turbine-powered, as are the vast majority of the approximately 2,000 regional aircraft. Other types of aircraft include rotorcrafts (helicopters) and balloons, gliders, and blimps.

A License to Fly

In 1998, 618,298 people had licenses to fly in the United States, down from 622,261 in 1996. Of that number, 97,736 held student licenses and were learning to fly. Approximately 247,000 had private licenses that permitted them to fly the smaller, private planes. Another 122,053 had commercial licenses which allowed them to fly the smaller airplanes owned by the airlines. More than 134,000 pilots held airline transport licenses, which permit them to fly the big jets owned by the airline companies. Nearly 7,000 had licenses for helicopters, and 9,402 for gliders.

The Top Airlines

As shown in Table 7.2, in 1998, Delta (105 million), United (nearly 87 million), and American (81 million), led the industry in numbers of passengers carried. Federal Express carried, by far, the largest number of freight ton kilometers (FTKs), followed by Lufthansa Cargo and United Parcel Service (UPS). American Airlines, Federal Express, Delta, and United had the most operating planes (fleet size).

Yield — or fares per passenger per mile — is rising. In 1988, airlines received an average yield of

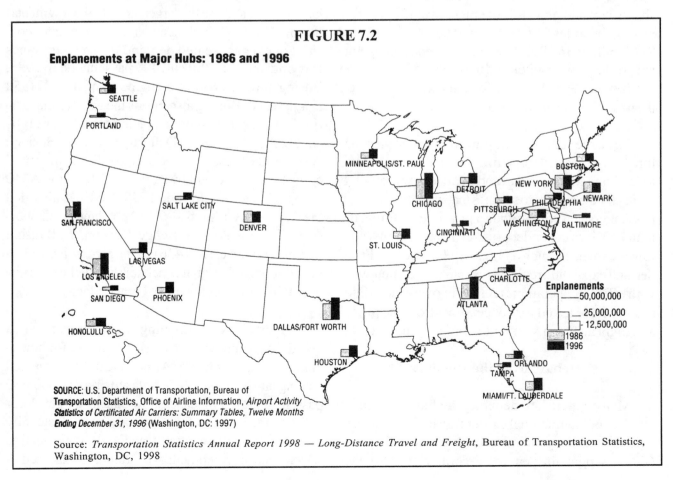

FIGURE 7.2

Enplanements at Major Hubs: 1986 and 1996

SOURCE: U.S. Department of Transportation, Bureau of Transportation Statistics, Office of Airline Information, *Airport Activity Statistics of Certificated Air Carriers: Summary Tables, Twelve Months Ending December 31, 1996* (Washington, DC: 1997)

Source: *Transportation Statistics Annual Report 1998 — Long-Distance Travel and Freight*, Bureau of Transportation Statistics, Washington, DC, 1998

11.9 cents per passenger mile; in 1997 and 1998, the yield was 13.1 cents per passenger mile. Freight and express yield — revenue per ton mile — have decreased. In 1988, the average yield was 78.4 cents; by 1997, it had dropped to 58.3 cents, and in 1998, it was nearly unchanged at 58.8 cents per ton mile. (See Table 7.3.)

Employment

The U.S. airlines employed 621,058 people in 1998, up 29 percent from 480,553 in 1988 (Table 7.4). At one time, airlines experienced a glut of employees in several categories, particularly pilots and airplane technicians. In fact, many pilots were flying for free for small airlines in order to build up enough hours of flying time so that they could apply for jobs at the big airlines. However, the rapid growth of the industry in the past several years has largely eliminated those overages.

When jet airplanes became part of the air passenger industry in 1958, pilots were largely recruited from the armed forces. These were men (exclusively) with prior military flight training and experience. Although pilots are private employees of the airline for which they fly, they are subject to the mandatory FAA-imposed retirement at age 60. The pool of military pilots has shrunk, and the rising cost of private pilot training has discouraged many would-be students. Many pilots now begin their careers with regional or cargo airlines in order to get enough required flying hours, hoping to move to the majors as vacancies appear.

Some pilots have tried to overturn the mandatory retirement age. The ruling, made over 30 years ago, was intended to reduce the danger of an older pilot suffering a heart attack or stroke while flying. Opponents of the ruling cite recent medical advances that greatly reduce this risk. Their main argument, however, is that older pilots have accumulated a vast store

TABLE 7.5

U.S. REGIONALS/COMMUTERS FORECAST ASSUMPTIONS

FISCAL YEAR	AVERAGE SEATS PER AIRCRAFT			AVERAGE PASSENGER TRIP LENGTH			AVERAGE PASSENGER LOAD FACTOR		
	298-C CARRIERS (Seats)	FORM 41 CARRIERS (Seats)	ALL CARRIERS (Seats)	298-C CARRIERS (Miles)	FORM 41 CARRIERS (Miles)	ALL CARRIERS (Miles)	298-C CARRIERS (Percent)	FORM 41 CARRIERS (Percent)	ALL CARRIERS (Percent)
Historical*									
1993	26.7	33.9	28.2	197.1	203.4	198.7	47.5	51.0	48.4
1994	27.1	35.8	29.1	205.9	210.5	207.2	49.6	52.3	50.4
1995	27.7	36.1	30.3	215.2	211.0	213.6	48.6	50.4	49.3
1996	27.8	35.0	30.5	224.3	220.7	222.7	51.5	53.4	52.3
1997	28.1	37.3	31.3	234.0	226.0	230.6	52.9	54.6	53.6
1998E	28.9	40.8	33.1	245.9	237.0	241.8	55.1	58.4	56.5
Forecast									
1999	29.6	41.5	34.2	253.9	240.0	246.9	55.1	58.8	56.8
2000	30.5	42.5	35.2	259.1	245.5	252.2	55.4	59.1	57.2
2001	31.5	43.5	36.2	264.3	251.0	257.6	55.7	59.4	57.5
2002	32.2	44.2	37.0	269.5	256.5	262.9	56.0	59.7	57.8
2003	32.9	44.9	37.7	274.8	262.0	268.3	56.3	60.0	58.1
2004	33.6	45.6	38.5	280.1	267.5	273.7	56.6	60.3	58.4
2005	34.3	46.3	39.2	285.4	273.0	279.1	57.0	60.6	58.7
2006	35.0	47.0	40.0	290.7	278.5	284.4	57.3	60.9	59.1
2007	35.6	47.5	40.6	296.0	284.0	289.8	57.6	61.2	59.4
2008	36.1	48.0	41.1	301.2	289.5	295.2	57.9	61.5	59.7
2009	36.7	48.5	41.7	306.5	295.0	300.5	58.2	61.8	60.0
2010	37.2	49.0	42.2	311.7	300.5	305.9	58.5	62.1	60.3

* Source: Forms 298-C and 41, U.S. Department of Transportation

Source: *FAA Aerospace Forecasts, Fiscal Years 1999-2010*, Federal Aviation Administration, Washington, DC, 1999

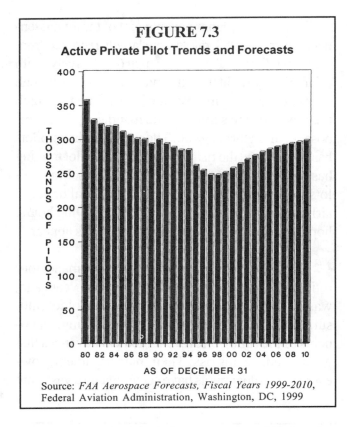

FIGURE 7.3

Active Private Pilot Trends and Forecasts

THOUSANDS OF PILOTS

AS OF DECEMBER 31

Source: *FAA Aerospace Forecasts, Fiscal Years 1999-2010*, Federal Aviation Administration, Washington, DC, 1999

there were 102 operating U.S. carriers, down from a high of 246 in 1981. Passenger enplanements, including Alaska and foreign territories, totaled almost 66.1 million in 1998, a gain of 7.2 percent over 1997.

The regionals and the commuter industry have created niches in the market tailored to the specific needs of their customers. While the fleet once consisted of a variety of small general-aviation aircraft, the planes are increasingly state-of-the-art, including a growing number of small, but comfortable jet aircraft, and the airlines now offer services similar to those of the commercial carriers.

The regional airlines became an essential element of the hub-and-spoke structure (see below) of the majors. Many have routes and schedules designed to mesh with major carriers at hub cities. They funnel passengers from smaller cities to flights outbound from the hub and relay arriving passengers to their final destinations. (See Figure 7.2 for the largest hubs in the United States.)

The regional airlines have become an important component in the airline industry, leading some of the majors to buy their connecting regionals to ensure continued operation and cooperation. For example, AMR (parent company of American Airlines) owns Simmons and other commuter airlines. The regionals also provide a training ground for pilots with backgrounds in military or general aviation who wish to fly eventually for one of the major airlines.

The regional/commuter industry is growing faster than the larger commercial carriers. Table 7.5 illustrates the forecasted passenger growth through the year 2010. The regional/commuter airlines will have more seats per plane and carry more passengers farther.

Regional/commuter air carriers are separated into two groups. One group reports traffic data to the U.S. Department of Transportation's (DOT) Office of Airline Information on DOT Form 298-C. The carriers in this group operate only commuter aircraft of 60 seats or less and are known as Form 298-C carriers. The second group reports traffic data to the DOT Office of Airline Information on Form 41. These carriers,

of experience during their many years of flying that classroom training cannot duplicate. The FAA, however, has stood by its decision and indicates that it intends to maintain the age limit. The Ninth Circuit Court of appeals agreed in *Western Air Lines, Inc. v. Criswell et al.* (709 F.2d 544, 1984), when it decided that the airlines could retire pilots at age 60.

The Regional/Commuter Airlines

In response to deregulation, the regional, or commuter, airlines underwent dramatic changes. Previously restricted almost exclusively to planes with fewer than 12 seats, which had severely hampered growth, deregulation freed the regional airlines to increase passenger capacity and passenger revenue miles. As the major airlines converted to larger turbojets suitable for high-capacity, long-haul flights, the regionals moved into the gap left in the low-density, short-haul market.

Since 1969, when the commuter lines received formal industry recognition, more than 600 different carriers have been in operation at one time or another. However, the consolidation that occurred among the major airlines also affected the regionals. In 1998,

104

known as Form 41 carriers, operate both large aircraft over 60 seats and smaller commuter aircraft. In 1998, a total of eight carriers (American Eagle — including Flagship, Simmons, and Wings West — Atlantic Southeast, Continental Express, Executive, Horizon, Mesaba, Trans States, and United Feeder Service) reported for all, or a part of the year, on DOT Form 41.

GENERAL AVIATION

Since flights by individuals in privately owned airplanes produce no revenue, the state of general aviation is reported in terms of numbers of private pilots, hours flown, fleet composition, and aircraft shipments by the manufacturers of general aviation aircraft. The total number of private pilots has decreased from 360,000 in 1980 to 247,226 in 1998. Figure 7.3 shows, however, that the number of private pilots is expected to increase to about 300,000 by 2010.

For FAA reporting purposes, the active general aviation fleet consists of those private airplanes that have been flown at least one hour during the previous year. As of 1997, the active fleet numbered 192,414

aircraft (Table 7.6), down from 210,266 airplanes in 1989.

Since 1978, the total number of general aviation aircraft shipments has been declining. In 1978, almost 18,000 general aviation aircraft were shipped; by 1994, fewer than 1,000 general aviation aircraft were shipped. The major cause for this decline was manufacturer liability. Up to that time, any time a general aviation plane crashed, no matter how old or how poorly maintained it had been, and regardless of the ability of the pilot, the manufacturer was at least partly responsible. It became too financially risky to manufacture aircraft. In 1994, following a virtual shutdown of the general aviation industry, Congress passed the General Aviation Revitalization Act (PL 103-298) limiting the manufacturers' liability and the amount of time during which they could be held legally liable.

The act states that "no civil action for damages for death or injury to persons or damage to property arising out of an accident involving a general aviation aircraft may be brought against the manufacturer of the aircraft or the manufacturer of any new component,

TABLE 7.6

U.S. FLEET AND FLIGHT HOURS BY TYPE AND USE

Number of Active General Aviation and Air Taxi Aircraft By Type and Primary Use—1997
(Excluding Commuters)

Aircraft Type	Active GA Aircraft	Public Use	Corporate	Business	Personal	Instruc-tional	Aerial Applica-tion	Aerial Observa-tion	Sight-Seeing	External Load	Other Work	Air Taxi	Other
ALL AIRCRAFT–TOTAL	192,414	4,130	10,411	27,716	115,630	14,663	4,858	3,311	677	186	679	4,777	5,250
PISTON–Total	156,056	1,980	3,036	25,940	99,482	13,363	3,606	2,682	416	6	606	2,350	2,511
One-Engine	140,038	1,717	1,080	20,095	94,317	12,801	3,569	2,619	381	6	528	843	2,021
Two-Engine	15,938	260	1,956	5,845	5,162	562	28	63	35	0	78	1,491	441
Other Piston	79	3	0	0	3	0	9	0	0	0	0	16	49
TURBOPROP–Total	5,619	300	2,423	494	425	49	399	19	0	0	8	1,221	274
One-Engine	650	11	46	43	61	2	376	4	0	0	0	80	11
Two-Engine	4,939	280	2,366	451	364	47	16	15	0	0	8	1,141	261
Other Turboprop	29	9	11	0	0	0	7	0	0	0	0	0	2
TURBOJET–Total	5,178	214	4,283	142	72	16	0	0	0	0	0	271	148
Two-Engine	4,638	214	3,837	133	60	12	0	0	0	0	0	265	122
Other Turbojet	539	0	446	9	12	4	0	0	0	0	0	6	26
ROTORCRAFT–Total	6,786	1,595	473	390	899	611	759	488	38	180	30	782	497
Piston	2,259	119	28	197	590	501	512	174	34	38	28	0	41
Turbine	4,527	1,476	445	193	309	110	247	314	4	142	2	782	456
One-Engine	3,762	1,447	270	190	287	110	247	303	4	74	2	510	276
Two-Engine	764	29	175	3	22	0	0	11	0	68	0	272	180
GLIDERS–Total	2,016	33	4	16	1,484	295	0	2	21	0	0	2	162
LIGHTER-THAN-AIR–Total	2,075	0	1	35	1,626	77	0	0	200	0	33	0	100
EXPERIMENTAL–Total	14,680	9	9	698	11,644	253	57	117	2	0	3	150	1,558
Amateur	10,261	0	0	356	8,813	108	0	1	1	0	0	0	980
Exhibition	1,798	0	0	38	1,143	117	0	0	0	0	0	44	458
Other	2,620	9	9	304	1,688	28	57	116	1	0	3	106	120

Note: Row and column summation may differ from printed totals due to estimation procedures, or because some active aircraft did not report use.   Source FAA

Source: *General Aviation 1999 Statistical Databook*, General Aviation Manufacturers Association, Washington, DC, 1999

FIGURE 7.4

Annual New U.S. Manufactured General Aviation Unit Shipments/Billings

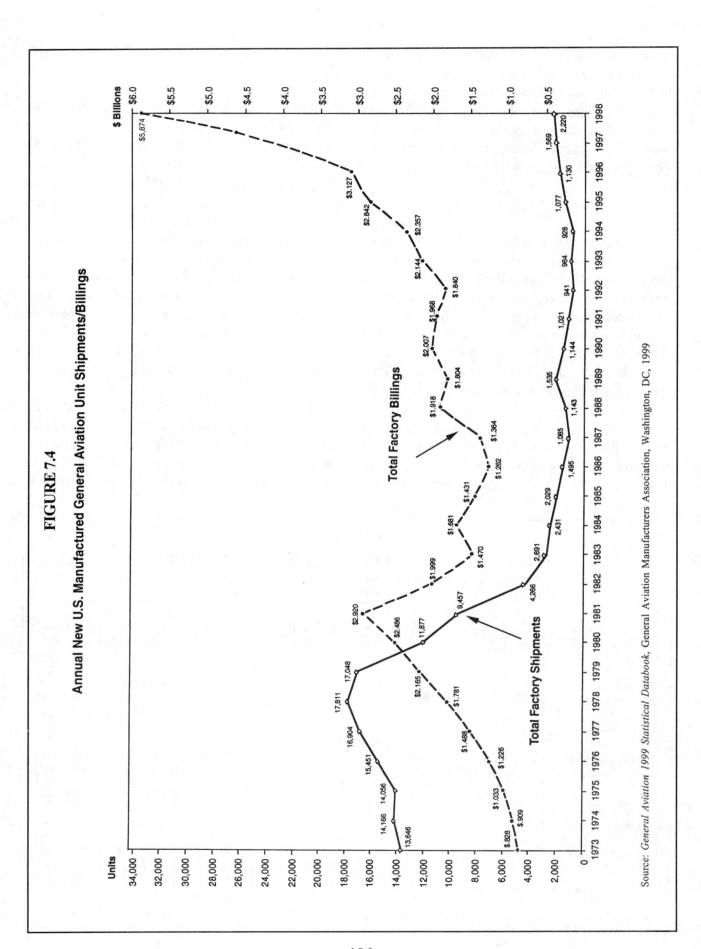

Source: *General Aviation 1999 Statistical Databook,* General Aviation Manufacturers Association, Washington, DC, 1999

TABLE 7.7

Annual New U.S. Manufactured General Aviation Airplane Shipments By Type of Airplane

Year	Grand Total	Single-Engine	Multi-Engine	Total Piston	Turboprop	Jet	Total Turbine
1962	6,697	5,690	1,007	6,697	0	0	0
1963	7,569	6,248	1,321	7,569	0	0	0
1964	9,336	7,718	1,606	9,324	9	3	12
1965	11,852	9,873	1,780	11,653	87	112	199
1966	15,768	13,250	2,192	15,442	165	161	326
1967	13,577	11,557	1,773	13,330	149	98	247
1968	13,698	11,398	1,959	13,357	248	93	341
1969	12,457	10,054	2,078	12,132	214	111	325
1970	7,292	5,942	1,159	7,101	135	56	191
1971	7,466	6,287	1,043	7,330	89	47	136
1972	9,774	7,913	1,548	9,446	179	134	313
1973	13,646	10,788	2,413	13,193	247	198	445
1974	14,166	11,579	2,135	13,697	250	202	452
1975	14,056	11,441	2,116	13,555	305	194	499
1976	15,451	12,785	2,120	14,905	359	187	546
1977	16,904	14,054	2,195	16,249	428	227	655
1978	17,811	14,398	2,634	17,032	548	231	779
1979	17,048	13,286	2,843	16,129	639	282	921
1980	11,877	8,640	2,116	10,756	778	326	1,104
1981	9,457	6,608	1,542	8,150	918	389	1,307
1982	4,266	2,871	678	3,549	458	259	717
1983	2,691	1,811	417	2,228	321	142	463
1984	2,431	1,620	371	1,991	271	169	440
1985	2,029	1,370	193	1,563	321	145	466
1986	1,495	985	138	1,123	250	122	372
1987	1,085	613	87	700	263	122	385
1988	1,143	628	67	695	291	157	448
1989	1,535	1,023	87	1,110	268	157	425
1990	1,144	608	87	695	281	168	449
1991	1,021	564	49	613	222	186	408
1992	941	552	41	593	177	171	348
1993	964	516	39	555	211	198	409
1994	928	444	55	499	207	222	429
1995	1,077	515	61	576	255	246	501
1996	1,130	530	70	600	289	241	530
1997	1,569	905	80	985	236	348	584
1998	2,220	1,436	98	1,534	271	415	686

Source: *General Aviation 1999 Statistical Databook*, General Aviation Manufacturers Association, Washington, DC, 1999

system, subassembly, or other part of the aircraft, in its capacity as a manufacturer if the accident occurred ..." following an agreed-upon, specified time, which starts on the date of delivery to the original buyer or lessee if the aircraft is delivered directly from the manufacturer. Similarly, if the aircraft is delivered to a sales person or company, no civil action for damages may be brought against the manufacturer if the accident occurs beyond an agreed-upon, specified time after that sales person or company receives the aircraft. The same conditions hold true for any new or replacement component, system, subassembly, or other part which was added to or replaced on the aircraft and which is supposed to have caused death, injury or damage.

After 1994, as the economy improved and aircraft manufacturers could buy more reasonably priced insurance, because of the passage of the act, shipments began to slowly increase. A total of 1,569 planes were shipped in 1997 and 2,220 in 1998. (See Figure 7.4.) Table 7.7 shows the number of purchases of single-engine and multi-engine piston, turboprop, and jet planes between 1962 and 1998.

ROTORCRAFT

As of December 31, 1997, the FAA reported a total of 6,785 active civil rotorcraft (helicopters and gyrocopters) in the United States. Jet-powered (turbine) helicopters accounted for 66.7 percent of the active helicopters, while piston engines powered the rest. Most rotorcraft are used for sightseeing, agricultural applications, law enforcement, fire fighting, personal transportation, emergency medical services,

TABLE 7.8

U.S. Civil and Joint Use Airports, Heliports, Stolports, and Seaplane Bases On Record
By Type Of Ownership—December 31, 1998

FAA	Total Facilities	TOTAL FACILITIES, BY OWNERSHIP		AIRPORTS OPEN TO THE PUBLIC				
				PAVED AIRPORTS[1]		UNPAVED AIRPORTS[1]		Total Airports
		Public	Private	Lighted	Unlighted	Lighted	Unlighted	
GRAND TOTAL	18,770	5,155	13,615	3,611	292	384	785	5,072
UNITED STATES—Total*	18,700	5,103	13,588	3,586	289	384	772	5,032

[1]Includes all airports open to the public, both publicly and privately owned.

*Excludes Puerto Rico, Virgin Islands, and South Pacific.

South Pacific includes American Samoa, Guam, Trust Territories, and Northern Mariana Islands.

Source: FAA

Source: *General Aviation 1999 Statistical Databook*, General Aviation Manufacturers Association, Washington, DC, 1999

transporting personnel and supplies to offshore oil rigs, traffic reporting, electronic news gathering, corporate or business transportation, and heavy lift for the oil, utility, and lumber industries.

AIRPORTS

Orville Wright's runway was a sand dune; Charles Lindbergh's, an open field. (Lindbergh made the first nonstop solo flight from New York City to Paris in 1927.) The first airline passengers walked to hangars or fields to board the parked planes. These arrangements soon proved inadequate. Larger planes, heavier loads, and increased traffic required paved runways and lighting for night flights and some sort of formal gathering place for passengers.

Government interest in airport development lagged behind its support for the industry as a whole. Federal aid was eventually granted under the Federal Airport Act of 1946 (60 Stat 170), the 1970 Airport and Airways Development Act (PL 91-258) (which, like the Highway Trust Fund after which it was patterned, levied taxes on airline users), and the 1982 Airport and Airway Improvement Act (PL 97-248). Most airports are now owned and operated by the city or municipality in which they are located, with funding provided locally and, to a lesser extent, by the federal government.

In 1998, planes could take off and land at 18,770 airports, heliports, and seaplane bases. Most of these airports are not big international airports with towers and multiple runways. Many are privately located in remote rural areas and may be only unlit grass strips. (See Table 7.8.) Table 7.9 shows the busiest U.S. airports in 1998. Atlanta (73 million), Chicago O'Hare (72 million), Los Angeles (61 million), and Dallas/Fort Worth (60 million), served the largest number of passengers in the United States. The route with the most passengers in the United States is from New York to Los Angeles. Eight of the 10 busiest routes originate or end in New York City (Table 7.10).

Local Impact

An airport has an enormous effect on the communities in its vicinity and can be a major benefit to the local economy. Quick, direct access increases business activity. Many companies are attracted to cities with large airport facilities. An airport may employ hundreds and even thousands of people and local industries, from food to real estate, to serve the needs of both the airport and its employees.

Ideally, an airport is located reasonably close to a community's business district but far from its residential areas. Often, this is not the case or is impossible. Population growth can overtake an airport that was once "out in the country." Smaller airports, built before the advent of jets in 1958, may have been able to coexist with suburban neighbors, but more flights and bigger planes have led to major complaints about noise and concerns about safety in populated areas. The FAA limits the noise which airliners can produce. Some airports impose additional restrictions on noise emissions, operating hours, or flight paths to reduce the discomfort of nearby residents.

Demand Exceeds Capacity

Air traffic is reaching critical levels as passenger numbers increase. Additional airports, or expansion of existing airports, may be part of the solution. The FAA expects that, in 1999, 623.9 million people will fly, and by the year 2010, the number of airline passengers will reach 931.1 million.

Building or expanding a major airport requires enormous capital expenditures and large areas of land. Further investment is needed for operation and maintenance. The airports must hire personnel for traffic forecasting, baggage handling, security, and public relations.

The popularity of air travel means that cutting back the number of flights is unlikely, even though this would relieve crowding of the nation's air space. Some restrictions, however, have been made at O'Hare Airport in Chicago, National Airport in Washington, DC, and at both La Guardia and Kennedy Airports in New York City. The "slots," authorizations to land and take off at particular times, have become valuable commodities at these airports and are bought and sold among carriers.

Since the airline industry was deregulated over 20 years ago, no new airports were built in the United States until 1992, when Pittsburgh International Airport opened its new terminal building. The $1.06 billion facility, the nation's most expensive airport at that time, represented a new age of efficiency and convenience. Designed to accommodate the increased traffic of the hub-and-spoke system (see below), it was equipped with innovative security checkpoints, baggage handling, and "smart" computer terminals for

---

TABLE 7.9

TOP-20 U.S. AIRPORTS — 1998

(In thousands)

Passengers (Arriving & Departing)

1	Atlanta	73,474	11	New York Kennedy	31,044
2	Chicago O'Hare	72,370	12	Houston	31,026
3	Los Angeles	61,216	13	Las Vegas	30,218
4	Dallas/Ft. Worth	60,483	14	St. Louis	28,640
5	San Francisco	40,060	15	Minneapolis/St. Paul	28,532
6	Denver	36,818	16	Orlando	27,749
7	Miami	33,935	17	Boston	26,416
8	Newark	32,521	18	Seattle	25,826
9	Phoenix	31,772	19	Philadelphia	24,231
10	Detroit	31,544	20	Charlotte	22,948

Cargo Metric Tonnes (Enplaned & Deplaned)

1	Memphis	2,369	11	Indianapolis	814
2	Los Angeles	1,861	12	Dallas/Ft. Worth	802
3	Miami	1,793	13	San Francisco	770
4	New York Kennedy	1,761	14	Oakland	707
5	Chicago O'Hare	1,440	15	Toledo	537
6	Louisville	1,395	16	Honolulu	502
7	Anchorage	1,388	17	Philadelphia	494
8	Newark	1,207	18	Denver	447
9	Atlanta	907	19	Boston	440
10	Dayton	887	20	Seattle	427

Source: Airports Council International.

Source: Reprinted from the *Air Transport Association 1999 Annual Report* with permission of the Air Transport Association of America, Inc., 1301 Pennsylvania Avenue, NW, Washington DC, 20004

---

ticket information in order to avoid the congestion typical of older airports.

Denver International, which opened in 1995, stirred controversy because of its $4 billion price tag, its two-year overrun on completion, its 23-mile distance from the city, and doubts whether traffic volumes would justify its cost. Internal difficulties with the baggage-handling system only added to the problems. Detroit plans a $1 billion terminal that will have anti-terrorism safeguards built into the facility.

AIR TRAFFIC SERVICES

Air Traffic Control

The air traffic control (ATC) system is a huge, nationwide network that controls the movements of airplanes in the United States. (See Figure 7.5.) The ATC system is made up of five types of facilities:

TABLE 7.10

TOP-30 DOMESTIC AIRLINE MARKETS*

Passengers — Outbound plus Inbound

(Twelve months ended December 1998, in thousands)

1	New York	Los Angeles	3,625		16	Honolulu	Lihue, Kauai	1,637
2	New York	Chicago	3,069		17	New York	West Palm Beach	1,560
3	New York	Miami	2,834		18	Honolulu	Kona, Hawaii	1,467
4	New York	San Francisco	2,683		19	Chicago	Atlanta	1,467
5	New York	Boston	2,651		20	Los Angeles	Oakland	1,459
6	Honolulu	Kahului, Maui	2,541		21	Chicago	Detroit	1,458
7	New York	Orlando	2,521		22	New York	Dallas/Ft. Worth	1,457
8	New York	Atlanta	2,377		23	Los Angeles	Phoenix	1,344
9	New York	Washington	2,372		24	Boston	Washington	1,340
10	Dallas/Ft. Worth	Houston	2,213		25	Los Angeles	Honolulu	1,335
11	Los Angeles	Las Vegas	2,055		26	Chicago	Dallas/Ft. Worth	1,329
12	Los Angeles	San Francisco	2,020		27	Chicago	Minneapolis/St. Paul	1,278
13	New York	Ft. Lauderdale	1,808		28	Los Angeles	Seattle	1,246
14	New York	San Juan	1,798		29	New York	Detroit	1,229
15	Chicago	Los Angeles	1,680		30	Chicago	San Francisco	1,193

* Includes all commercial airports in a metropolitan area. Does not include connecting passengers.

Source: DOT *Passenger Origin-Destination Survey.*

Source: Reprinted from the *Air Transport Association 1999 Annual Report* with permission of the Air Transport Association of America, Inc., 1301 Pennsylvania Avenue, NW, Washington DC, 20004

- Flight service stations — usually used by private aircraft for flight plan filing and weather report updates.

- Air traffic control towers — control aircraft on the ground and before landing and after take-off within five nautical miles of the airport and up to 3,000 feet over the airport.

- Terminal radar approach control (TRACON) stations — line up and separate aircraft as they approach and leave busy airports, five to 50 miles from the airport, up to 10,000 feet above the ground.

- En route centers — control aircraft while in flight over the continental United States. The 20 en route centers usually control commercial aircraft above 18,000 feet.

- Oakland and New York (oceanic) en route centers — control in the same way as the other 20 en route centers, but also control aircraft over the ocean, using radar for up to 225 miles offshore.

Thereafter, they use radio contact to learn aircraft location over the ocean.

Run by the FAA, the ATC system provides safe, orderly, and efficient air travel. However, the increase in air traffic in the past two decades has put a strain on the ATC system. To correct this problem, in 1981, the FAA began to modernize its hardware, software, and communications equipment. The $34 billion program has over 200 separate projects and will be completed by the year 2003.

FAA Air Traffic Services

The FAA provides the aviation community with three distinct air traffic services:

- Air traffic control tower service at selected airports (288 FAA towers and 161 contract towers as of September 30, 1998).

- Traffic surveillance and aircraft separation by air route traffic control centers, which oversee air traffic movement that is enroute and between airports.

- Flight planning and pilot briefings at flight service stations.

All four aviation system user groups — air carriers, commuter/air taxi, general aviation, and military — use these FAA operational services to maintain the flow and safety of aviation traffic.

Air Traffic Controllers

In 1981, a strike by air traffic controllers, employees of the FAA, was broken when President Ronald Reagan fired 11,400 striking controllers. Their number has since returned to pre-strike levels, but there is still a shortage of experienced controllers, especially in busy East Coast airports. Training new controllers takes two-and-a-half to three years. Congress sets the controllers' salaries, and neither the FAA nor union negotiations can change them. However, realizing the great need for qualified personnel, the FAA has begun paying 20 percent bonuses to some controllers at the busier airports and authorizing overtime pay.

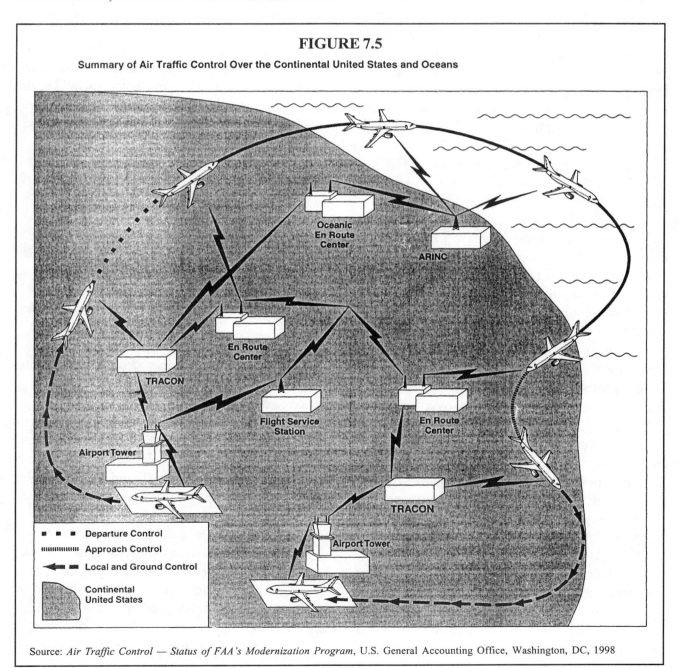

FIGURE 7.5

Summary of Air Traffic Control Over the Continental United States and Oceans

Source: *Air Traffic Control — Status of FAA's Modernization Program*, U.S. General Accounting Office, Washington, DC, 1998

The growing number of aircraft and flights makes an air traffic controller's job very stressful, but some relief may be on the way. New technological developments are in various stages of planning or testing, including advanced computer automation, navigation, and landing systems. These new technologies use the Defense Department's highly accurate global positioning system satellites, microwave landing systems, and on-board anticollision devices. Whether they can completely solve existing problems remains to be seen.

Congress often reduces or delays expenditures from the Airport and Airway Trust Fund to help reduce the federal deficit, thus postponing improvements in the air traffic control system. (See section on Federal Legislation below.) Air traffic controllers report that equipment (technology and computers) is outdated, resulting, they claim, in a dangerous situation. Computers at major hubs such as Chicago's O'Hare International are 30 years old. In July 1995, Chicago's computers broke down, requiring use of the back-up system, which, controllers claimed, was inadequate and a safety risk.

In January 1994, the FAA reported that an increasing number of aircraft were flying too close to other planes because of errors made by air traffic controllers. The required distances of separation were breached 757 times in 1993, the year of the study. Controllers attribute the increase in plane separation errors to increased air traffic, overburdened airports, and stressed and tired controllers. In New York and other crowded airports, chronic shortages of air traffic controllers are being eased by overtime and by delaying flights. In addition, controllers are being recruited from other parts of the country where crowding is less of a problem. On the other hand, some observers believe that the required distances between planes, established many years ago when planes were much less sophisticated, are much too great and could be reduced.

For the most part, since the early 1990s, the number of pilot-reported near-midair collisions have decreased. In 1997 there were 239 near-midair collisions, up from 194 in 1996, but down significantly from the 311 that occurred in 1992.

Proposals for Free Flight

In response to the crisis in air traffic control, some experts have proposed a method known as "free flight" to replace the existing system. Free flight is exactly what the term implies — pilots take off and land when they want and fly to their destinations by whatever routes they desire. The system is based on the assumption that most aircraft will be equipped with flight management systems that can guide them on a 4-dimensional track. That is, the systems can predict where the aircraft will be at any given time until it reaches its destination.

On the ground, the key to free flight is a "conflict probe," a software package that examines all tracks within its sector and detects contact that would result between two aircraft. Advocates of the system believe free flight will yield massive savings for airlines and reduce congestion and delays.

A REMARKABLE SAFETY RECORD — BUT THE LARGER THE SAFER

The crash of a wide-bodied jumbo jet is a major disaster. Hundreds of lives may be lost in a single incident. Nonetheless, flying on a scheduled air carrier is one of the safest ways to travel, and the risk of death or injury is far less than when riding the same distance in a car.

Consumer advocates are concerned that deregulation has created intense competition that has led to dangerous cost-cutting. Airline mechanics complain of an erosion of maintenance standards. Some airline critics believe that the old direct-route system was less dangerous than the hub-and-spoke system because the latter involves more takeoffs and landings, when most accidents occur.

Many recent airplane accidents have been attributed to flight or ground crew failures. These include, for example, failure to de-ice airplanes properly, improper setting of flaps and slats, misjudgment of weather (including "wind shear") poor navigation, pilot fatigue, and improper maintenance or parts replacement. Airlines are working with the FAA to improve the training and teamwork of both flight and ground crews. Table 7.11 shows the accident and fatality figures for scheduled aircraft from 1992 through 1997.

Despite statistics that find it safer than most forms of transportation, the American public sometimes feels that air travel has become less safe. In 1994, after several crashes of small commuter planes known as ATRs, the National Transportation Safety Board called for study of those aircrafts and the crashes in order to determine if commuter planes should be held to the same safety requirements as the larger aircraft. It concluded that the commuter airlines' rapid expansion has outpaced regulation. Original regulation of commuter aircraft dated from the 1950s, when small planes were not a major segment of the transportation system.

As Table 7.11 illustrates, the commuter's safety record steadily improved from 1992, when there were seven fatal accidents and 21 fatalities, to 1995, with two fatal crashes and nine fatalities. Figures for 1996 show only one fatal accident, which accounted for 14 deaths. However, preliminary figures for 1997 show five fatal accidents accounting for 46 deaths. (The 1997 figures indicate that, for large air carriers, 8 people died in a total of four air crashes — 0.03 fatalities occurred for every 100,000 hours flown.)

TABLE 7.11

TOTAL SYSTEM ACCIDENT DATA BY SEGMENT
1992 through 1997

Segment	YEAR	FLIGHT HOURS	TOTAL	ACCIDENTS FATAL	ACCIDENTS FATALITIES	ACCIDENT RATE TOTAL	ACCIDENT RATE FATAL
Large Air Carrier	1992	12,359,715	18	4	33	0.15	0.03
	1993	12,706,206	23	1	1	0.18	0.01
	1994	13,124,315	23	4	239	0.17	0.03
	1995	13,510,066	36	3	168	0.27	0.02
	1996	13,962,892	38	5	380	0.27	0.04
	1997P	15,290,000	49	4	8	0.32	0.03
Commuter	1992	2,335,349	23	7	21	0.94	0.30
	1993	2,638,347	16	4	24	0.61	0.15
	1994	2,784,129	10	3	25	0.36	0.11
	1995	2,625,329	11	2	9	0.42	0.08
	1996	2,540,864	12	1	14	0.47	0.04
	1997P	1,120,000	16	5	46	1.43	0.45
Air Taxi	1992	2,000,000	76	24	68	3.80	1.20
	1993	1,700,000	69	19	42	4.06	1.12
	1994	1,900,000	85	26	63	4.47	1.37
	1995	1,740,000	75	24	52	4.31	1.38
	1996	2,000,000	89	29	63	4.45	1.45
	1997P	1,980,000	82	16	40	4.14	0.81
General Aviation	1992	24,800,000	2073	446	857	8.35	1.79
	1993	22,800,000	2038	398	736	8.93	1.74
	1994	22,240,000	1995	404	730	8.96	1.81
	1995	23,930,000	2055	412	734	8.57	1.71
	1996	24,100,000	1905	359	631	7.90	1.49
	1997P	24,700,000	1854	350	646	7.51	1.42

Data Source: NTSB

Rates are per 100,000 hours flown

Suicide/Sabotage cases are included in "Accidents" and "Fatalities" but not in "Accident Rates"

P - Preliminary Data

Source: *Aviation Safety Statistical Handbook,* Federal Aviation Administration, Washington, DC, 1998

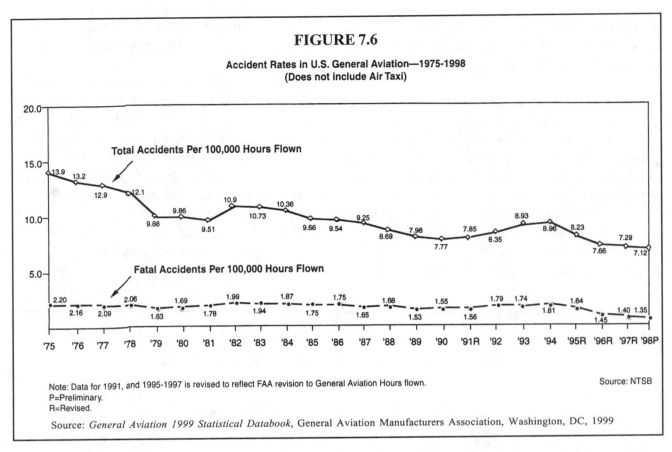

FIGURE 7.6

Accident Rates in U.S. General Aviation—1975-1998
(Does not include Air Taxi)

Note: Data for 1991, and 1995-1997 is revised to reflect FAA revision to General Aviation Hours flown.
P=Preliminary.
R=Revised.

Source: NTSB

Source: *General Aviation 1999 Statistical Databook*, General Aviation Manufacturers Association, Washington, DC, 1999

In comparison, the accident and fatality rates of the general aviation fleet, in which the majority of the aircraft are small, single-engine piston planes and pilot training and testing are less stringent, are far worse than that of large jets. As shown in Figure 7.6, the rate of accidents and fatalities declined sharply from 1975 to 1979 and then have fallen much more slowly over the past two decades. Figure 7.7 shows the number of fatal accidents in U.S. General Aviation between 1975 and 1998.

Wearing Out

No matter how well designed, properly handled, and carefully maintained, machines eventually wear out, and airplanes are no exception. Even though the FAA has increased its inspection staff by almost 75 percent since 1985, their workload has grown even faster. More planes are in the air, and a large number are growing very old. Adding to the problem are the slow delivery and expense of new airplanes, which has forced some airlines to buy and fly used, usually older, aircraft. In addition, many new airlines have chosen to buy older aircraft. Although not as efficient as the newer planes, their low purchase price makes them very attractive. It is not unusual for a plane to be 25 years or older.

Accidents attributed to structural failure appear to be on the rise. Both the airline industry and government agencies are seeking solutions. Proposals include more frequent and thorough inspections, stepped-up preventive maintenance, and a scheduled program of mandatory repairs or parts replacement.

The average age of a commercial airliner is now 13 years. The average age of North America's fleet will decline through the 1990s, dropping to 11.3 years by 1999, as new aircraft meeting improved federal standards for noise reduction, safety issues, and technical requirements replace older machines. Thereafter, the fleet's age will gradually rise to 14.7 years by 2014.

FEDERAL LEGISLATION

Unlike the railroads, the airline industry was heavily regulated almost from its beginning. The rapid growth

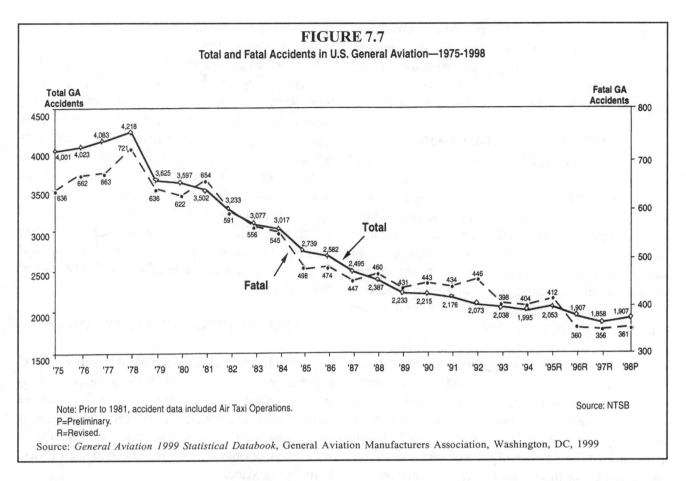

FIGURE 7.7

Total and Fatal Accidents in U.S. General Aviation—1975-1998

Note: Prior to 1981, accident data included Air Taxi Operations.
P=Preliminary.
R=Revised.

Source: NTSB

Source: *General Aviation 1999 Statistical Databook*, General Aviation Manufacturers Association, Washington, DC, 1999

of airplanes and air services in the early 1920s prompted legislation both to support and to control the growing industry. The transport of mail, initially the province of the federal government, was opened to private operators by the Kelly Air Mail Act of 1925 (45 Stat. 594). The U.S. government used air mail contracts to subsidize commercial airlines. The Air Commerce Act of 1926 (44 Stat. 568) promoted air safety. It authorized the Secretary of Commerce to register aircraft and certify pilots, established air traffic rules, and required the government to supply and maintain lighted airways.

The Civil Aeronautics Act of 1938 (72 Stat. 731) created the Civil Aeronautics Authority (CAA) to provide economic regulation, investigate accidents, and administer airport construction and maintenance. Economic regulation and safety functions were turned over to the newly formed Civil Aeronautics Board (CAB) in 1939. The Federal Airport Act of 1946 (60 Stat. 170) provided financial assistance for airport development.

The Airways Modernization Board was formed to study a national air navigation and traffic control system. The Federal Aviation Act of 1958 (PL 85-726) brought its work under the jurisdiction of the new Federal Aviation Agency. It became part of the Department of Transportation (DOT) in 1966 when DOT was created, and the Agency was given its present-day name, the Federal Aviation Administration (FAA). Air safety functions were taken over by the new National Transportation Safety Board (NTSB).

The Airport and Airway Development Act of 1970 (PL 91-258) provided increased financial support for airport development. Taxes and fees on air travelers and airlines have been collecting in a trust fund. To make the federal budget deficit appear smaller, Congress has appropriated these dedicated funds far more slowly than the FAA or the airlines would like, thus delaying the improvement of the air traffic system.

The aviation trust fund was one of the issues dealt with by Congress in 1999. The aviation trust fund is expected to have large balances in the future unless spending from the fund is increased. This situation may pave the way for a new budgeting process for aviation if there is enough support from Congress. As of the second half of 1999, nothing had been decided.

AIRLINE DEREGULATION — THE BEGINNING

Prior to 1978, an airline company needed government approval to enter the market, merge with another company, engage in foreign commerce, establish a new route, abandon an existing route, or set or change fares. While this regulation of airlines ensured service to almost all cities, it discouraged competition on the basis of price. Airlines, instead, vied for market share by attempting to provide the best service.

In 1978, the Airline Deregulation Act (PL 95-504) eliminated many government restrictions and permitted competition between airlines. Many Americans think that government intervention in any industry restricts free competition and is thus detrimental to the public interest. Critics of airline regulation had pointed out during the 1970s that airlines which operated entirely within a state and thus escaped Civil Aeronautics Board (CAB) regulation charged far lower fares for routes of the same distance than CAB-regulated carriers. On the other hand, the existing airlines and labor unions feared the cost pressure of competition and opposed deregulation.

The act lifted government restrictions on many aspects of the airline industry and led to the elimination of the CAB in 1984. It intended to increase competition in the domestic airline industry by easing the requirements for new airlines entering the market, reducing 40 years of restrictions on routing and scheduling, and eliminating price controls. Its supporters believed that competition and "free market forces" would benefit both the industry and the public with lower fares, better service, and increased passenger loads.

The 1978 Deregulation Act dealt primarily with domestic, not international, air transportation. The United States shares authority over international air service with all other nations, with each country controlling its own territory. An American airline can enter or leave a foreign airport only with the consent of the foreign country, and it must obey the aviation rules of that country. As a result, the United States and other nations have a large number of intergovernmental agreements that control international air service. Many foreign countries regard their airlines as important vehicles to represent them and promote international business and tourism. Therefore, these governments often own and subsidize their airlines, and they frequently regulate or restrict commercial competition from other countries. On the other hand, a number of other nations have also deregulated and/or privatized their airlines.

AIRLINE DEREGULATION TODAY

What has happened to the industry since the Deregulation Act was passed in 1978 shocked many people, including those in the airline industry. Some airlines, such as Braniff, Pan American, and Eastern, which had been household names, went out of business, and Continental Airlines has been in and out of bankruptcy twice.

Deregulation was intended to create more choices for passengers and to decrease air fares as a result of the emergence of new, more efficient carriers. While more flights are available and fares are lower, 118 of the 150 airlines that started operations after 1978 have either failed or have been forced to merge with other carriers. Deregulation thus appears to have failed, so far, to produce the intended plurality, although airlines such as Frontier, Vanguard, and Western Pacific continue to pop up to challenge the established airlines. Of the 614.2 million passengers who flew in the United States in 1998, 45 percent flew on Delta, United, and American, and 71 percent flew on the six largest airlines.

Advocates of deregulation apparently did not foresee how effectively the largest airlines would use their size advantage to thwart the smaller airlines and the numerous newcomers to the market. They also did not predict that intense fare competition would make it difficult for new entrants to finance their growth. Instead, the industry has become more concentrated, with only a small number of major carriers able to survive in such a competitive environment.

One airline has prospered under deregulation. Southwest Airlines was able to extend a strategy, which succeeded in Texas, to most of the southern states, and more recently to California, some mid-Atlantic states, and a few northeastern locations. Southwest differs from most other carriers by offering low-ticket prices but with no reserved seating and little in-flight service. Its frequent flights to markets in which business travelers dominate have contributed to its success. Many of its competitors have adopted this "no frills" approach, with major airlines such as American, Delta, and United serving fewer and smaller meals with fewer flight attendants. Some have introduced more major-city-to-major-city flights although none has indicated it will drop the hub system.

The Hub-and-Spoke Network

The major airlines gained passengers — and revenue — by offering an increased number of connections through use of *hub-and-spoke networks*. Under this scheduling system, passengers boarding at many different locations arrive nearly simultaneously at one of the nation's 24 large hub airports. Connecting flights then redistribute them, through the spokes, to their final destinations. Approximately two-thirds of all air travelers go through a hub to reach their destinations. (See Figure 7.2.) Many low-demand routes are no longer served by nonstop flights.

On the one hand, travelers benefit since the hub systems allow them to travel to more destinations and have a wider choice of arrival and departure times. However, the time required for connection at the hub means flight times are longer than for direct flights. Airline consultant Theodore P. Harris estimates that the average trip of under 2,000 miles now takes twice as long as it did prior to deregulation and the use of the hub system.

The hub-and-spoke system can also cause frequent and long flight delays. Most of the major airlines schedule hub departures and arrivals during the peak time periods — early morning and early evening. When too many jets are scheduled to leave at the same time, the airplanes are forced to line up on the tarmac and wait. Bad weather at a large hub can cause chaos throughout the network. The problems of congestion and delays at the hubs have displeased passengers. The Air Transport Association of America, which represents the airline industry, estimates that these long waits at major hubs cost the nation's air travelers about $2 billion a year in lost time.

Robert Crandall, former chairman of American Airlines, defends the hub-and-spoke system. He believes that, even though customers prefer nonstop service, they like frequent service and time-of-day choices even more. Therefore, they prefer to accept the option of many flights from their cities to a hub airport rather than to wait several hours for less-frequent, nonstop service. Crandall feels that the intense competition between airlines offering more frequent flights to major hubs does a better job of providing what airline passengers want most — a wide variety of departure and arrival times.

For the airlines, the hub system, along with the introduction of sophisticated systems (see below) and a booming economy has allowed a dramatic increase in passenger load factor. During the 1990s, load factor increased from 62.4 percent in 1990 to 70.9 percent in 1998. (See Table 7.1.) This is a huge increase reflected in growing airline profits. It also has been reflected in some of the consumer complaints. The widespread belief that the seats are smaller (very unlikely) is apt to be a product of increasingly crowded flights and the decreasing likelihood of keeping the center seat free. In fact, most frequent-flier miles are not used to visit Paris or some other exotic destination, but to upgrade to first class or business class and escape the crowded conditions in coach class.

Yield Management

Deregulation produced a dizzying array of new fare categories, and fares swing sharply from season to season and, sometimes, day to day. Even the most sophisticated traveler can become confused by the multitude of ticket prices offered. These prices result from the airlines' efforts to obtain maximum revenue from each planeload.

The increasing power and sophistication of computer systems have allowed the airlines to develop a strategy called "yield management" or "revenue control." The point is to sell the mix of low-, medium-, and high-priced coach tickets that will earn the most money from each flight. Yield management leads the major airlines to introduce many discount fare categories, each with its own set of restrictions.

Business travelers are the airlines' favorite customers since they must travel and since companies often pay full fare. There are, however, not enough business travelers to fill the airplanes, and they usually buy seats at the last minute. Airlines attempt to fill the remaining seats at lower prices with leisure travelers. An estimated 41 percent of persons fly for business and 59 percent for pleasure. The point of yield management is to charge business travelers, with the least flexibility, the highest fares. The airlines can profit by then using the most heavily discounted fares to fill seats that would otherwise be empty. This is because the additional cost of serving one more passenger, even at a deep discount, is little more than the price of a small meal, the ticket taxes, and the cost of a slight amount of additional fuel. The "yield management" strategy has been a major factor in the increase of passenger load factor from 62.4 percent in 1990 to 70.9 percent in 1998, discussed above.

Discount fares attract vacation travelers. Restrictions that apply to reduced fares, such as advance-purchase requirements and travel extending through Saturdays, inhibit the use of these fares by business travelers and thus serve to maintain profit margin. Fully refundable tickets, standard before deregulation, are now less common. Most tickets also have a charge for refund or exchange.

Frequent-Flier Plans — Wooing the Travelers

The intense competition resulting from deregulation caused major changes in airline marketing strategies. One technique, aimed primarily at the higher-paying business traveler, the so-called frequent-flier (mileage bonus) program, is used by nearly all airlines. Such plans offer future free trips as a reward for accumulating trip mileage on a specific airline, encouraging brand loyalty among those who fly often. Frequent-flier plans also offer seasonal discounts and coupons that the passenger can use to upgrade from a coach seat to the more desirable first-class or business-class sections, as well as other promotions. Since the larger carriers with their extensive number of routes offer the most attractive destinations for flyers when they cash in their mileage bonus points, this marketing tool gives them a special edge in the era of deregulation. On the other hand, fare-based competition produces only a temporary advantage, as other carriers rapidly match any changes.

The first frequent-flier plan was started by American Airlines in 1981 as the American AAdvantage program and was intended to be temporary. Its success as a marketing strategy led other airlines to start their own plans. *Inside Flyer* magazine estimates total frequent-flier membership in the United States and Canada at about 60 million in 1999. The program was considered a marketing success because it worked. Now many planes are too full to make room for frequent flyers, and this has caused the airlines to tighten up the rules, raising redemption levels and combining them with expiration deadlines. In July 1999, American Airlines announced that it would do away with expiration deadlines and that AAdvantage program members would have 36 months in which to show any activity — from booking a flight to simply making a purchase on an AAdvantage credit card — to keep the miles indefinitely. United Airlines made similar changes to its program, and other airlines are expected to follow suit.

Customer Dissatisfaction

Deregulation has received mixed reviews from consumers. After an initial period of extremely low fares, ticket prices have risen on many routes, especially to areas served by only one or two carriers. Ridership has, nonetheless, increased, suffering only a slight setback in the early 1980s. Even so, many observers believe that current prices are near the ceiling of consumer tolerance and that further increases may result in reduced passenger travel. The airlines counter that airline ticket prices have lagged well behind the Consumer Price Index and are a good buy. (See Figure 7.8.)

After deregulation, customer complaints about flight delays and cancellations, overbookings, airline food, cramped seating conditions, and lost luggage skyrocketed as new carriers entered the market and airlines began to experience cost pressures. Passengers today are flying on more crowded airplanes, waiting in more congested hub airports, facing more delayed take-offs, and putting up with more stopovers en route to their destinations. Many find service less satisfactory overall than before deregulation.

Nonetheless, a significant part of the problem is not because the industry is no longer being closely regulated. From 1980 to 1998, the number of domestic passenger miles more than doubled from 204.4 billion to an estimated 459.7 billion and is forecasted to reach 737 billion by 2010. Also, the number of aircraft used by certified air carriers more than doubled from 2,818 to 5,961. These are huge increases in a short period of time. While airports have expanded, they have not kept up with this rapid growth. Furthermore, the FAA, which controls the movement of these aircraft, still works with outdated equipment, some of which is decades old and inadequate to the task.

Finally, there no longer is the feeling that flying is something special. Few people look out the windows anymore. Airlines used to serve relatively decent meals because it was part of a special event — a flight in the clouds.

Now an airline flight is a rapid way to get from here to there. Southwest Airlines' success has been predicated on a "no frills" policy, getting passengers on and off as quickly as possible and turning the plane around in a dozen minutes. Most airlines have adopted as much of this strategy as possible.

Most business people recognize that an airline is just a mode of transportation. Recreational travelers often consider the airplane trip as part of their vacation and, therefore, something special. They are bound to be disappointed. An airline and a bus are similar forms of transportation, but the airplane is much faster.

GOING GLOBAL — ASIAN AND EUROPEAN MARKETS

Under the (Jimmy) Carter Administration, Congress passed the International Air Transportation Competition Act of 1979 (PL 96-192), intended to create a more competitive international system of airline travel.

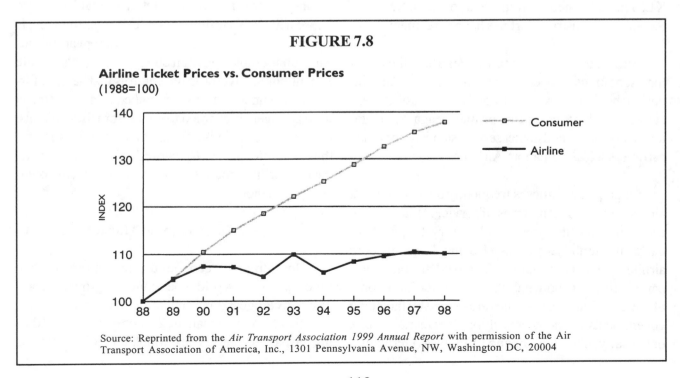

FIGURE 7.8

Airline Ticket Prices vs. Consumer Prices
(1988=100)

Source: Reprinted from the *Air Transport Association 1999 Annual Report* with permission of the Air Transport Association of America, Inc., 1301 Pennsylvania Avenue, NW, Washington DC, 20004

Despite concern among many foreign governments about the new law, a few governments — mainly those that realized their national airlines had more to gain than to lose — edged partly toward the U.S. "open skies" objective (the easing of market restrictions between the United States and other countries).

In 1995, the United States signed an open-skies agreement with Canada for full open-sky service, after a three-year phase-in period. The value of the agreement to the economy has been estimated at about $15 million per year.

Open-skies agreements have also been reached with 32 countries in Europe, Asia, Latin America, and the Middle East. The United States and Japan updated a previous bilateral agreement that will permit a 50 percent increase in flights between the two countries. The United States is talking to other countries in these regions about easing the market restrictions. More agreements over the next few years could significantly increase the level of activity between United States carriers and foreign flag carriers.

The FAA expects the industry to continue toward globalization through agreements. The number of alliances has recently increased: Air France has made agreements with Delta and Continental; Northwest and KLM have formed an alliance; and Delta, Swissair, Sabena, and Austrian Airlines have agreements.

While strong industry alliances are at the top of the list of industry needs, the immediate priorities involve labor issues, ownership, and cost control. American carriers have competed primarily against the far lower labor costs and higher service standards of Asian carriers, such as Singapore Airlines.

Singapore Airlines is frequently cited as the best airline in the world in terms of service. While a U.S. carrier may profitably carry only 10 or 12 flight attendants on a jumbo jet such as a Boeing 747, Singapore airlines can carry as many as 22 attendants on a comparable flight at about half the cost. In addition, some of the large European airlines are owned by their own governments, either completely, such as Iberia (Spain), or partially, like Swissair and Lufthansa (Germany).

Whether these countries will improve efficiency, or even privatize their airlines, remains an important question.

International Deregulation — The European Connection

International air travel competition between the United States and Europe is quite different from that between the United States and Asia. Despite a population larger than that of the United States, Europe accounts for just 28 percent of the world's airline traffic. Air travel in Europe is complicated by certain structural factors. An outdated air traffic control system limits capacity. Restrictions on over-flights (the right to fly over another country's territory) mean that some flights between countries in Europe use more time and fuel than would otherwise be necessary. Many European airports are at capacity, thus discouraging new service. Most Europeans prefer to travel by train, particularly for shorter distances. Train fares are often much lower than air fares, seating on European trains is more comfortable than the typical coach seat on any jumbo jet, and trains generally drop the passenger off downtown where most business and recreational activities occur in European cities.

With well over 30 million passengers flying between the United States and Europe annually, trans-Atlantic service is the largest international market for U.S. airlines. Teaming up, or forming alliances, is emerging as one way American and European airlines can gain footholds on each other's continents in spite of continuing governmental controls that hamper foreign competition. Although smoother, "seamless" travel for passengers is claimed to result from these unions, the greatest benefit is a financial one for the airlines, that of greater access to markets. Under such pacts, the two airlines operate as one to avoid foreign ownership limitations.

The International Market

Most long-term economic indicators are positive for the industry. Worldwide economic growth is forecast to average 3.3 percent annually through 2014, significantly higher than the 2.7 percent achieved during the past 20 years. The outlook for jet fuel prices is

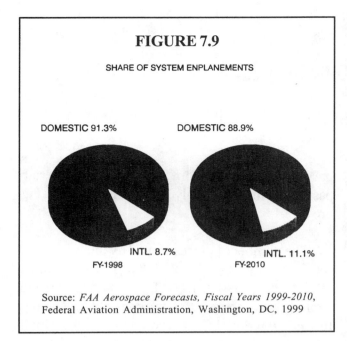

FIGURE 7.9

SHARE OF SYSTEM ENPLANEMENTS

DOMESTIC 91.3%   DOMESTIC 88.9%

INTL. 8.7%   INTL. 11.1%

FY-1998   FY-2010

Source: *FAA Aerospace Forecasts, Fiscal Years 1999-2010*, Federal Aviation Administration, Washington, DC, 1999

flat, with no increases in real terms. Global passenger traffic is projected to grow at an average annual rate of 5.9 percent over the next 20 years. The FAA forecasts that international enplanements will grow at a faster rate than domestic enplanements. In 1998, 91.3 percent of enplanements were domestic. This will likely drop to 88.9 percent in 2010. (See Figure 7.9.)

Passenger capacity requirements are expected to rise by 5.6 percent annually. In order to satisfy those projected needs, it will be necessary to expand the world's passenger jet fleet to nearly 18,600 aircraft by 2014, roughly doubling today's active fleet. Approximately 4,800 active jetliners will be permanently retired. Most of these will be short- and medium-range narrow-body aircraft.

Of the more than 614.2 million U.S. domestic and international passengers enplaned on U.S. scheduled airlines in 1998, nearly 59 million were on international routes. International freight (revenue ton miles) surpassed domestic shipments, reflecting the increasing importance of international air cargo and foreign trade.

International aviation is increasingly important to U.S. airlines. In 1998, the FAA estimated that U.S. and foreign flag carriers conveyed a total of 126.1 million passengers between the United States and the rest of the world, a number that is expected to increase to 230.2 million in 2010, an average annual growth rate of 5.1 percent. Passenger traffic is forecasted to increase by 6.3 percent annually in Latin American markets, 5.8 percent in Pacific markets, 4.4 percent in Atlantic markets, and 3.3 percent between the United States and Canada.

CHAPTER VIII

BUSES*

The American scheduled intercity (between cities) bus system has been in decline since the end of World War II, when automobiles began to be more readily available to the public. By the late 1960s and early 1970s, bus ridership had dwindled to about 400 million riders annually. Historically, buses had played a significant role in the nation's transportation system, connecting small towns that did not have railway or airline service with other towns and cities. When privately owned passenger trains stopped running in the 1970s, the bus system became even more important for the nation's small towns.

GROWING COMPETITION

The building of the national highway system, beginning in earnest in the 1950s, enabled people to drive long distances and promoted America's love affair with the automobile. At the same time, airline fares were becoming cheaper, and travelers were enjoying the convenience, speed, and comfort of air travel. Amtrak, the national passenger railroad system, was created in 1971. Because the federal government supported the new system, it could offer cheaper fares to its riders. Finally, the number of people living in rural areas, which were served mostly by buses, was dropping.

SOME GOOD NEWS
BUT MOSTLY BAD NEWS

As a result of these events, in the 1960s and 1970s, the number of people using buses continued to drop. Later, over the decade from 1987 to 1997, intercity bus traffic increased from 333 million to 351 million, a rise of just 5.3 percent; however, the bus share of the passenger transportation market declined. As a percentage of intercity passengers, the number of bus passengers dropped from 30.7 percent of intercity passengers in 1987 to only 27.3 percent in 1997 (Figure 8.1).

The number of places served by intercity buses fell from about 17,000 in 1968 to 11,820 places in 1982 and to 5,690 in 1991. By the spring of 1996, intercity buses served or stopped at only 4,274 cities. In 1997, intercity buses accounted for 29.6 billion passenger-miles (the cumulative sum of the distances ridden by each passenger), just 1.2 percent of domestic intercity miles traveled (Figure 8.2).

Greyhound Lines

In 1997, there were 124,538 registered private and commercial buses in the United States. About half (52 percent) of interstate bus companies have six or fewer buses; only one percent (161) have 100 or more buses. Greyhound Lines, Inc., is the largest of all the private bus companies and is the only remaining nationwide provider of scheduled, regular-route intercity bus service (Figure 8.3). During 1997, Greyhound operated 252 million miles of regularly scheduled service within the continental 48 states. In 1998, it carried about 60 percent of bus passengers; regional carriers carried the rest. In 1998, Greyhound provided service to 2,600 destinations and scheduled over 18,000 departures daily across North America.

The decades of industry decline culminated in Greyhound's filing for bankruptcy protection in 1990. Although it came out of bankruptcy in 1991, Greyhound continues to battle for survival and has undergone major restructuring. In 1998, Greyhound reported net income of $35.2 million, or $0.50 per share — the first full-year profit realized by the company since 1993.

---

* See Chapter IX for information on mass transit buses.

Struggling with years of declining ridership, bankruptcy, and a poor image, many bus lines have taken measures to attract the public back to bus service. Greyhound has renovated bus stations and increased security at terminals. In addition, Greyhound has instituted airline marketing techniques such as mail delivery of tickets and computerized reservations. A smoking ban keeps the air fresher; express routes between big cities lessen travel time; and plans are underway to make rental cars available at terminals, just like at airports.

New services being offered by Greyhound include casino trips to popular gambling destinations around the country. In 1998, its casino ridership contributed over $30 million to the company's revenues. Bus-to-air travel service is a recent option offered by Greyhound. Started in the mid-1990s at Hartsfield Airport in Atlanta, Greyhound now serves 13 airports around the country. The bus company provides pickup and drop-off service to terminals at selected airports. A similar service is available to various Amtrak stations.

In 1998, Greyhound formed joint ventures with several Mexican bus carriers to create Autobuses Americanos and Autobuses Amigos. The two new companies, operating under a Greyhound subsidiary, Sistema Internacional Transporte de Autobuses, Inc. (S.I.T.A.), will provide cross-border bus service between five southwestern states and several cities in Mexico.

In 1999, Greyhound plans to test a new communications system on 250 buses. Called On-Guard™ Tracker System, it is a satellite/cellular personal security and vehicle tracking system. The two-way communication and tracking system allows drivers to contact an emergency center or a Greyhound dispatcher by pushing a button. If the test run is successful, Greyhound will install the system on all its 2,400 buses.

1999 Changes at Greyhound

Greyhound has been in the shipping business since 1930. In February 1999, Greyhound expanded its shipping services when it acquired On Time Delivery, a Minnesota-based courier company. In June 1999, the company further expanded shipping in the Mid-

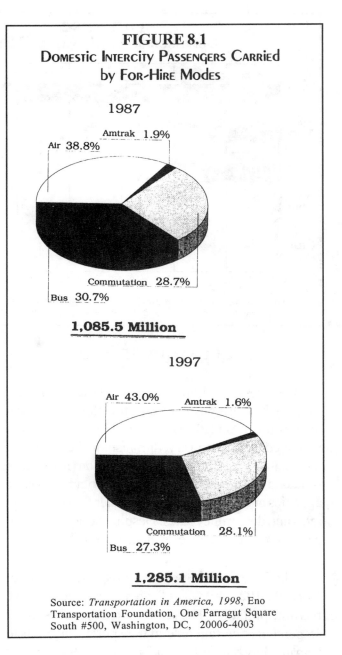

FIGURE 8.1
DOMESTIC INTERCITY PASSENGERS CARRIED by FOR-HIRE MODES

1987

Air 38.8%
Amtrak 1.9%
Commutation 28.7%
Bus 30.7%

1,085.5 Million

1997

Air 43.0%
Amtrak 1.6%
Commutation 28.1%
Bus 27.3%

1,285.1 Million

Source: *Transportation in America, 1998*, Eno Transportation Foundation, One Farragut Square South #500, Washington, DC, 20006-4003

west with the acquisition of Larson Express, a Chicago-area courier. The two acquisitions will allow Greyhound to rebuild its package express service in the Midwest. The two courier companies will provide Greyhound with pickup and delivery services for its shipping customers. Today, shipping constitutes only 4 percent of the company's total revenues.

In March 1999, Greyhound became a wholly owned subsidiary of Laidlaw, Inc., based in Burlington, Ontario, Canada. The merger makes Laidlaw the largest provider of school and intercity bus, municipal transit, patient transportation, and emergency department management services in North America.

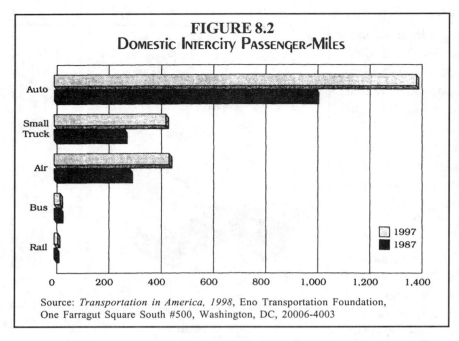

FIGURE 8.2
Domestic Intercity Passenger-Miles

Legend: 1997, 1987

Categories: Auto, Small Truck, Air, Bus, Rail

X-axis: 0, 200, 400, 600, 800, 1,000, 1,200, 1,400

Source: *Transportation in America, 1998*, Eno Transportation Foundation, One Farragut Square South #500, Washington, DC, 20006-4003

CHARTER OR TOURIST BUSES

A *charter* bus is rented for a special reason. If, for example, students at a school want to attend a museum or special event, they may rent, or charter, a bus for a day. If the students are visiting a distant city, they might choose to buy a ticket on a sightseeing bus that will show them city landmarks and sights. A bus used for this purpose is called a *tourist* bus.

Only 20 years ago, intercity passenger traffic was a major function of the bus system. Today, only a small part (10.9 percent) of all bus traffic is made up of scheduled buses carrying people from town to town. The remainder of the bus traffic is for charter (66.6 percent) or tourist (22.5 percent) use. In 1997, according to the Office of Motor Carriers, there were about 124,538 registered private and commercial buses in the United States, most of them used by charter or tourist companies.

While some of the regional carriers are making a profit, most are not. Charter and tourist bus companies are doing better; in fact, some are quite profitable. There is little likelihood, however, that the nation's scheduled bus system will ever fully recover.

WHO RIDES THE BUS?

According to a 1996 Greyhound survey, 49 percent of riders traveled 200 miles or less on the bus; 56 percent travel for pleasure. Most travelers were alone (73 percent) and did not own an automobile (64 percent). Most of the passengers were female (56 percent) and single (70 percent). The ages of travelers were fairly evenly spread from 18 years of age to 65 and older. Thirty-six percent of riders were employed full time, 22 percent were high school graduates, and 33 percent had had some college. Nearly 30 percent lived alone, 51 percent were White, 24 percent were African-American, and 11 percent were Asian.

REGULATORY REFORM

Congress had hoped to reverse the downward trend in the bus industry by enacting the Bus Regulatory Reform Act (PL 97-261) in 1982. This act deregulated the bus industry, diminishing the role of the federal Interstate Commerce Commission (ICC); since replaced by the Office of Motor Carriers) and state agencies and giving bus firms greater freedom to set rates and determine routes. Despite the act, bus companies continued to face declining profits.

The Intermodal Surface Transportation Act of 1991 (PL 102-240) was a further attempt to improve bus transportation. The law required the states to use 15 percent of certain federal transportation grants to help intercity bus traffic. For fiscal years 1992 through 1997, the act set aside about $122 million in federal grant funds for states to use specifically for intercity bus service. However, a state did not have to use the funds if the governor certified that the state's bus needs were being met by local or passenger funds.

In 1998, Congress passed the Transportation Equity Act for the Twenty-first Century (TEA-21; PL 105-178). It included funding for improved rural (city to city) bus service and for new buses that operate on cleaner fuel, such as natural gas. The Blue Bird Corporation of Macon, Georgia, has already begun manufacturing school buses that run on natural gas.

FIGURE 8.3
Intercity Bus

Source: Greyhound Bus Lines

BUILDING BUSES

Today, there are seven manufacturers of buses in the United States, none of which are American-owned (MCI, Dina, Neoplan, Eagle, Prevost, Van Hool, and Setra). In 1996 (latest figures available), 2,650 intercity coaches were either built or sold in North America, a 25 percent increase over 1995.

Many buses made today are not built for bus companies. Some of them are made for private companies. These buses may be very fancy, with comfortable chairs, and some have beds for sleeping. Some buses are built to be used as mobile medical clinics for delivering vaccinations, health screenings, or taking blood donations. Entertainers and performers who tour from city to city also use customized buses.

In addition, buses are built as recreational homes for retired persons who want to live in the bus and travel the country. These buses are often luxurious and have many features of home, such as bathrooms and kitchens, televisions, compact disk (CD) players, etc. Some very expensive motor-home buses can cost as much as $850,000. Industry sources estimate that there are more than 5,000 of these recreational buses traveling the roads of the United States.

Until the mid-80s, buses were often seen on the campaign trail, but fell out of favor when candidates decided they needed faster modes of transportation. In 1999, some candidates for public office are turning to buses once more to visit small cities and towns across the country. These campaign buses are equipped with multiple telephone lines, faxes, and satellite phones. One candidate uses a bus that converts quickly into a rolling television studio when needed.

Cost

The American Bus Association reports that the average cost of a new 40-foot motorcoach (more than 90 percent of motorcoaches are 40 feet or longer) is approximately $273,000 to $285,000, which includes $5,000 to $25,000 for video equipment. The operating cost for a motorcoach is $1.46 per mile, including driver and fuel.

CHAPTER IX

MASS TRANSIT AND COMMUTING

THE BEGINNINGS OF MASS TRANSIT

In 1827, a 12-passenger, horse-drawn carriage began carrying passengers along Broadway in New York City, marking the debut of mass transportation. For most of the century, the cars were pulled by horses, but in 1887, Frank Sprague built and profitably ran an electric streetcar (trolley) company in Richmond, Virginia. Electric current delivered by overhead trolley lines connected to a central power source powered the cars.

Sprague's success led to a veritable explosion in electric car lines, and by 1895, approximately 850 electric car lines were running over 10,000 miles of track. In 1897, Boston officials came up with the innovative idea of putting the electric cars underground, and in 1904, New York City also began subway service.

In such cities as New York, Chicago, and Boston, the electric streetcar and subway offered a major advance in comfort and relatively pollution-free transportation. Previously, these cities had built overhead railroads or "els," for elevated railways. However, these "els" were expensive to construct and shut out light to the streets. Furthermore, the small steam engines that usually pulled three or four cars proved to be hazardous because they dropped soot and hot coals on the pedestrians below.

The electric train was far cleaner and safer in comparison. Many cities introduced cable cars during the latter part of the nineteenth century, but only San Francisco's cable car system remains active today, as much to amuse tourists as to serve the city's citizens. In 1905, the first motor bus company began operating in New York City.

The term "mass transportation" encompasses a wide range of vehicles but generally includes transport by bus, rail, or other conveyance, either publicly or privately owned, which provides service to the public on a regular and continuing basis. However, mass transportation can also include less formal arrangements known as "ridesharing," the voluntary association of individuals in a variety of conveyances including vanpools, carpools, and shared-ride taxis.

While the motor bus is the most widely used mass transit vehicle, a variety of fixed-guideway modes (steel wheel or rubber tires on a set path) operate in U.S. cities. These modes include rapid rail, light rail, commuter rail, subway, trolleys, cable cars, ferryboats, and tramways. Table 9.1 shows the array of vehicles and types of infrastructures that make up the U.S. transit system.

TRENDS IN MASS TRANSIT RIDERSHIP

Transit ridership has gone through several major cycles of growth and decline over the past century. For the first three decades (1900 to 1929), mass transit grew steadily in popularity. By the late 1920s, more than 1,000 cities and towns had trolley systems operating nearly 63,000 streetcars over about 40,000 miles of track. During the Great Depression (from 1929 through the 1930s), there was a steep decline in the number of transit riders. Unemployed people were no longer traveling to work, and money was scarce for many persons, making pleasure trips infrequent.

World War II (1939-1945) brought about another surge of interest in mass transit because gasoline and rubber tires were strictly rationed and automobile manufacturers were making fewer cars and more military equipment, such as jeeps and tanks. During the war years, employment was high, especially among the growing female labor force, and public ridership shot up 80 percent. The number of transit passengers peaked at an all-time high of over 23 billion in 1946.

Following the war, a number of factors contributed to the decline in ridership on transit systems. Low-cost, tax-deductible mortgages, a growing number of highways, and inexpensive fuel prices made suburban living and car ownership extremely attractive. The returning soldiers began buying the increasingly available new cars, starting families, and buying houses in less congested areas. The rapid growth of suburban living contributed to a decentralization of employment, shopping, and recreation.

The popularity and affordability of the automobile and the increasing development of new highways led many Americans to rely more heavily on their own personal cars. Cars promised a wonderful world of speed, freedom, and convenience, taking drivers and passengers in comfort and privacy wherever they wanted to travel. American's love affair with the car has never waned. (For further information on automobiles, see Chapter IV.)

Government officials began seeing public transportation as a relic from an earlier time and,

consequently, gave it less support. As a result of these changing American attitudes, private transit systems were faced with a deadly spiral of increasing costs, deferred maintenance, rising fares, declining ridership, shrinking profits, deteriorating equipment, and decreasing quality of service. Mass transit became an increasingly unappealing alternative to the private automobile. These factors combined to produce a steep decline in the public's

TABLE 9.1

Mass Transit Active Fleet and Infrastructure 1995

	Areas >1 Million	Areas <1 Million	Total
Vehicles			
Buses	40,962	17,443	58,405
Rapid Rail	10,157	0	10,157
Light Rail	917	38	955
Self-Propelled Commuter Rail	2,645	0	2,645
Commuter Rail Trailers	2,382	20	2,402
Commuter Rail Locomotives	565	5	570
Vans	12,751	5,573	18,324
Other (Including Ferryboats)	261	64	325
Rural Service Vehicles	0	12,450	12,450
Special Service Vehicles	4,400	24,931	29,331
Total Active Vehicles	**75,040**	**60,524**	**135,564**
Infrastructure-Track			
Rapid Rail	2,073	0	2,073
Light Rail	678	23	701
Commuter Rail	6,717	68	6,785
Other Rail	21	2	23
Total Miles of Track	**9,489**	**93**	**9,582**
Infrastructure-Stations			
Rapid Rail	989	0	989
Light Rail	441	37	478
Commuter Rail	1,097	7	1,104
Other Rail	42	7	49
Total Transit Rail Stations	**2,569**	**51**	**2,620**
Infrastructure-Maintenance Facilities			
Rapid Rail	53	0	53
Light Rail	20	3	23
Commuter Rail	42	0	42
Ferryboat	4	15	19
Bus	281	220	501
Demand Responsive	23	45	69
Other	8	0	8
Rural Transit Maintenance Facilities	0	450	450
Total Maintenance Facilities	**431**	**734**	**1,165**

Federal Transit Administration National Transit Database (NTD)

Source: *Condition and Performance: 1997 Status of the Nation's Surface Transportation System*, U.S. Department of Transportation, Washington, DC, 1998

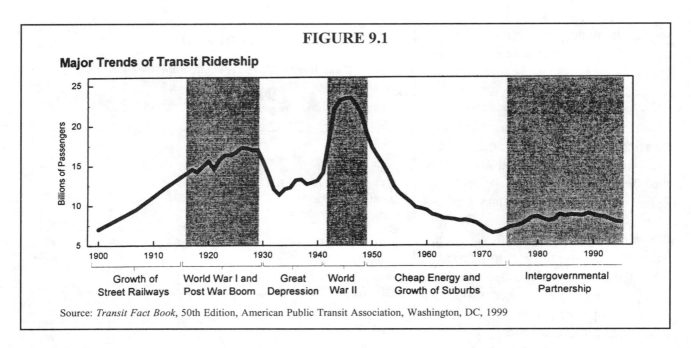

FIGURE 9.1

Major Trends of Transit Ridership

Source: *Transit Fact Book*, 50th Edition, American Public Transit Association, Washington, DC, 1999

interest in using mass transit. In 1973, transit ridership reached an all-time low of only about 7 billion passengers. (See Figure 9.1.)

A RENEWED INTEREST — THE GOVERNMENT BECOMES INVOLVED

Not until the 1960s and 1970s did serious interest again develop in mass transit. Urban and suburban growth led to frequent traffic jams. Noise and air pollution became an increasing worry. Rising fuel prices provided further incentive to seek alternatives to cars. In 1961, Congress included a $25 million mass transit pilot demonstration grant in the Housing and Urban Development Act (PL 87-117). Three years later, in 1964, Congress approved the Urban Mass Transportation (UMT) Act (PL 88-365). Passed mainly to help public authorities take over ailing private transit systems, the bill also called for improved mass transit. The UMT Act established federal matching grants (two-thirds federal, one-third local) for repairing, improving, or developing mass transit. A 1966 amendment to the UMT Act directed the Secretary of Transportation to establish a comprehensive research plan.

The Urban Mass Transportation Act of 1970 (PL 91-453) created the Urban Mass Transportation Administration (UMTA). It also permitted a more reliable 12-year federal funding plan instead of year-to-year financing. Other provisions promoted a greater commitment to urban transit construction. The Federal Aid Highway Act of 1973 (PL 93-87) made highway trust monies available for urban mass transit. It increased the matching grant to an 80 percent federal, 20 percent local share basis.

In 1974, transit ridership began to rise again as the increasing cost and shortage of gasoline caused by the Organization of Petroleum Exporting Countries (OPEC) oil embargo left many motorists either waiting in long lines at the gas stations or with empty gas tanks. This crisis prompted the National Mass Transportation Assistance Act of 1974 (PL 95-503), which allocated federal aid for capital expenses and permitted assistance for operating expenses.

The Federal Public Transportation Act of 1978 (PL 95-599) established a $16.4 billion grant and loan program for public transit capital and operating assistance through 1982, the largest commitment ever. Ridership rose until about 1980 and has since leveled off.

Not a Federal Government Responsibility

The Ronald Reagan Administration (1981-1989) did not believe it was the responsibility of

TABLE 9.2

Operating Funding Sources, Millions of Dollars

CALENDAR YEAR	DIRECTLY GENERATED FUNDS (c)			GOVERNMENT FUNDS				TOTAL PUBLIC FUNDS (e)	TOTAL
	PASSENGER FARES (a)	OTHER	TOTAL	LOCAL (c)	STATE	FEDERAL	TOTAL		
1984	4,447.7	780.5	5,228.2	5,399.1 (b)	(b)	995.8	6,394.9	6,394.9	11,623.1
1985	4,574.7	701.8	5,276.5	5,978.5 (b)	(b)	939.6	6,918.1	6,918.1	12,194.6
1986	5,113.1	737.3	5,850.4	4,244.5	2,305.6	941.2	7,491.3	7,491.3	13,341.7
1987	5,114.1	776.6	5,890.7	4,680.6	2,564.6	955.1	8,200.3	8,200.3	14,091.0
1988	5,224.6	840.7	6,065.3	4,893.1	2,677.1	905.1	8,471.3	8,471.3	14,536.6
1989	5,419.9	836.7	6,256.6	4,995.4	2,796.3	936.6	8,728.3	8,728.3	14,984.9
1990	5,890.8	895.0	6,785.8	5,326.8	2,970.6	970.0	9,267.4	9,267.4	16,053.2
1991	6,037.2	766.8	6,804.0	5,373.4	3,199.5	955.9	9,728.8	9,728.8	16,532.8
1992 (d)	6,152.5	645.9	6,798.4	5,268.1	3,879.5	969.1	10,116.7	10,116.7	16,915.1
1993	6,350.9	764.0	7,114.9	5,490.6	3,704.2	966.5	10,161.3	10,161.3	17,276.2
1994	6,756.0	2,270.6	9,026.6	4,171.2	3,854.4	915.6	8,941.2	10,570.3	17,967.8
1995	6,800.9	2,812.2	9,613.1	3,980.9	3,829.6	817.0	8,627.5	10,171.7	18,240.6
1996	7,416.3	2,928.2	10,344.5	4,128.5	4,081.8	596.4	8,806.7	10,502.1	19,151.2
1997 P	7,599.3	2,961.7	10,561.0	3,956.0	3,878.8	578.1	8,412.9	10,242.9	18,973.9
1997 % of Total	40.1%	15.6%	55.7%	20.9%	20.4%	3.0%	44.3%	54.0%	100.0%

P = Preliminary
(a) Includes fares retained by contractors; beginning 1991 includes fare subsidies formerly included in "other".
(b) "Local" and "state" combined.
(c) "Local" includes taxes levied directly by transit agency and other subsidies from local government such as bridge and tunnel tolls and non-transit parking lot funds. Beginning 1994, such funds reclassified from "local" to "other".
(d) Beginning 1992, "local" and "other" declined by about $500 million due to change in accounting procedures at New York City Transit Authority.
(e) Includes "Total Government Funds" plus that portion of "Other Directly Generated Funds" included in "Local Government Funds" beginning in 1994 consisting of transit agency-raised taxes, tolls, and other dedicated funds.

Source: *Transit Fact Book*, 50th Edition, American Public Transit Association, Washington, DC, 1999

the federal government to subsidize mass transit. The use of federal funds, the administration claimed, contributed to local inefficiencies, such as underused routes and unrealistically low fares. Consequently, with every budget proposal, the Reagan Administration tried to phase out operating subsidies, although the Transportation Assistance Act of 1982 (PL 97-424) authorized continued operating subsidies through 1986. Even though President Reagan attempted to reduce the actual authorizations, mass transit continued to receive subsidies for capital purchases (buses, railway cars, stations) because the legislation mandated that one penny of the nickel-a-gallon gasoline tax increase be used for mass transit.

Legislators from urban areas most directly affected by the proposed cuts successfully prevented the Reagan Administration from eliminating federal subsidies. Under the George Bush Administration (1989-1993), Congress passed the Federal Transit Act Amendments, extending transit assistance through 1997 at higher levels than before, to be used for the modes of transportation best suited to individual areas and states.

In 1997, while passengers and other directly generated funds contributed 55.7 percent to transit revenue, federal (3 percent), state (20.4 percent), and local assistance (20.9 percent) supplied the remaining funds needed to operate the systems. Note that local funding (20.9 percent) contributed about half as much to mass transit revenue as passenger fares (40.1 percent). In contrast, the federal government contributed the lowest proportion, only 3 percent. (See Table 9.2.)

ADVANTAGES OF MASS TRANSIT

Transit and Basic Mobility

Mass transit offers many advantages and may be the only alternative for many people. It gives mobility to those who cannot afford to purchase or maintain an automobile; it offers greater mobility to the handicapped, the young, and older Americans, freeing family and friends from the obligation of providing transportation for these individuals. It also gives the commuter the opportunity to leave the frustrations of driving in heavy traffic to someone else. Inner city residents use public transportation most often.

Mass transit often provides only minimal service to outlying suburbs where job growth is the greatest. Therefore, this vital link between central city workers without cars to suburban jobs is weak or, sometimes, nonexistent. The Urban Mass Transportation Administration does not expect this situation to improve.

Dollar Comparisons

For many commuters, mass transit can be more economical than driving to work alone. Annual transit costs can range from $189 to $2,077, depending on such factors as the number of miles traveled and transfer fees. In 1998, the American Automobile Association (AAA) estimated that the cost for a single-occupant driver ranged from $4,660 for a small car to $9,441 for a sport utility vehicle, depending on the number of miles driven. Table 9.3 compares costs for a daily ten-mile trip. Gasoline, oil, maintenance, and tire costs are based on AAA data. Average parking costs and transit commuting fares are American Public Transit Association (APTA) estimates.

Congestion and Land Use

Public transportation reduces congestion on the nation's highways, most notably during the already over-crowded "rush hours." Cities dependent on the automobile must set aside more land for streets, highways, and parking lots. Consequently, they tend to become more spread out. For example, streets and highways take up 68 percent of the land in Los Angeles. On the other hand, in downtown Chicago, which has an extensive bus and rail system, roadways account for only 36 percent of land use. Not only do roadways cause the city to spread out, but they can also lower the tax base since land used by public highways does not generate taxes.

TABLE 9.3

Daily Costs for a Ten-Mile Trip

	Daily Cost (Dollars)
Walking to transit stop and taking transit	
Fares ($1.50 each way)	$ 3.00
Driving alone	
Gasoline & oil ($0.06/mile)	$1.20
Maintenance & tires ($0.04/mile)	0.80
Parking (APTA estimate)	5.00
Total	7.00
Driving 3 miles to a park-and-ride lot and using transit for the remainder of the trip	
Fares	$3.00
Gasoline & oil	0.36
Maintenance & tires	0.24
Total	3.60

Source: *Transit Fact Book*, 50th Edition, American Public Transit Association, Washington, DC, 1999

TABLE 9.4

Cities with Highest Percentage of Workers Using Public Transportation, 1990

CITY	PER CENT USING PUBLIC TRANSPORTATION
New York, NY	53.4
Hoboken, NJ	51.0
Jersey City, NJ	36.7
Washington, DC	36.6
San Francisco, CA	33.5
Boston, MA	31.5
Chicago, IL	29.7
Philadelphia, PA	28.7
Atlantic City, NJ	26.2
Arlington, VA	25.4
Newark, NJ	24.6
Cambridge, MA	23.5
Pittsburgh, PA	22.2
Baltimore, MD	22.0
Evanston, IL	20.9
Atlanta, GA	20.0
White Plains, NY	19.1
Camden, NJ	18.1
Oakland, CA	17.9
Hartford, CT	17.1
New Orleans, LA	16.9
Idaho Falls, ID	16.5
Minneapolis, MN	16.0
Seattle, WA	15.9
Berkeley, CA	15.2
Albany, NY	15.1

U.S. Census Bureau, *1990 Census, Journey to Work, Characteristics of Workers in Metropolitan Areas*

Source: *Transit Fact Book*, 50th Edition, American Public Transit Association, Washington, DC, 1999

The Federal Highway Administration (FHWA) reports that congestion on the urban Interstate System seems to have stabilized at a level of about 54 percent and on the urban National Highway System at about 45 percent. (See Chapter III, Figure 3.5.) The closer the congestion levels get to 100 percent, the more crowded the roadway. Anything over 80 percent is considered congested.

The relationship between ridership and service helps to explain the huge differences between mass transit's usage in some mid-size cities and its role in the nation's largest cities. The metropolitan area of New York City has only 6.4 percent of the total nation's population, yet it generates half of the total U.S. mass transit use. Half the people of New York use mass transit to get to work, followed by more than one-third of workers in Washington, DC, San Francisco, and Boston and about one-fifth in Pittsburgh and Atlanta. Table 9.4 also shows the other American cities where significant proportions of workers take mass transit.

Economic Considerations

Since most downtowns were built before the explosion in automobile ownership and the migration to the suburbs, few can supply enough parking spaces to make shopping convenient. In addition, the growth of the suburbs has made downtown shopping very distant from potential suburban shoppers. As a result, downtown stores have been losing out to suburban shopping centers and malls. In fact, the so-called "Main Streets" of 50 years ago have been replaced in most suburbs by malls. Teenagers, young mothers, workers, and the elderly go the local malls to shop, eat, and see movies.

Effective public transport has helped to support some downtown business or, as in the case of BART (Bay Area Rapid Transit) in San Francisco, to revitalize it, but this is the exception, not the

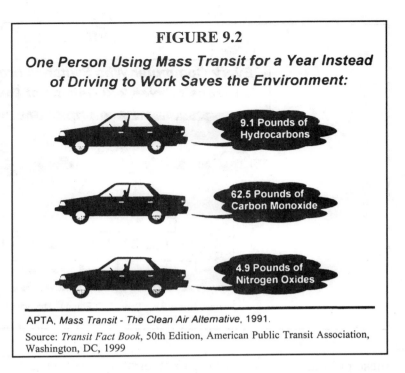

FIGURE 9.2

One Person Using Mass Transit for a Year Instead of Driving to Work Saves the Environment:

9.1 Pounds of Hydrocarbons

62.5 Pounds of Carbon Monoxide

4.9 Pounds of Nitrogen Oxides

APTA, *Mass Transit - The Clean Air Alternative*, 1991.

Source: *Transit Fact Book*, 50th Edition, American Public Transit Association, Washington, DC, 1999

rule. In fact, very few of the urban rail projects have achieved even 50 percent of the passenger volume they had predicted.

Those who support mass transit claim it is not enough to add up direct financial costs when assessing whether or not a public transit system justifies the expenditure. A simple profit and loss statement does not take into account benefits to society, such as increased mobility, increased employment, less congestion, better land use, increased downtown economic growth, and less pollution and energy use. These factors not only benefit society generally, but also have a real financial value that can justify considerable public support through financial subsidies.

Environmental Pollution

Half of all air pollution comes from transportation sources, most by automobiles. Denver, Colorado, is a prime example of the environmental hazard represented by cars. Once known for its clean air, Denver is now second only to Los Angeles in air pollution. This pollution has been linked to Denver's mountain setting, which makes it easier for pollutants to be trapped in the valleys, and to its high automobile usage. High concentrations of

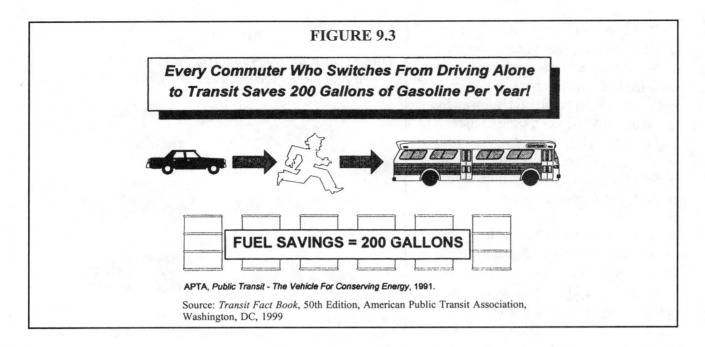

FIGURE 9.3

Every Commuter Who Switches From Driving Alone to Transit Saves 200 Gallons of Gasoline Per Year!

FUEL SAVINGS = 200 GALLONS

APTA, *Public Transit - The Vehicle For Conserving Energy*, 1991.

Source: *Transit Fact Book*, 50th Edition, American Public Transit Association, Washington, DC, 1999

these pollutants can contribute to respiratory diseases and cancer. But the most pervasive and underestimated effects of pollution are headaches, eye irritation, blocked sinuses, and general malaise. Noise pollution, another problem created by traffic, can lead to headaches, high blood pressure, ulcers, and general stress.

Proponents of mass transit point out that hydrocarbons and carbon monoxide emissions are reduced dramatically (more than 99 percent) on a trip by rail compared to the average trip by car. Nitrogen oxide emissions are reduced more than 60 percent. (Figure 9.2 shows the reduction in contaminants by using mass transit for a year.) Riding the bus also promotes cleaner air. Taking the bus to work instead of driving a car cuts hydrocarbon emissions by almost 90 percent and reduces carbon monoxide fumes by about 75 percent.

Energy Use

The 1991 invasion of Kuwait and the Persian Gulf War again focused the nation's attention on its continued dependence on foreign oil and the huge amount of oil Americans consume. According to the American Public Transit Association (APTA), an international organization representing the transit industry, both national security and economic stability are directly tied to energy use and sources of supply. The APTA points out that transportation (of all types) uses 63 percent of all oil consumed in the United States. The APTA further notes that imported oil accounts for almost 45 percent of the total amount. Personal cars or light trucks are primarily responsible for the extraordinary expense and dependence on foreign oil. The average American household owns two vehicles, uses about 1,014 gallons of gas each year, and spends almost 19 percent of its total income on transportation, second only to housing costs.

If more people used mass transit, the nation would use less energy. The APTA thinks the answer to the promotion of energy conservation and energy independence lies in encouraging a move back to mass transit. It believes that for every commuter who uses mass transit instead of a car, 200 gallons of gasoline would be saved every year (Figure 9.3). Mass transit is also environmentally cleaner than cars, although buses emit high levels of nitrogen oxides into the air.

**TRANSIT SYSTEMS —
A VARIETY OF TYPES**

In 1997, 5,975 transit agencies were moving people in the United States. (See Table 9.5.) The

TABLE 9.5

Number of Transit Agencies by Mode

MODE	NUMBER
Aerial Tramway	1
Automated Guideway Transit	6
Bus	2,250
Cable Car	1
Commuter Rail	18
Demand Response	5,214
Ferryboat (b)	25
Heavy Rail	14
Inclined Plane	5
Light Rail	22
Monorail	2
Trolleybus	5
Vanpool	55
TOTAL (a)	5,975

(a) Total is not sum of all modes since many agencies operate more than one mode.
(b) Excludes international, rural, rural interstate, island, and urban park ferries.

Source: *Transit Fact Book*, 50th Edition, American Public Transit Association, Washington, DC, 1999

following is a list of the most common types in service today.

- *Transit Bus* — a generic term for a rubber-tired vehicle with front and center doors and a rear-mounted diesel engine, usually designed for frequent-stop service. It is not equipped with luggage storage or restroom facilities.

- *Heavy Rail* — an electric transit railway with the capacity for a heavy volume of traffic and characterized by multi-car trains, high speed, rapid acceleration, and exclusive rights-of-way. Heavy rail systems are also known as "subways," "elevated railways," or "metropolitan railways" (metros).

- *Light Rail* — a type of electric transit railway with a "light volume" of traffic compared to "heavy rail." Generally, light rail includes streetcars (trolley cars) and tramways.

- *Commuter Railroad* — a "main line" railroad (not electric) that involves passenger train service between a central city and adjacent suburbs. Commuter railroad service typically is characterized by multi-trip tickets, specific station-to-station fares, and normally only one or

two main stations in the central business district. It is also known as a "suburban railroad."

- *Demand Response Service* — a type of non-fixed-route bus or van service that typically picks up and drops off passengers at any location within the transit provider's service area. The vehicles provide services at times requested by the passengers.

- *Ridesharing* — an informal and voluntary association of individuals in a variety of vehicles, including vanpools, carpools, and shared-ride taxis.

About 8.6 billion trips were made in 1997. Three of 5 (60.7 percent) were by bus; 28.4 percent by heavy rail; 4.2 percent, commuter rail; 3.1 percent, light rail; and 1 percent each by demand response and trolley bus. (See Table 9.6.) About 54 percent of these trips were for work; 15 percent for school; 9 percent, shopping; 9 percent, social; and 5.5 percent, medical.

In 1997, mass transit passengers traveled 43 billion miles. About half (47 percent) was by bus; 27.8 percent by heavy rail; 18.6 percent, commuter rail; 2.4 percent, light rail; and the rest by demand response and trolley bus. (See Table 9.7.)

By 1998, 72.4 percent of all buses were wheelchair accessible, as were 93 percent of demand response vehicles. Nearly three-fourths (71.9 percent) of commuter rail cars could accommodate wheelchairs, as could 94.2 percent of heavy rail cars and 73.2 percent of light rail cars.

The Suburbanization of Employees and Jobs

Families were not the only ones heading to the outlying areas. Businesses were also in pursuit of the increasing number of two-income families. Between 1960 and 1980 alone, the growing suburbs doubled in size and received approximately two-thirds of all job growth. This explosion and shifting of growth is a major factor in the future of commuting.

TABLE 9.6

Passenger Trips by Mode, Millions

CALENDAR YEAR	BUS	COMMUTER RAIL	DEMAND RESPONSE	HEAVY RAIL	LIGHT RAIL	TROLLEY BUS	OTHER	TOTAL (a)
1977 (b)	4,949	---	---	2,149	103	70	---	7,286
1978	5,142	---	---	2,285	104	70	---	7,616
1979	5,552	---	---	2,381	107	75	---	8,130
1980	5,837	280	---	2,108	133	142	67	8,567
1981	5,594	268	---	2,094	123	138	67	8,284
1982	5,324	259	---	2,115	136	151	67	8,052
1983	5,422	262	---	2,167	137	160	55	8,203
1984	5,908	267	62	2,231	135	165	61	8,829
1985	5,675	275	59	2,290	132	142	63	8,636
1986	5,753	306	63	2,333	130	139	53	8,777
1987	5,614	311	64	2,402	133	141	70	8,735
1988	5,590	325	73	2,308	154	136	80	8,666
1989	5,620	330	70	2,542	162	130	77	8,931
1990	5,677	328	68	2,346	175	126	79	8,799
1991	5,624	318	71	2,172	184	125	81	8,575
1992	5,517	314	72	2,207	188	126	77	8,501
1993	5,381	322	81	2,046	188	121	78	8,217
1994	4,871	339	88	2,169	284	118	80	7,949
1995	4,848	344	88	2,033	251	119	80	7,763
1996	4,887	352	93	2,157	261	117	81	7,948
1997 P	5,199	357	95	2,430	263	121	93	8,558
1997 % of Total	60.7%	4.2%	1.1%	28.4%	3.1%	1.4%	1.1%	100.0%

--- Data not available; no data were collected for these modes in years indicated.
(a) Excludes modes with "---" entries.
(b) Beginning 1977, data are for unlinked passenger trips, which are not comparable to prior years.

TABLE 9.7

Passenger Miles by Mode, Millions

CALENDAR YEAR	BUS	COMMUTER RAIL	DEMAND RESPONSE	HEAVY RAIL	LIGHT RAIL	TROLLEY BUS	OTHER	TOTAL
1984	21,595	6,207	349	10,111	416	364	382	39,424
1985	21,161	6,534	364	10,427	350	306	439	39,581
1986	21,395	6,723	402	10,649	361	305	369	40,204
1987	20,970	6,818	374	11,198	405	223	360	40,348
1988	20,753	6,964	441	11,300	477	211	434	40,580
1989	20,768	7,211	428	12,030	509	199	458	41,603
1990	20,981	7,082	431	11,475	571	193	410	41,143
1991	21,090	7,344	454	10,528	662	195	430	40,703
1992	20,336	7,320	495	10,737	701	199	453	40,241
1993	20,247	6,940	562	10,231	705	188	511	39,384
1994	18,832	7,996	577	10,668	833	187	492	39,585
1995	18,818	8,244	607	10,559	860	187	533	39,808
1996	19,096	8,351	656	11,530	957	184	604	41,378
1997 P	20,357	8,038	928	12,056	1,039	189	699	43,306
1997 % of Total	47.0%	18.6%	2.2%	27.8%	2.4%	0.4%	1.6%	100.0%

P = Preliminary

Source of both tables: *Transit Fact Book*, 50th Edition, American Public Transit Association, Washington, DC, 1999

A closer balance between the number of work opportunities and employees in a given suburb does not necessarily mean, however, that there will be less commuting to work — many workers will still have to commute many miles from one suburb to another in large metropolitan areas. In fact, the most common commuter pattern is now the trip from one suburb to another. Suburb-to-suburb trips represent about 33 percent of all metropolitan commuting and the largest work trip growth over the last 20 years. About twice as many workers commute from suburb to suburb than commute from suburb to downtown.

The Boom in Automobile Commuting

Commuting to and from suburbs heavily favors the use of the private automobile. (Auto commuting refers not only to cars, but also to light trucks, vans, and sport utility vehicles.)

The number of cars per household has risen steeply since 1960, and the number of available vehicles per person has almost doubled. In fact, the majority of households of every size have more vehicles than workers. The Federal Highway Administration (FHWA) reported in 1995 that 40 percent of American households owned two vehicles, while those households owning three or more vehicles totaled nearly 20 percent. (See Figure 9.4.) The doubling of the number of cars available for travel has meant that commuting by car rose at the same time that mass transit use declined.

In contrast, according to FHWA, the number of households with no access to private transportation shrank to 8.1 percent in 1995 (Figure 9.4.) Two-thirds of the households without vehicles also had no workers, and another 28 percent had only one worker. Zero-vehicle households are usually very small and are located in large central cities. The New York City area leads the list with 20 percent of its households having no personal vehicle.

The Car Commute — Shorter and Faster

As more and more companies have located in the suburbs, following the changes in population growth, shorter commutes have resulted because the jobs are now often much closer to the workers' homes. In fact, the suburb-to-suburb trip to work is about 50 percent shorter than the traditional ride to work from a suburb to the central city. As a result, nationwide, the time spent traveling on various types of public transit, which usually goes from suburb to city, is about twice as long as commuting by car.

In the country's largest cities, however, with higher mass transit use, the average travel time is 1.7 times the amount of time spent behind the wheel of a private car. Nonetheless, American employees generally prefer commuting in their own cars to using mass transit.

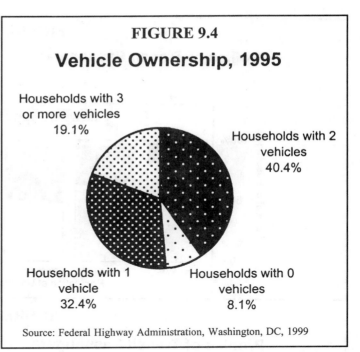

FIGURE 9.4

Vehicle Ownership, 1995

Households with 3 or more vehicles 19.1%

Households with 2 vehicles 40.4%

Households with 1 vehicle 32.4%

Households with 0 vehicles 8.1%

Source: Federal Highway Administration, Washington, DC, 1999

Carpooling — We Want to Be Alone

Despite energy issues, pollution, and traffic congestion, most motorists shun carpooling. Campaigns to persuade people to carpool or vanpool have generally failed. Among the reasons motorists prefer to "go it alone" are the ability to come and go at will, freedom to run errands with their own autos, and the ability to depart immediately in the case of family emergencies. Also cited are the choice of radio stations, privacy, and, most importantly, an unfettered, go-as-you-please American individualism.

Nationwide, the number of people who carpool has been declining over the past decade. The Regional Plan Association, a nonprofit research organization, observed that carpools are disrupted when riders change jobs or residences. Half of all Americans change jobs or residences every five years. The organization claimed that carpools could be made to work better by use of incentives, such as cheaper tolls for group travel or corporate monetary incentives to those who participate.

When Congress passed the Clean Air Act Amendments of 1990 (PL 101-549), it intended to address such incentives. In certain polluted regions,

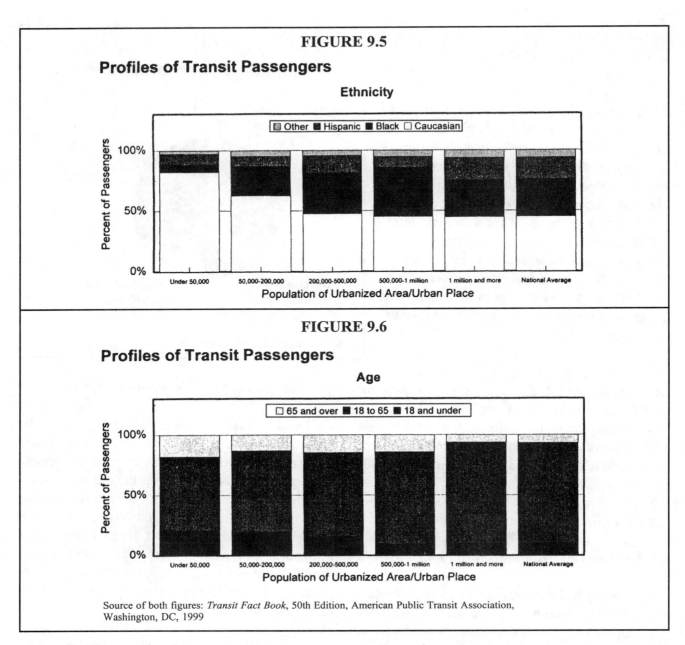

FIGURE 9.5

Profiles of Transit Passengers

Ethnicity

Legend: ▨ Other ▩ Hispanic ■ Black □ Caucasian

Percent of Passengers: 100%, 50%, 0%

Population of Urbanized Area/Urban Place: Under 50,000 | 50,000-200,000 | 200,000-500,000 | 500,000-1 million | 1 million and more | National Average

FIGURE 9.6

Profiles of Transit Passengers

Age

Legend: □ 65 and over ■ 18 to 65 ■ 18 and under

Percent of Passengers: 100%, 50%, 0%

Population of Urbanized Area/Urban Place: Under 50,000 | 50,000-200,000 | 200,000-500,000 | 500,000-1 million | 1 million and more | National Average

Source of both figures: *Transit Fact Book*, 50th Edition, American Public Transit Association, Washington, DC, 1999

such as New York, Southern California, and the Chicago area, companies employing more than 100 people at a single site must develop plans to increase the number of employees using mass transit or carpooling. The amendments include fines against companies that have not drawn up such plans.

A LOOK AT TRANSIT RIDERS

The Federal Highway Administration (FHWA) reported that the vast majority (87 percent) of people travel to work by car, van, or motorcycle. In fact, three-fourths (73 percent) drive to work alone in their cars. About 10.5 percent ride with one other person, while less than 3 percent ride in a carpool or vanpool with three or more other people. Only 5 percent ride mass transit to work.

FHWA considered characteristics of mass transit users based on the size of the city where they lived. It found that approximately 50 percent were non-Caucasian, especially in cities with a population over 200,000 (Figure 9.5). It also found that young people and those over 65 years of age made up nearly equal portions (10 percent and 7 percent, respectively) of transit users in cities with populations under 500,000 persons (Figure 9.6).

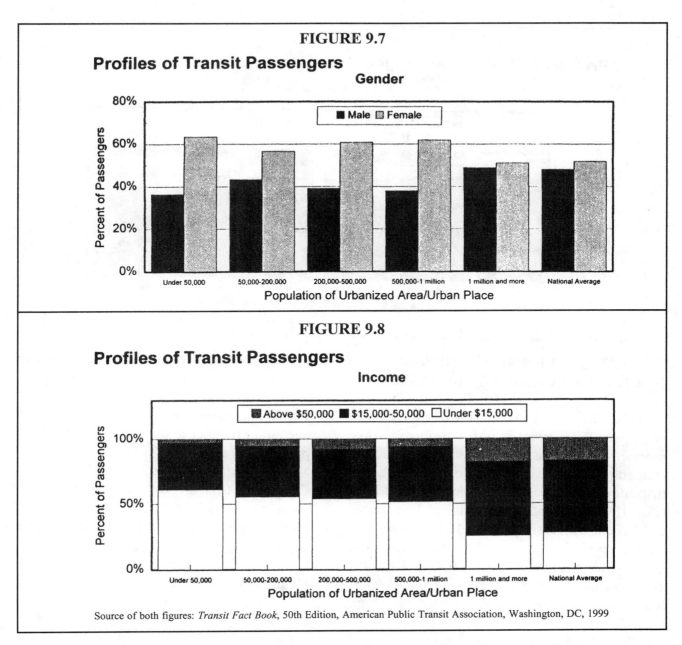

FIGURE 9.7

Profiles of Transit Passengers
Gender

Population of Urbanized Area/Urban Place

FIGURE 9.8

Profiles of Transit Passengers
Income

Population of Urbanized Area/Urban Place

Source of both figures: *Transit Fact Book*, 50th Edition, American Public Transit Association, Washington, DC, 1999

Women were more likely to use public transportation, especially in cities under 1 million people (Figure 9.7). Poorer Americans were the heaviest users of mass transit in cities under 1 million people. However, in cities of 1 million people or more, middle- and upper-income people made up a majority of those using public transportation (Figure 9.8).

In smaller cities with populations under 200,000, people used public transportation for many reasons, including work, school, going to the doctor, and social activities. In the larger cities, however, people used mass transit mainly to get to work or school (Figure 9.9).

In an effort to lure a number of commuters to mass transit, cities are considering innovations — unusual design including futuristic architecture, use of art work, and decoration with color murals and lighting — color, fantasy, and whimsy that planners hope will be "magnets" to commuters. Some cities that have experienced loss of riders on subways and buses, such as New York City, are proposing restructuring fare schedules to allow riders to transfer from subway to bus and are planning better connecting routes for such transfers.

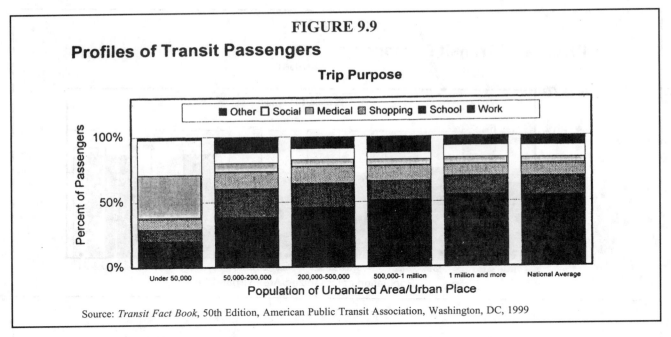

FIGURE 9.9

Profiles of Transit Passengers

Trip Purpose

Legend: ■ Other □ Social ▦ Medical ▨ Shopping ■ School ■ Work

Y-axis: Percent of Passengers (0%, 50%, 100%)

X-axis categories (Population of Urbanized Area/Urban Place): Under 50,000; 50,000-200,000; 200,000-500,000; 500,000-1 million; 1 million and more; National Average

Source: *Transit Fact Book*, 50th Edition, American Public Transit Association, Washington, DC, 1999

THE GOVERNMENT HOPES TO CHANGE COMMUTER BEHAVIOR

Urban traffic congestion imposes large costs on society. Time spent in traffic results in lower productivity, excess fuel consumption, and increased pollution. The federal government, under mandate of the Clean Air Act Amendments of 1990 (PL 101-549), the Intermodal Surface Transportation Efficiency Act (ISTEA; PL 102-240) of 1991, the Transportation Equity Act for the Twenty-first Century, which reauthorizes ISTEA (TEA-21; PL 105-178), and other state and local regulations, is attempting to discourage drive-alone commuting.

The ISTEA (through September 1997) and TEA-21 (from 1998 through 2003) authorize special funding for projects likely to reduce vehicle miles traveled, decrease fuel consumption, or otherwise reduce congestion and improve air quality. The Clean Air Act requires employers in 11 states (Arizona, Georgia, Minnesota, Oregon, Virginia, Washington, California, Connecticut, Maryland, New Jersey, and Texas) to reduce drive-alone commuting among employees by providing incentives to employers. Some of the efforts include

- Transit vouchers programs — employers provide employees with vouchers for free or reduced fare to use for mass transit.

- Taxing employers for parking space — taxing parking could also affect government revenues.

- Zoning changes — changing zoning laws to encourage transit use and reduce the supply of parking spaces.

- Cash returns for the value of parking spaces — offering employees cash equivalent to the market value of parking spaces instead of the use of that space.

- Higher gasoline taxes.

- Congestion pricing — charging drivers for the use of congested roads.

TEA-21 retains the basic structure of the federal transit programs authorized under ISTEA. TEA-21 provides $41 billion, $36 billion of which is guaranteed, in transit funds between 1998 and 2003. (The guaranteed amount is protected in the budget process and can only be allotted for transit uses, subject to annual appropriation by Congress.) The money will be spent in both rural and urban areas. New transportation systems will be built, and existing ones will be improved and modernized. The Rail Modernization Program will increase the proportion of new funds for newer fixed-guideway (steel wheel or rubber tires on a set path) systems.

Some funds will be spent to improve the chances of success for the 2002 Salt Lake City (Utah) Olympics.

Another benefit of TEA-21 is a $100 per month tax-exempt employee allowance that will be available for workers who use public transit, effective December 31, 2001. Prior to TEA-21, the maximum benefit was $65 per month.

Two new programs were created under TEA-21. The Clean Fuels Formula Grant program provides funds for adoption of clean fuel technologies, including purchase or lease of clean fuel buses and facilities. The Job Access and Reverse Commute Program funds projects designed to help welfare and low-income families and others who do not own cars get to and from higher-paying jobs in suburbs without bus service, or to travel to and from off-hour jobs when other forms of public transportation have stopped running. The program authorizes $50 million for 1999, of which $10 million is set aside for "reverse commuting" projects. Funding up to $150 million annually for five years may become available.

BUILDING COMMUNITIES
FRIENDLY TO TRANSIT

Many American neighborhoods and communities are hostile environments to transit users and pedestrians. Campus-style office parks, walled-in residential divisions, and mega-malls are often designed so that it is difficult to access them or get around by any means other than the private automobile.

In recent years, some experts have called for the redesign of America's suburbs so they are more conducive to transit riding, walking, and bicycling. These developments would include residential areas within a one-quarter-mile radius of a rail transit station built to tie into the transit system through easy walking or shuttle access. The rail transit stations differ considerably — the designs used mainly on the East Coast are primarily high rise; on the West Coast, they are three to four stories in height; in the southwest, they are often single-story buildings.

More and more communities are asking their elected officials to work together with transportation agencies to begin to develop transportation plans for the future. Such a plan might include new land use development, high-density mixed-use areas with good pedestrian access to transit stations, landscape improvements, security lighting, and new zoning laws. The public is involved in the process, and the project goes through many steps in an effort to create the best transit-oriented plan for the individual community.

TRANSIT SAFETY

The Transportation Department is now taking steps to monitor U.S. mass transit workers for drug and alcohol use. Congress mandated the testing program, the largest of its kind in the United States, in 1991 in response to a series of accidents involving alcohol. Among them were the *Exxon Valdez* oil spill in 1989, which was partly attributed to the captain's drinking, and the derailment of a subway train that killed five people in New York City in 1991, in which the motorman's drinking was blamed.

The transportation industry had long held that testing was an invasion of privacy, but federal courts, in *Skinner, Secretary of Transportation et al. v. Railway Labor Executives' Association et al.,* (839 F.2d 575, Ninth Circuit, 1989), decided that safety considerations can override privacy concerns, as in the decision to require drug testing of transportation employees.

The new regulations apply to truck drivers, school bus drivers, railroad employees, pilots and air traffic controllers, merchant mariners, and others involved in "safety sensitive" jobs. New employees will be tested, and random tests of those already employed will be conducted. The Transportation Department estimates that the rules will save nearly 1,200 lives and avert 21,000 injuries over 10 years.

TABLE 9.8

Light-Rail Lines in Comparable Metro Areas: 1998

	Length of Line	Open	Cost	Average Weekly Ridership
Dallas	20 miles	1996 and 1997	$860 million	35,000
Denver	5.3 miles	1994	$116.5 million	16,000
Portland	15 miles	1986	$214 million	33,000
Sacramento	18 miles	1987	$176 million	27,500
Salt Lake City	15 miles (under construction)	2000 (projected)	$322 million	20,000 expected
St. Louis	17 miles	1993	$464 million	44,000

Source: Minneapolis *Star Tribune*, March 29, 1998

Drug and alcohol abuses are not the only causes of accidents. Sometimes, trains are not equipped with the latest safety features. Following a February 1997 accident that took three lives in New Jersey when a transit train ran a red light and collided with another train, New Jersey Transit was ordered to install Automatic Brake Control (an automatic braking system) on every transit train.

The braking system automatically stops trains that run a red light. The system was designed to prevent the type of human error that was blamed for the crash in 1997. Automatic Brake Control is expensive; it can cost over $100 million, depending on the size of the rail network. However, a spokesman for a network that has installed the system claims that results are nearly guaranteed, since the Automatic Brake Control enables the train to stop itself.

Overly long work shifts are often responsible for contributing to fatigue and human error. Split shifts — extended work periods of up to fourteen and one-half hours with only a four-hour break in the middle — have been blamed for several accidents. One such case involved a shift that began at 6 p.m. and finished at 8:30 a.m. the following day with a four-hour break during the night. In this accident, three people were killed and more than 160 were injured.

THE FUTURE

Light Rail Systems

Many U.S. cities have successfully introduced light-rail lines. Although such systems are expensive to build and to operate, and most do not make a profit, ridership is higher than expected, and six major cities have recently begun expanding their systems. (See Table 9.8.)

Portland, Oregon, has extended its original 15-mile track by adding another 18 miles. About 33,000 people ride the line per week. Voters in Denver, Colorado, rejected a system-wide expansion in 1997, but the city has started to extend its 5.3-mile light-rail system piece by piece. Average weekly ridership on Denver's transit system is 16,000. In Sacramento, California, where 27,500 persons use the light-rail system weekly, 18 miles of track will increase to 39 miles by 2002. In Salt Lake City, Utah, a 15-mile line is currently being built, and another line is being planned for the 2002 Winter Olympic Games. Weekly ridership on the completed system is expected to amount to 20,000. Dallas, Texas, recently added light-rail to its existing bus routes, and now has 20 miles of track and an average weekly ridership of 35,000 people.

On the other hand, not all systems run smoothly. St. Louis, Missouri, has a strong ridership of 44,000 per week and plans to build another light-rail line. However, the city is having difficulty paying its operating subsidy. Los Angeles, California, built too many rail lines too quickly and now has a $50 million deficit and relatively few riders.

Light Rail in the Grand Canyon

In 1901, visitors to the Grand Canyon in Arizona took the Santa Fe Railroad to see the south rim of the canyon. Now, nearly 100 years later, mass transit is once again planned. Ground was broken recently for the first light rail to service a national park. Work will begin during the summer of 1999 on a $100 million light-rail system designed to cut vehicle traffic by 80 percent. Nearly 5 million visitors are expected to travel to the Grand Canyon in 1999.

Hybrid Buses

A new hybrid bus is being used as a shuttle between terminals at Logan Airport in Boston. The vehicle hums at a constant tone, never emits visible exhaust, and runs on about half the horsepower used by a compact car. The bus is 30 feet long, is powered by two electric motors — one for each rear wheel — and has a natural gas engine. The bus, made of more fiberglass than steel, is two-thirds as heavy as a regular bus. The prototype costs about $1 million, while a comparably sized bus costs between $225,000 and $275,000. However, with other bus designers moving in the same direction, the cost of the hybrid model is expected to drop.

New York City has been using five hybrid buses with conventional steel bodies since September 1998 and plans to purchase 10 more. According to a spokesman for New York City Transit, the hybrid buses afford a great reduction in energy use; when the bus stops, the brake pedal turns the drive motors into generators, slowing the bus and converting the energy into electricity that flows back into the battery.

A conventional New York City bus the same size as the hybrid would require a 190-horsepower diesel engine, while the hybrid uses a 68-horsepower engine. The New York City hybrid bus has two electric motors powered by batteries charged continuously by a generator, which in turn is powered by the small natural gas engine.

IMPORTANT NAMES AND ADDRESSES

Air Traffic Control Association, Inc.
2300 Clarendon Blvd., #711
Arlington, VA 22201
(703) 522-5717
FAX (703) 527-7251
ATCA@worldnet.att.net

Air Transport Association of America
1301 Pennsylvania Ave. NW, #1100
Washington, DC 20004
(202) 626-4000
FAX (202) 626-4166
www.air-transport.org

American Automobile Association
1440 New York Ave. NW, #200
Washington, DC 20005
(202) 942-2050
FAX (202) 783-4798
www.aaa.com

American Bus Association
1100 New York Ave. NW, #1050
Washington, DC 20005
(202) 842-1645
FAX (202) 842-0850
www.buses.org
abainfo@buses.org

American Public Transit Association
1201 New York Ave. NW, #400
Washington, DC 20005
(202) 898-4000
FAX (202) 898-4070
www.apta.com

American Trucking Associations
2200 Mill Rd.
Alexandria, VA 22314
(800) 282-5463
FAX (703) 684-5720
www.truckline.com

Association of American Railroads
Economics and Finance Department
50 F St. NW
Washington, DC 20001
(202) 639-2555
FAX (202) 639-2868
www.aar.org

Bicycle Federation of America, Inc.
1506 21st St. NW, #200
Washington, DC 20036
(202) 463-6622
FAX (202) 463-6625
www.bikefed.org
askbfa@aol.com

Bureau of Transportation Statistics
400 7th St. SW, Rm. 3430
Washington, DC 20590
(202) 366-DATA
FAX (202) 366-3640
www.bts.gov

Cargo Airline Association
1220 19th St. NW, #400
Washington, DC 20036
(202) 293-1030
FAX (202) 293-4377
cargoair@aol.com

Department of the Army
Corps of Engineers
20 Massachusetts Ave. NW
Washington, DC 20314
(202) 761-0010
FAX (202) 761-1803
www.usace.army.mil

Eno Transportation Foundation, Inc.
One Farragut Square South, #500
Washington, DC 20006-4003
(202) 879-4700
FAX (202) 879-4719
www.enotrans.com

Federal Aviation Administration
800 Independence Ave. SW
Washington, DC 20591
(202) 267-8521
FAX (202) 267-5039
www.faa.gov

Federal Highway Administration
400 7th St. SW
Washington, DC 20590
(202) 366-0660
FAX (202) 366-7239
www.fhwa.dot.gov

Federal Transit Administration
400 7th St. SW
Washington, DC 20590
(202) 366-4319
FAX (202) 366-3472
www.fta.dot.gov

General Aviation Manufacturers
Association
1400 K St., #801
Washington, DC 20005
(202) 393-1500
FAX (202) 842-4063
www.generalaviation.org

Highway Loss Data Institute
1005 N. Glebe Road
Arlington, VA 22201
(703) 247-1600
FAX (703) 247-1678
www.highwaysafety.org

Motorcycle Industry Council, Inc.
2 Jenner St., #150
Irvine, CA 92718
(949) 727-4211
FAX (949) 727-4217
www.msf-usa.org

National Bicycle Dealers Association
777 N. 19 St., Suite O
Costa Mesa, CA 92627
(949) 722-6909
FAX (949) 722-1747
www.nbda.com
bikeshops@aol.com

National Highway Traffic Safety
Administration
400 7th St. SW, #5232
Washington, DC 20590
(202) 366-9550
(800) 424-9393
FAX (202) 366-9562
www.nhtsa.dot.gov

National Railroad Passenger
Corporation (Amtrak)
60 Massachusetts Ave. NE
Washington, DC 20002
(202) 906-3860
(800)-USA-RAIL
FAX (202) 906-3306
www.amtrak.com
service@sales.amtrak.com

National Safety Council
1121 Spring Lake Dr.
Itasca, IL 60143
(630) 285-1121
FAX (630) 285-1315
www.nsc.org

National Transportation Safety Board
490 L'Enfant Plaza East SW, 6th floor
Washington, DC 20594
(202) 314-6000
FAX (202) 314-6178
www.ntsb.gov

Recreational Vehicle Industry
Association
1896 Preston White Dr.
P.O. Box 2999
Reston, VA 22090
(703) 620-6003
FAX (703) 620-5071
www.rvia.org

Regional Airline Association
1200 19th St. NW, #300
Washington, DC 20036
(202) 857-1170
FAX (202) 429-5113
www.raa.org
raa@dc.sba.com

U.S. Department of Transportation
400 7th St. SW
Washington, DC 20590
(202) 366-5580
FAX (202) 366-5583
www.dot.gov

RESOURCES

The U.S. Department of Transportation (DOT) is an excellent source of information about all types of transportation. DOT prepared the *1997 Status of the Nation's Surface Transportation System: Conditions and Performance*, which provides current data on transportation and projects transportation needs for the future. The Bureau of Transportation Statistics, another DOT agency, publishes several excellent annual compendia, including *Transportation Statistics Annual Report* (1998) and *National Transportation Statistics* (1997).

The Federal Highway Administration (FHWA), also part of DOT, publishes data on the state of the nation's highways and bridges, including *Our Nation's Highways: Selected Facts and Figures 1998* (1998). FHWA also published *Large Truck Crash Profile: The 1997 National Picture* (1998). The National Highway Traffic Safety Administration, a department of DOT, prepared *Traffic Safety Facts 1997* and many other pamphlets.

The Federal Aviation Administration (FAA), a DOT agency, in its *FAA Aviation Forecasts — Fiscal years 1999-2010* (1999), provides valuable information on the nation's aviation system, including not only present conditions but also forecasts for the future. The FAA also published *The Aviation Safety Statistical Handbook: 1997 Annual Report* (1998), which reports on accident data.

Air Transport 1999, Annual Report, prepared by the Air Transport Association of America, the airline trade association, is a very useful source for statistics on many facets of the air travel industry. (Complete copies of the annual report are available by calling 800-497-3326 [U.S. and Canada] or 301-490-7951.) The General Aviation Manufacturers Association provided its *Statistical Databook* (1999). *Air Transport World* magazine's annual "The World Airline Report" (vol. 34, no. 7, July 1997) is an invaluable survey of the world's airline industry.

The U.S. General Accounting Office, an investigative agency of the U.S. government, published several reports on the rail industry, including *Intercity Passenger Rail: Outlook for Improving Amtrak's Financial Health* (1998*), Intercity Passenger Rail: Financial Performance of Amtrak's*

Routes (1998), and *High Speed Rail Projects in the U.S.* (1997).

Waterborne Commerce of the United States (1997), prepared by the Department of the Army Corps of Engineers, reports on the commercial shipping of both foreign and domestic cargo and the condition of the nation's waterways and harbors.

The American Public Transit Association's *1999 Transit Fact Book* (1999) supplies invaluable data on mass transit. The Association of American Railroads, the industry's trade group, furnishes data on the nation's freight trains in its annual *Railroad Facts (*1998).

The *1998 Motorcycle Statistical Annual*, prepared by the Motorcycle Industry Council, Inc., provided information on motorcycles and motorcycle owners. The National Bicycle Dealers Association was the source of data on bicycle usage and the U.S. bicycle market. The Recreational Vehicle Industry Association, in its annual *Year in Review*, supplied valuable information on the various types of recreational vehicles and their owners.

Information Plus thanks the American Trucking Associations for allowing the use of information from *American Trucking Trends, 1999 Edition* (1999), which gives the current status of the trucking industry. *Ward's Automotive Yearbook 1998* (Ward's Communications, Southfield, MI, 1998), furnished complete information on the production and sales of the nation's cars and trucks.

Information Plus would also like to thank the National Safety Council, which publishes the annual *Accident Facts. Transportation in America* (1998), prepared by the Eno Foundation for Transportation, Inc., is an excellent resource for the entire field of transportation.

Information Plus appreciates the information on buses received from the American Bus Association and Greyhound Lines. We also thank Dun & Bradstreet, The Polk Company, the American Automobile Association, Runzheimer International, and DuPont Automotive, which permitted use of information from their surveys.

INDEX